P9-CFO-966

"I [have] accepted Evelyn Ryan as my personal savior."

—Salon.com

"Ryan inherited her mother's way with words and has written this loving and upbeat—and very funny—memoir. Because of that, we are all winners."

—*The Dallas Morning News*

"If all the world loves a winner, get ready to swoon over Evelyn Ryan. . . . With her brevity and wit, Evelyn Ryan sparkles like a down-home Ogden Nash."

—*The Cleveland Plain Dealer*

"This book is a well-aimed kick in the pants for anyone who says they don't have time to pursue their passion."

—*The Calgary Herald*

"The wonderfully wacky story of Terry's mom, Evelyn Lehman Ryan, is a kitsch spin on the classic victim-turned-victor that Hollywood so loves."

—*The Daily Telegraph* (London)

"An experience that is both understated and intensely powerful."

—*Chicago Tribune*

"An affectionate, wonderfully funny tribute."

—*St. Petersburg Times*

"*Prize Winner* is the most charming and inspirational book I've read in a long time. It bursts with stories of soul, humanity, cunning, courage, and humor in the face of desperate times."

—Anne Lamott, author of *Plan B: Further Thoughts on Faith*

"Terry Ryan's story of her amazing, prize-winning mother is simply fabulous. *The Prize Winner of Defiance, Ohio* is a wonderful snapshot of mid-twentieth-century America—a heart-warming, marvelous story that deserves its place alongside the best nonfiction in modern literature."

—Patricia Cornwell

"Nabs first prize in the memoir genre."

—*People* (Book of the Week)

"An unforgettable account . . . In its delicate balance of the comic, the tragic, and the occasionally insane, Ryan's book leaves a sense of wistfulness at never having met her amazing mother."

—*San Francisco Chronicle*

"Inspirational."

—*USA Today*

The Prize Winner

of Defiance, Ohio

HOW MY MOTHER RAISED
10 KIDS ON 25 WORDS OR LESS

Terry Ryan
Foreword by Suze Orman

POCKET STAR BOOKS
New York London Toronto Sydney

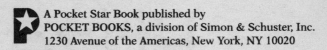 A Pocket Star Book published by
POCKET BOOKS, a division of Simon & Schuster, Inc.
1230 Avenue of the Americas, New York, NY 10020

Copyright © 2001 by Terry Ryan

Cover art ™ and © 2005 DreamWorks Productions LLC &
Revolution Studios Distribution Company. All rights reserved.

Originally published in hardcover in 2001 by Touchstone

ISBN-13: 978-1-4165-1081-9
ISBN-10: 1-4165-1081-8

This Pocket Star Books paperback edition September 2005

10 9 8 7 6 5 4 3

POCKET STAR BOOKS and colophon are registered
trademarks of Simon & Schuster, Inc.

Cover photo credit: Michael Gibson

Printed in the U.S.A.

For information regarding special discounts for bulk purchases,
please contact Simon & Schuster Special Sales at 1-800-456-6798
or business@simonandschuster.com.

For my mother, Evelyn Lehman Ryan

(and the little bit of Evelyn in all of us)

CONTENTS

Foreword by Suze Orman xi

FOREWORD BY SUZE ORMAN

I never met Evelyn Ryan, but I feel an uncanny kinship with this remarkable woman, thanks to her daughter Terry's rollicking, painful, hilarious—and often instructive—remembrance.

Here is the true story of an "average housewife" whose life is not so average at all. Evelyn is the mother of ten children and married to an alcoholic, sometimes violent husband. She regularly faces eviction, poverty, and even near-starvation in the small Midwestern town aptly named (in her case) Defiance, Ohio.

At a time, in the 1950s and 1960s, when women were discouraged from taking jobs and made to feel powerless in the face of adversity, it's not difficult to imagine how a mother like Evelyn Ryan might find it impossible to help her children keep fear at bay.

How could such a woman show her children that life is not cruel, but bountiful? How could she possibly keep them, all ten of them, afloat, much less teach them abundance, grace, and courage in the face of grinding poverty and adversity?

Well, if the potential for true wealth resides, as I believe it does, deep in the spirit of each and every one of us, Evelyn Ryan draws from the depths of her spirit many times. With a gift for writing jingles, poems, and 25-words-or-less compositions, she wins hundreds of contests that save her family from destitution, and she does it with incredible humor and joy.

And what a magnificent winner is Evelyn! Regularly awarded cash, shopping sprees, automobiles, trips to Europe, gold watches, color televisions, radios, a refrigerator, a freezer, a washer-dryer, and bicycles, she stores the smaller prizes in what the family calls "Mom's Legendary Closet": Here are toys, clocks, sporting goods, toasters, silverware, record players, fans, jewelry, and (as though a sign of the times were needed) not one but three pairs of Arthur Murray shoes.

It would be a mistake to think that Evelyn is "saved" by her gift for writing, unique though it is. What emerges as the driving element in this story is the courage of this indefatigable mom as she faces creditors and overcomes her husband's anger when there isn't a penny in the family coffers.

So this would be an amazing story, funny and poignant, if Terry Ryan only listed her mother's thousands of entries, each one worthy of Ogden Nash or Dorothy Parker or Erma Bombeck, that result in enough cash to pay this large family's many bills in the nick of time.

But it is that and much more. To me, the real story of *The Prize Winner of Defiance, Ohio* is the lesson of pride and possibility that Evelyn Ryan teaches her kids time after time.

Even scraping together suppers of rice and milk—or, to her children's horror, soup with bugs she insists are "spices"—Evelyn knows that thoughts of never having enough money are thoughts of impoverishment. She prefers to think of succeeding at great contests ("Win a Producing Oil Well!" "Win Your Weight in Gold!"), while relishing the small treasures that keep the family running, right down to the $1 she receives for every inventive poem published by her local newspaper.

One might read this book and think, well, maybe Evelyn Ryan is just lucky. Maybe it's luck to have such a quirky talent in a quirky postwar era when she can put that talent to use. But think about the strength of character and persistence it takes to enter contest after contest, to put aside despair and summon up words of cheer, time and time again.

Richness of the spirit can dwell in the most desolate places, and it pervades Evelyn's household like a healing balm. It will touch you as well, when you read her story. For this is a saga that resonates like—well, a jingle from the 1950s, but profoundly.

The Prize Winner
of Defiance, Ohio

 PART ONE

CHAPTER ONE

The Contester

*T*he ordinarily sleepy town of Defiance, Ohio, emitted an industrious hum on hot days, a subtle pulse of activity—like the buzzing of distant bees. It was late Indian summer, a little too warm for an October day, in 1953. Most of the rust-red and golden leaves still held fast in the towering maple trees that lined our block on Latty Street. You could feel the moisture in the air seeping up from the muddy, slow-moving Auglaize River a few blocks away.

My mother, Evelyn Ryan, had sent six of her nine children outside to play while she and my sixteen-year-old sister, Lea Anne, made lunch. As usual, all the school-age kids in the family came home at noontime, and we crammed as much recreation into the hour as we could.

As a seven-year-old, I sat on the porch steps reading comic books with my brothers Mike, five, and Bruce, who had just turned nine. My oldest brother Dick, fourteen, his arm still in a cast from a bicycle accident, played one-armed catch with my thirteen-year-old brother, Bub, on the sidewalk in the sun. Rog, two years younger than Bub, roller-skated in the street, hoping to get a free ride by grabbing on to the bumper of a passing car. My baby sisters, three-year-old Barb and one-year-old Betsy, were somewhere inside the house with Lea Anne and Mom, who was pregnant with my brother Dave at the time.

Just as Rog decided that little or no traffic would pass the house on the quiet little street and clumped up the steps to remove his skates, a sleek jet-black Pontiac Chieftain pulled up to the curb in front. It was so new we could see ourselves reflected in the side panels. The chrome grille glistened expensively in the sun. Even the aerodynamic hood ornament— a small amber-colored bust of Chief Pontiac—looked valuable, more like a misplaced jewel than an auto accessory.

So few visitors ever stopped at our house that we all turned to stare. When three men wearing dark pinstripe suits got out of the car and started up the walk, Bruce and I raced into the house to tell Mom that some very well-dressed strangers were about to knock on the door. Because of the suits, we thought that someone must have died.

Our middle-America town of Defiance was big enough to be the county seat and small enough to need only three traffic lights on Clinton, the main street. Visitors arriving in a quasi limousine were unheard of. Not that we weren't getting used to surprises. In the late 1940s my mother had begun to enter the many contests of skill that had sprung to life in the post–World War II economic boom. Poems, limericks, and statements of the "25 words or less" variety had been pouring out of her for the past five years. She was now winning small prizes with some frequency—the Benrus ladies' watch she wore everywhere, even to bed; the Bulova watch she saved for special occasions, like Sunday Mass; $95 in cash (from multiple contests); an automatic coffeemaker; frying pans, a Westinghouse blender, basketballs, footballs, Rog's roller skates, and—by my reckoning, the best prize of all—an entire case of Almond Joy candy bars.

"Contesting" was a relatively new outlet for Mom, though she had been writing her whole life. The poems she submitted to magazines or poetry contests tended to be short, pithy, and unexpectedly humorous. The dollar she received for "But Excuse Us" went a long way in 1953:

Folks endowed with
Luck, or virtue,
Get the tissue
To the kerchoo.

She began her contesting career simply enough, with Burma-Shave roadside rhymes. In the 1950s you couldn't drive down a highway without passing a Burma-Shave roadside billboard campaign, six signs spaced at hundred-yard intervals down the road, one line to a sign, the last always "Burma-Shave." The verses were clever and meant to amuse, their content ranging from shaving to safe driving and current culture. My mother's submissions added to those topics an occasional touch of irony:

> *Race little roadster,*
> > *Fairly fly.*
> > > *You'll be*
> > > > *Used parts*
> > > > > *By and by.*
> > > > > > *Burma-Shave.*

Successful Burma-Shave jingles inserted a not-so-hidden advertisement into the mix, and in one entry Mom went for broke—if you don't shave close enough, you could kill yourself:

> *Hairpin turn,*
> > *Hotrod ditched.*
> > > *Lost control,*
> > > > *His whiskers*
> > > > > *Itched.*
> > > > > > *Burma-Shave.*

Our family was often surprised at Mom's uncanny knack for working complex political issues into something as simple as a Burma-Shave jingle. I doubt anyone would have accepted the premise of a Korean War veteran who survived combat only to be killed because he foolishly passed another car on a hill. But the poem she sent in was quick-witted and timely enough to hit just the right note:

> *Passed on a hill,*
> > *Lived through*

> *Korea.*
> *Met a guy*
> *With the same idea.*
> *Burma-Shave.*

By the age of five, I had grown used to seeing Mom, pencil behind her right ear, spend hours each day at the ironing board. She often said that she did her best work while ironing, her hands working on one chore, her head on another. On the squared end of the board, where the iron stood upright, Mom kept an open notebook of current contest jingles and entries in various stages of completion. A basket of pre-sprinkled clothes rested at her feet. The iron hissed on the board as she scribbled. "Even Steven" won a poetry contest in the Toledo *Blade*, earning her at least $25, a veritable windfall in our family.

Who'd trade
Peace of mind
(To most rich men
Denied)
For all of their
Worrisome money?
I'd.

Each evening after the last supper dish had been washed and put away—never an easy task since we used every plate in the house—Mom would grab her notebook and sit down at the end of the couch to produce more entries. Inevitably she fell asleep after a few minutes, notebook on her lap, postage stamps and other effluvia of contesting slipping out of the pages and onto the floor. Each new year, Mom started a new notebook to fill with entries that might go nowhere or all the way to the top.

She used her writing skills to win some of the necessities our large family couldn't afford to buy. Ours was one of the poorest families in Defiance. Mom was far too busy with the family and housework to take on an outside job, and Dad's take-home pay from Serrick's Screw Machine Shop—where he made nuts, bolts, screws, screwdrivers, pliers, hammers, and an occasional pair of tweezers for home use—was about $90 a week, barely enough to pay for food and rent. His nightly liquor consumption— a fifth of Kessler's whiskey and a six-pack of Pabst Blue Ribbon beer—came to $30 a week, sapping his paycheck of any real buying power.

In the days before credit cards, few people in Defiance had a checking account. Bills were paid in cash and in person. Our family finances worked like this: Dad cashed his weekly paychecks at the bank, and at the end of the month, he drove all over town to pay the mortgage and bills at the gas and electric, telephone, and doctor's offices. Whatever was left by the time he got home usually remained in his wallet, getting distributed bit by bit for groceries, clothes, and incidentals (newspapers, the milkman).

Medical bills were paid in erratic installments, if ever. We relied on the Lions Club to pay for eyeglasses for Lea Anne, Rog, Bruce, me, Mike, Barb, and Betsy. We got much of our clothing from more well-to-do relatives as they outgrew them. Most of the food we ate was bought by our generous aunt Lucy.

So Mom, like a surprisingly large number of housewives in the 1950s and 1960s, turned to contesting for a living. Of course, thousands of contestants competing for a small pool of prizes made for long odds. But Mom won a great deal of the time, and any prize she received (with the possible exception of the free accordion lessons she won for Mike in 1958, Barb in 1961, and Betsy in 1963) usually filled a pressing household need.

The contests Mom entered required word skills, wit, and originality. "Luck," she always said, "has nothing to do with it." An average contest might ask for a rhymed jingle, the last line of a five-line limerick, or 25 words or less on a specific product. In 1955, for example, she won $10 for this submission to Dial soap:

I'm glad I use Dial
Though my reign's in the kitchen
I needn't pour perfume
To keep quite bewitchin'.

The same year, she won an RCA Victor AM/shortwave radio with this jingle:

Kraft's Parkay won't tear fresh bread.
Even ice-cold, it will smoothly spread.
It tastes as delicious as can be—
No "seasonable" facsimile.

Mom worked on her entries day and night, honing them until the rhyme or the sentiment, in her mind, perfectly fit the sponsor's expectations. She never submitted just one entry when she had enough ideas for ten or eleven. She learned to use every variation on her own name (Mrs. Evelyn Ryan, Mrs. Evalyn Ryan, Mrs. Evalynn Ryan, Mrs. Evelyn L. Ryan, Mrs. Evelyn

Lenore Ryan, Mrs. E. L. Ryan, Miss Evelyn Ryan, Mrs. Leo J. Ryan, Mrs. L. J. Ryan, Mrs. Kelly Ryan, Mrs. Kelly J. Ryan, Mrs. K. J. Ryan); used fictitious middle initials (Mrs. Evelyn A., B., C., D., E., F., G., H., I., J., K., M., N., O., P., R., S., T., U., V., W., X., Y., and Z. Ryan); made up names (Eva Ryan, Donna Bea Ryan, Bud Ryan); used relatives' names (Dad's, Aunt Lucy's, Aunt Enie's, Lea Anne's, Dick's, Bub's, Rog's, Bruce's, mine, Mike's, Barb's, Betsy's, Dave's). When she ran out of names, she changed the address (adding a letter to the house number, changing "Avenue" to "Street"). All these variations allowed her to submit numerous entries for any contest, and also let her know which entry won when one did win.

Companies sponsored contests for two reasons: to acquire new advertising ideas from the public, and to sell more products. Most contest entry blanks had to be accompanied by a "proof of purchase" (labels on cans and jars, box tops, "freshness seals," bottle caps, candy and cigarette wrappers). Fifty thousand contest entries represented fifty thousand purchases that might not have occurred otherwise. Contesting was big business, for both sponsors and winners. Entrants felt almost patriotic to be a part of it.

Our kitchen cabinets were crammed with shoeboxes full of entry blanks and labels that Mom was saving for future use—one for cereals and other boxed foods (Kellogg's, Wheaties, Cheerios, Jell-O), one for canned and bottled foods (Spam, Del Monte, Heinz), one for candies (Peter Paul, Tootsie Roll, Pom Poms), one for soaps (Duz, Lux, SweetHeart), one for soft drinks (Dr Pepper, Coca-Cola, Hires), and one for any product not fitting those categories (Alcoa Wrap, Motorola, General Electric). No empty can or jar was tossed in the garbage until the label had been soaked off in the sink, a process that sometimes took days.

It didn't matter if the product manufacturer had never sponsored a contest. Mom saved the proofs of purchase just in case. "If Tang doesn't offer a contest one of these days," she said one morning, "I'm going to have to move you kids out of the bedroom to make room for the labels."

My mother had so many box tops, labels, and wrappers put aside that finding the right one could take an entire day. As a last resort, she'd remove a label from an unopened package or can and put the unmarked container back in the cupboard. The process inspired this poem:

✏️

Hmn! Wonder What This Is
A Contester's life is full of woe!
She parts with her box tops, then doesn't know
If she's washing with Surf or with Oxydol;
Might be Fab. Might be Duz. It could even be All,
Once her soap's poured in cans.
(Isn't yours, Contest fans?)
But the food she prepares is exciting, gay fare!
There's always an aura of mystery there,
For labels are long gone from fruit, fowl and fish,
So whatever she cooks is a real surprise dish.

Whoever happened to be passing the ironing board at the moment of Mom's inspiration was pressed into service. We loved to listen and collaborate with her, but sometimes—unless the entry rhymed or was funny in a conventional way—we would just stare at her, slack-jawed. We wondered how in the world she ever won a single contest with entries that sounded so indecipherable. Some of them seemed closer to Greek than English—underlined, italicized, polysyllabic verbal tangles studded with clusters of capital letters. This submission won a brand new Schwinn bicycle from a Champion spark plugs contest:

➤

Champion KNOWHOW puts MOST in SPARK PLUG to get the MOST (power, mileage) out of a CAR—a powerFULL "plug" for a spark plug!

Mom had a reason for producing such deliberate gobbledygook. Contesting, as she always said, required more than collecting box tops and being clever. There was *form* to consider (some contests required the use of specific words, or gave points for the use of product-related words in an entry), *product focus* (was it aimed at families, at young men, at children?), and *judges*. The advertising agency hired by the sponsoring company to judge the contest was always a more important consideration for entrants than the sponsor or the product. Each agency had its preference for rhyme or prose, for humorous or straight material.

So did the Ryan family. We considered some of Mom's entries just plain boring, or complete exaggerations. In a contest sponsored by the Plough pharmaceutical company, contestants wrote 25 words or less in praise of the local drugstore, in our case Kuntz's Drugs in Defiance.

➤

Kuntz's compounds hand-to-the-'Plough' dedication,

what-you-don't-see,-ask-for informality, what-we-
don't-have,-we'll-get-you accommodation.

This cheery, welcoming scenario was so unlike the
real drugstore, whose owner—some people thought—
treated many of his customers like potential shop-
lifters, that when my sister Barb read the entry,
she blurted out, "This glorified place is *Kuntz's*?" The
toaster Mom won for her entry arrived just two days
after the previous toaster expired. Truth was always
secondary when a new appliance was needed.

For every entry we couldn't understand or appreciate, there were far more that we could. A Real-Kill
pesticide contest required the entrant to think up a
name for the company's new bug spray and write a
rhymed description of it. Mom submitted at least
thirteen entries, using her usual aliases and alter-
nate addresses. To those of us passing the ironing
board, four of them seemed promising:

One, Two—
Today's bug's dead, tomorrow's too!

Inning—
A game life's bugs won't be winning!

Blend—
As bug sprays go, "the LIVING end"!

Blight 'em—
From bugs you're free ad finitum!

Even Mom wasn't sure which entry won, but one
of them did. As with the toaster, her timing seemed

almost divinely inspired. The prize was a top-of-the-line RCA color television set, which arrived just days after our old TV stopped working for good. Mom had won the old General Electric TV from *The Ed Sullivan Show* for this jingle on Mercury automobiles:

With power-endowed wizardry,
Nice "going" M-phatically!

We didn't understand this entry either, or why it was good enough to win such a big prize. The judges must have liked Mom's double entendre (*nice "going"*) and *M-phatically* (with the *M* signifying Mercury).

Whenever she won a major prize (to us, anything worth over $25), Mom wrote a personal thank-you note to the sponsoring company. Her intentions were sincere, but she believed as well that a letter of thanks just might give her an edge the next time around. "Evelyn C. Ryan" wrote the following letter to Ed Sullivan after receiving the TV:

A thousand pardons. I hope you'll forgive me for being so tardy to acknowledge receipt of the beautiful G.E. portable TV awarded me in the recent Mercury contest. We are all overjoyed.

I was aiming, I'll admit, for a brand new Mercury to replace our decrepit '46 Chevy, which runs nowadays only when it chooses, and seldom does.

You may be interested to know that the new portable entertains a family of twelve—Pop, Mom, twenty-, eighteen-, sixteen-, fourteen-, twelve-, ten-, eight-, six-, four-, and three-year-olds, so the superiority of the G.E. line will doubtless be broadcast far and wide.

We are very grateful, and are biding our time until next year, so please *do* have another Mercury contest! Huh?

Happily and hopefully yours, (Mrs.) Evelyn C. Ryan

Mom didn't win a prize in every contest she entered, of course. (And though she tried, she *never* won a sweepstakes contest, where winners were picked at random.) In the 1950s, Pepsodent, one of the more popular brands of toothpaste, saturated radio and TV airwaves for at least a decade with its familiar singsong jingle, "You'll wonder where the yellow went / When you brush your teeth with Pepsodent." When Pepsodent sponsored a contest asking *"where the yellow went,"* Mom's entries, all four of them, went nowhere, though we thought they showed her typical humor and range:

The yellow escaped
By the skin of its teeth
When Pepsodent unveiled
The white underneath.

The yellow battled
As it went
(But it didn't make
A PepsoDENT).

Down the drain and
Over the dam

Pursued by the paste
with the whammy what-am!

It took to the bottle—
Wasn't Pepsodent-fond,
And what came out?
Peroxide-blonde!

Occasionally, months would go by without a single prize, and these were dark times indeed. We'd come home from school and spot Mom lingering at the front windows, watching "Pokey," as she called our slow-moving mailman, make his lumbering way up one side of Latty Street and back down the other to our house, endlessly chatting with milkmen and garbage collectors on the way. Big events in our house, even the little kids knew, had occurred because of Mom's contesting before. And most of them had begun with a simple envelope hand-carried by Pokey, like this January 1953 letter from NBC's *Bob Hope Show* in Hollywood:

Dear Mrs. Ryan:

Your contribution to the "Truth Is Funnier than Fiction" portion of the Bob Hope daytime radio show has been accepted for broadcast. It will be heard on the broadcast of Friday, February 6, 1953.

You may expect to receive your Bulova "American Girl" watch in the near future.

Yours very truly,
Marian H. Kate,
Assistant to the Producer

Enclosed in the envelope was a copy of the winning story Mom sent in:

Four-year-old Mike objected to getting his cowboy hat off the back porch after supper, explaining that he was afraid of the dark. "Mike," his father said, "God is out there, too." Thus emboldened, Mike opened the back door a crack and called out, "God, will you please hand me my hat?"

Mom hit a dry spell starting late in the summer of 1953, but that, it turned out, was the least of her worries. The tiny two-bedroom house we had rented for six years, we learned, would soon be the home of someone else. Granted, the house was far too small and cramped for a family of eleven. We had no bathtub and only two bedrooms. Mom and Dad had one; the kids slept in the other—nine of us in two double beds and three single cots.

As children we hardly noticed the crowded conditions. What kid wouldn't like waking up in a room with eight other boys and girls? It was life as we knew it, and it was grand. What the house lacked in size was more than mitigated by the enormous backyard, a large expanse of lawn we used as a baseball diamond, with built-in snacks as well: a fifty-foot grape arbor, twin peach trees, a cherry tree, and a giant old apple tree.

But now it seemed our life on Latty Street was over. The landlord told Mom that he wanted the house for his daughter, who was getting married in a few months. In short, we were being evicted. Dad didn't give this news much thought, assuming that a solution would appear in time. Mom had worried ever since about where we would relocate and how we'd get the money to do it.

Then Dick was hit by a car while delivering newspapers on his bicycle. Although he came through the accident with only a broken arm, the bike was destroyed. Just a month before, he had pitched a no-hitter, almost unheard of in Little League. The coach told Mom he had high hopes for Dick's future as a professional baseball player. When the police called from the hospital about the accident, they put Dick on the phone first, so my mother would know immediately that he wasn't seriously injured.

"Hi, Mom, it's me." Dick spoke so softly Mom could hardly hear him. "I got hit by a car on the northside bridge, but I'm okay."

"What?" Mom sat down before her knees could buckle. "Where are you? Are you hurt?"

"I'm at the hospital. I bounced off the guy's hood and broke my arm."

"You *what?*" wailed Mom. "Did they take X rays?"

"They did, Mom, and I'm okay. The only thing broken is my arm."

As she began to understand that he had indeed survived the accident, Mom paused to smile. "It's not your *pitching* arm, is it?"

"No." He laughed. "It's my left arm. The bike's smashed, though. The car drove right over it."

Without a bike, Dick lost his newspaper route to another boy who had a functioning bicycle. A few weeks later on a visit to the hardware store, Mom noticed an ad for a bicycle contest sponsored by Western Auto: "Kids! Complete this sentence in 25 words or less (Mom and Dad's help is encouraged): I

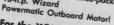

like the all-new 'X-53 Super' Western Flyer Bicycle because . . ."

Mom took home an entry blank, determined for the first time to win a contest for a specific need. Her goal was to win Dick one of the 101 new bikes that would be awarded to the grand prize winner and the hundred runner-ups. The entry she finally submitted seemed, to her kids, another of the slack-jawed variety, but we didn't say this out loud. There would be other contests, we thought, other bicycles:

✏️➤

I like the all-new "X-53 Super" Western Flyer Bicycle because *brand new ideas about safety, service, sleekness, combined with Western Flyer's old reliable construction make "X-53 Super" a stand-out in ANY bike rack!*

Nothing had come of the Western Flyer entry Mom had sent in during her dry spell, and we could tell she was becoming increasingly worried about that and our eviction notice by the time the three men in business suits pulled up in their gleaming Pontiac. They must have stifled laughter when they saw the scrappy Ryan kids staring at them open mouthed, until two of us broke ranks and ran in to announce their approach. As the men stepped up to the door and knocked, the remaining kids traipsed through ahead of them, leaving them alone on the porch.

Assuming the men were lost, Mom opened the screen door prepared to direct them elsewhere. Her sturdy five-foot six-inch frame came up to the knot in the tallest man's necktie, but she probably could

*P*ublicity photo taken after Mom (in Dick's name)
won the Western Auto bicycle contest, including
$5,000, in the nick of time. Back row, standing: Dad,
Rog, and Bub. Others, from left: Lea Anne, Bruce,
Barb (holding her favorite toy, an empty Vaseline
jar), Dick, Mom, Betsy (sitting on Mom's lap), me,
Mike (with toy gun). Brother Dave was born eight
months later.

have beaten him in arm wrestling. Years of hauling kids around had given her a body as solid as stone, her able shoulders visible at the edges of the square-cut top of her yellow sundress. She had high cheekbones and olive skin, remnants of the smattering of Indian blood rumored to have circulated in her mostly German ancestors. Her black eyes stared directly into the blue eyes of the tallest visitor and saw nothing but good news. She wiped her hands on her apron and smiled.

"Mrs. Ryan?" the blue-eyed man inquired.

She seemed intrigued that he knew her name. "Yes?"

"Is your son Dick here?"

"Yes," she said, grabbing Dick's shoulders from behind, "this is Dick. What's this about?"

The three of them erupted in a chorus. "Congratulations, Dick! You've just won five thousand dollars!"

In the first few mute moments that followed, the men introduced themselves as Mr. Forrest, Mr. Braby, and Mr. Kraber of Western Auto Supply Company and told Mom the news: Out of sixty-five thousand entries in the company's national bike contest, Dick's had won the grand prize, which included $5,000 (about $35,000 today), a new washer and dryer, and a brand-new Western Flyer bicycle.

Dick, who had no idea that Mom entered this contest in his name, was speechless. Mom, who realized instantly that the money was enough to solve our housing problem, began to weep with relief, which in turn made all the rest of us cry. The men in suits, perhaps having seen at a glance that ours

Dick accepting his new bike from Western Auto regional manager W. F. Clark at halftime of a Defiance High School football game. The stadium exploded in laughter when Mom accepted the check and someone yelled, "She'll need it with all those kids!" Others, from left: division manager J. W. Lockhart, Mom, Dad, and Defiance Western Auto dealer John Kraber.

was not an affluent household, were moved too, no doubt surprised and touched that their grand prize winner actually needed the prizes.

The next day (the very day Dick's cast was removed), they returned to take a photograph of the family for publicity purposes. In the picture, three-year-old Barb clutches her favorite toy, an empty Vaseline jar, and five-year-old Mike points a toy gun at the camera. Since Dave wasn't born until eight months later, the photo shows only nine of us and Dad clustered around Mom in our well-worn living room. The linoleum at her feet is so thin it is scarcely there at all. A dark splotch appears where pattern used to be. Dad stands in the background, a ghostlike specter at the edge of the family, neither in nor out of it. The look on his face seems to say, "See, Mother? I knew things would work out all right."

When both the Toledo *Blade* and the *Defiance Crescent-News* ran articles on Dick's big win, the headlines called him "Moneybags." Dad was not happy when both papers referred to the head of the family as "Leo P. Ryan" instead of Leo J. (his given name) or Kelly (his nickname), a typographical error the rest of us laughed at. Dad didn't.

A few weeks later, the prizes were awarded to Mom and Dick during halftime at a Defiance High School football game. When she was presented with the check for $5,000, a voice in the stands yelled out, "She'll need it with all those kids!" and a thousand people attending the game laughed. Mom and Dad used the money as a down payment on a sixty-year-old, two-story, four-bedroom house near the railroad tracks on Washington Avenue.

With his new X-53 Super Western Flyer, Dick got his newspaper route back. With the $5,000 for a down payment, we got a new house. With our mother, we began to suspect that we had a direct line to God.

CHAPTER TWO

Rhyme Does Pay

Moving across town and into a bigger home on Washington Avenue was a thrilling prospect. For one thing, this house had a bathtub, an entirely new concept for most of us. No more kids soaking in the kitchen sink after the dishes were done at night, in more or less public view.

Even Dad could appreciate this new privacy. The Saturday before we moved, he stood dripping wet and naked at the kitchen sink, giving himself a sponge bath, when our Latty Street neighbor Idawilma Masterson came flying through the back door, as she was wont to do, before anyone thought to stop her. If Dad jumped a mile, Idawilma jumped two.

"Idawilma!" Dad yelled. "Jesus Christ!"

"Kelly!" Idawilma screamed. "Lord A'mighty!"

Mom said later they sounded like "the dueling blasphemers of Defiance, Ohio."

Though our new house was only six blocks away, we said our good-byes to the neighbors on Latty Street—the Plassmans, the DeTrays, the Sorgs, and the Mastersons. (Defiance was half German, a quarter Irish, and a quarter everything else, including French.) "You think Idawilma will walk a mile to see me naked?" Dad asked, only half kidding.

We were excited to meet the new families on Washington—the Druhots, the Zipfels, the Bidlacks, and the McBrooms. The McBroom family, with nine kids, was almost as big as ours. With the two groups combined, we were an instant baseball game.

Knowing that Mom had made the down payment on this house herself with the prize money from the Western Auto contest made us feel rich. The new house had four small bedrooms—twice as many as the Latty Street house. Despite its compact size and proximity to the railroad tracks, 801 Washington seemed cavernous to us, palatial even, as we toured its empty rooms. "We'll never fill this one up," said Dad.

Mom knew better as she walked around dealing out sleeping arrangements. She and Dad would take the downstairs bedroom, along with baby Dave, whose bed would be a dresser drawer. Dick and Bub would share the small upstairs bedroom; Rog, Bruce, and Mike would sleep in a double bed in another ("the boys' room"); and Barb, Betsy, and I would be in the third upstairs bedroom ("the girls' room"). When Lea Anne, newly enrolled in nursing school, came home on the weekends, she would sleep on the living room couch.

I don't know where we got the beds to furnish the bedrooms, but certainly they were secondhand. Dick and Bub's bed may have been *third* hand, since one toss or turn too many slipped the wooden support slats off the ledges underneath. The first time the slats, springs, mattress, and bodies slammed to the floor in a heap, we thought the house had exploded. The second time, we shot up in bed before realizing the slats in Dick and Bub's room had given way again. After that, nobody heard a thing.

We learned early on to ignore other explosive nighttime eruptions, too. On the day we moved in, everyone noticed the double set of elevated train tracks just four houses up the street, but we never grasped how close they were until a fast-moving passenger train roared through at three o'clock the next morning. The sound began as a distant rumble in the west and quickly grew into a house-rattling, ear-splitting temblor that had us all standing wide-eyed in the hallway in a matter of seconds. Dad went right back to sleep, his snores seeping up through the floorboards to the second-floor bedrooms. After a few weeks, the trains lulled us all to sleep—they made us, in fact, feel safe.

Though we knew anything and everything would be turned into ammunition for Mom's contest-winning arsenal, shortly after our move to Washington Avenue, I was surprised to see her eyeing the small square of grass and dirt we called a front yard. It was partly green, partly balding due to the procession of shoes, skates, and baseball cleats that traversed it daily. The resulting poem brought in a

single but appreciated dollar bill from the Chicago
CBS radio program *Rhyme Does Pay:*

Lawn Time No See
When I survey
My barren plot . . .
Long stamping ground
For tyke and tot . . .
I must conclude
It's clear (alas!)
One cannot grow
Both kids and grass!

A lot of Mom's wins came in the form of prizes
with no resale value, but they were welcome nonethe-
less. She once won a set of Irish whiskey bottles
etched with the face of George Washington in various
shades of colored glass. Dad was disappointed that
they were empty, but Mom explained they were simply for decoration and set them in the front window
to catch the afternoon light.

She spent a lot of time standing at that window,
waiting for Pokey to bring cash prizes she could use
immediately to pay the milkman or newspaper boy.
As luck would have it, Pokey had put in for a trans-
fer to Washington, his home street. Pokey was even
slower on the Washington Avenue route than he had
been on Latty. Not only did he spend the entire
morning working the other side of the street, he
stopped for lunch and a nap at his house at the end
of the block before resuming delivery on our side of
the street. So Mom had to wait even longer for what
we all hoped were announcements of additional

*O*ur new house at 801 Washington Avenue had four small but (to us) luxurious bedrooms. For the first time, the Ryan kids didn't have to sleep nine to a room.

wins. More than once she would mumble, standing in the shafts of light reflected in the blue, green, lilac, and orange whiskey bottles, "We should have bought a house across the street."

Perhaps because the house was still sparsely furnished, we seemed to feel the bedlam of so many kids racing in and out more acutely than we had on Latty Street. Things went haywire on a regular basis, but if everyone was still standing at the end of the day, we considered ourselves fortunate. In one six-hour period, Mom made five trips to the hospital emergency room for various injuries: a bashed head from a thrown brick (me), a hand closed in a car door (Mike), a ripped ear (Bruce), a re-ripped ear (Bruce), and a fake pearl stuffed high into a nostril (Betsy).

For the most part, all the kids got along except for Rog and Bruce, two years apart in age and miles apart in opinion. They teased and taunted each other through the day, often exchanging blows. Even unconsciousness couldn't stop them. "Mom," said Bruce one morning, "Rog was sound asleep last night and socked me in the face."

Barb, seven years old, had the closest call of all. In the new house, Mom stashed snacks on a ledge above the back of the stove, safely out of reach of her children's hands. One night Barb climbed onto a chair next to the stove and leaned across the burners toward a plate of shortbread cookies, not realizing the cuff of her pajamas was resting too close to the pilot light. In an instant, the pajamas and Barb's arm were on fire, her screams piercing the household. Lea Anne, home from nursing school, was the first to react, bounding down the stairs in front of my mother while the rest of us stood still in shock. By the time we hurried after them, Lea Anne had smothered the flames and was administering to Barb's arm, which had first-degree burns up to the elbow. From that night on, Mom hid everything from doughnuts to bananas in the only place she knew her children would never look—the clothes dryer she had just won. More accurately, we knew the food was in there, but it was impossible to open the dryer door without making noise, and Mom would have been the first to know. She was also often the last to remember that she had hidden food in the dryer, opening the door at the end of a cycle, only to find the remains of a dozen doughnuts in there with the towels and sheets.

My own most harrowing night occurred the first time I was left in charge of the house. Mom, Dad, and the big kids were rushing out the door to attend a baseball play-off game. Dick and Bub would be pitching, and Dad was anxious to get good seats.

Even before they left, the day hadn't been a good one. At 7:00 A.M., a highway patrol officer knocked on the door to inform Mom that Bub had abandoned his junker of a car in the driveway of a grocery store across town, where it was currently holding up a long procession of beer, meat, bread, and Coke trucks. At 8:00 A.M., the washing machine stopped dead, followed by the dryer a few hours later—an emergency in any house with twelve people. About 11:00, Betsy got hit in the mouth with a swing board, loosening four front teeth, and at 12:00, Mike got beaned from behind by a baseball that raised a huge knot on his neck. That afternoon, I lost the monthly house and car insurance payment ($29). The envelope must have fallen out of my back pocket somewhere in my bike ride between home and the agent's office. Twenty-nine dollars was a lot of money for us. Without it our insurance would be canceled. I was mortified that I had lost the money, yet Mom still trusted me to baby-sit Mike, Barb, Betsy, and Dave. This made me feel somewhat better.

"Now, Tuff"—my nickname—"if anyone calls about finding that money," Mom said through the passenger-side window as our old blue Chevy backed out of the driveway, "be sure and take down the caller's name and number."

"Okay, Mom." Fat chance, I thought. Somebody was probably $29 richer already.

"And don't let Mike out of your sight."

Mike, with his fledgling scientific mind and growing fascination with explosive materials, could be trouble. A few weeks before, he found a bullet in the street and took it down to the basement for analysis. At first he tried to pry off the shell to get to the gunpowder inside, but that didn't work. So he held a burning match up to the bullet casing and blew a hole through the basement door.

"Okay," I said.

"And watch Betsy's eye patch."

Betsy had one strong eye and one weak eye that tended to cross. She didn't use the weak one because she couldn't see very much through it. The patch was meant to block the good eye so that she would use the weak eye and make it stronger. But whenever she thought no one was looking, Betsy switched the patch from the good eye to the bad eye so she could see better. You had to pay attention.

"Okay," I said.

"And don't let Davey upstairs by himself."

Dave, three years old at the time, had a habit of locking himself in the smallest bedroom upstairs. The lock was a simple up-down lever on the inside of the door. He loved to push the lever up to lock the door, but he was incapable of pulling the same lever down to open it. The only way to get him out of the locked room was to remove the metal air vent from the wall in the next room and pass Betsy's slim five-year-old body through the eight-inch-square opening. She was always so pleased to save Dave in this way, and Dave was always so pleased to be saved. Once inside, she would unlock the door and open it slowly to reveal the two of them beaming happily at all of us waiting out in the hallway.

"Okay," I said.

"And another thing," Dad said, leaning over Mom to make sure I heard him. "Don't let that godforsaken cat in the house." He meant Mammy, the black-and-white alley cat we had found living in the basement when we moved in. Dad couldn't abide the thought of a cat sharing a house with people, and Mammy seemed to sense this animosity, taking every opportunity to curl up on his side of the bed and shed copiously. No matter how many times someone picked her up and put her outside, she always managed to get back in. We could never figure out how.

"Okay." I felt confident on this one. I could see Mammy from where I stood—she was lying under the evergreen bushes in the front yard, staring sleepily at a moth dancing in the late afternoon light.

The Chevy had barely left the driveway when I

Harsh winter blizzards made the backyard a snowy playground for Mike, me, Betsy (snow-coated glasses), and Barb.

heard screams coming from upstairs. "Help! Tuffy, come quick!"

I raced up the stairs to find the bathroom filled with steam, the faucet roaring. Barb, Betsy, and Dave—the youngest kids, seven, five, and three—stood huddled in a little fat mass, as if they were a single body. "What's happening?" I yelled, although the roar of the water should have given me a clue.

"The hot-water handle fell in the bathtub!" said Barb. "It's too hot to get it out!"

The air in the bathroom was almost opaque, but I could see that the hot-water spigot on our ancient claw-footed tub was completely stripped—and no handle in sight. Barb had put the stopper in the drain, so the boiling-hot water was already roiling close to the brim of the tub. If I dipped my arm in to find the handle or pull the plug, I'd be scalded, but I had no idea how to turn off the faucet.

"Oh God, oh God, oh God!" I said this under my breath so as not to alarm the kids further, but my sotto voce didn't fool them. I was as panicked as they were, and they knew it. Running down the stairs, I collided with Mammy. "Who let the cat in?" I yelled to no one in particular, my screaming siblings following me down the stairs, through the living room, and out the front door like the tail on the end of a kite.

In less than a minute, we rocketed from door to door down half the block in search of an adult male with a set of tools:

"Hi, Mrs. Druhot." I attempted to sound calm. "Is Mr. Druhot home?" By the time Mrs. Druhot said that her husband was out, the four of us had already run halfway to the next neighbor's house.

"Hi, Mrs. Zipfel. Is Mr. Zipfel home?" No luck.

"Hi, Mrs. Bidlack. Is Mr. Bidlack home?" We were doomed.

Word traveled fast through the neighborhood that something was amiss at the Ryan house, and as heads of households ran out into the street to find out what the trouble was, somebody came up with a pair of pliers and barreled back to the house with us. By that time, the bathroom floor was under a half inch of water, with two throw rugs floating on top, but we got the water turned off and the crisis was over. Or so I thought.

As I toweled up the last of the overflow from the bathroom floor, a new set of screams suddenly exploded through the house, this time coming from the basement.

"Help! Tuffy! Help!"

I raced out of the bathroom and down the stairs to the first floor, even more alarmed this time because I smelled smoke. Faint puffs of chalky white were rising up through the cold air vents in the first floor as I ran past. "Oh God," I said. "Oh God, oh God, oh God!" At the top of the basement steps, I met Barb, Betsy, and Dave charging upward—their small bodies moving like a single unit with three heads, their voices merged into one continuous peal: "MIKE SET THE COT ON FIRE!"

"Betsy!" I yelled as the three of them ran by. "Move the patch back to your good eye!"

Plowing up the stairs behind them came Mike, his face bright with fear and adrenaline, his arms carrying a smoking mattress that had been molding away down there for years. He shot by me and leapt out the kitchen door to the backyard, where he dumped the mattress and doused it with the garden hose.

"Mike! What's the *matter* with you?" I screamed. "Why in the world would you set fire to a mattress?"

"It was an experiment!" he yelled. "I didn't think mold would burn!"

After all the hubbub, the five of us—Mike, Barb, Betsy, Dave, and I—settled in the living room to watch TV in an attempt to calm down. The theme music from *Bonanza* had just started when Mammy strolled through the room and stopped at the front door. Too pooped to care anymore about her unauthorized presence, we simply stared at her.

"Who keeps letting her in?" I asked.

"Not me," said Mike.

"I like her," said Barb, "but I didn't let her in."

Just then Mammy leapt up from a spot directly beneath the doorknob, grabbed it in midair with both paws, and twisted it to the left. As she dropped to the floor, the door opened. She walked out to the front porch. We followed, mesmerized, then watched as she repeated the procedure on the porch door.

"Okay," I said, after a moment's awed silence, "we can tell Mom, but we can never tell Dad."

By the time Mom and Dad got home, the house felt damp and smelled like toasted mildew. Mike was grounded for the rest of his life, but the bathtub episode didn't surprise my parents, considering the advanced age of the house. In the only good news, a woman did call to say that she found an envelope with our name on it and $29 inside. Honesty like this, even in a small Midwestern town like Defiance, was extraordinary. Oddly, Mom had almost forgotten about the lost money. She had been too caught up in the thrill of watching Bub pitch an almost perfect game—he had struck out twenty batters. She had also won a baseball that night during a pregame All-Star baseball trivia contest and was still thinking how close she had come to winning more. "I missed the question about who picks the league's best players," she said. "That darned Bub told me it was only the managers, but it's the managers *and* the fans. If I'd known that, I'd have probably gotten a glove or a ticket to the All-Star game."

She would have, too, and handed them out as birthday presents. We saw the light in her eyes as she talked about the near miss at the park. The loss didn't seem to deter her. Mom was like a catcher diving after a foul ball—just because she missed one didn't keep her from going after the next one.

CHAPTER THREE

Supermarket

Spree

Our new home at 801 Washington looked unfurnished even after we moved in. We had no money to buy appliances, let alone furniture. But in the months after winning the Western Auto contest, Mom entered a slew of other contests and won enough things to make the house seem functional: an automatic coffeemaker, a Deepfreeze home freezer, a Westinghouse refrigerator, a Motorola radio, two wall clocks, three wool blankets, a box of household tools, a set of kitchen appliances, and three pairs of Arthur Murray shoes.

Many of these prizes were not what Mom had been aiming for. The wall clocks, for example, were seventh prizes in a contest whose first prize was a station wagon. She was always trying to replace the dilapidated family Chevy with something a bit more dependable. Just to start the car most mornings required a ten-person push so Dad could pop the clutch and rumble off to work in a cloud of blue smoke. Even so, the two wall clocks didn't go to waste. Mom gave one to our aunt Lucy and hung the other in the dining room, where it covered a baseball-sized dent of missing plaster that no one would ever own up to.

The Westinghouse refrigerator, though, was a first prize in an aluminum foil contest, for which Mom submitted this 25-words-or-less entry on why she liked using Alcoa Wrap:

I like strong Alcoa Wrap because *Alcoa resists "all thumbs" handling—stays whole to keep juices and flavors IN, ashes OUT, of cookout meals; deserves merit badge for simplifying Scout cookery.*

The Deepfreeze home freezer, also a first prize, was gigantic—four feet high, five feet wide, and three feet deep—so big it would have been more appropriate in a restaurant or an army mess hall. It looked very empty with just a single gallon of ice cream sitting in the bottom of it. Most of us couldn't even reach the container without falling in. But my mother was ingenious. If we needed clothes, she made them. If we needed a freezer, she won one. If we needed food to fill the new freezer, she was going to win that too.

In a Seabrook Farms contest, Mom was awarded a shopping spree at the local Big Chief Supermarket. She submitted her 25-word entry in poem form:

Wide selections, priced to please her;
Scads of Seabrook's in their freezer;

Warmth that scorns the impersonal trend,
Stamps "Big Chief" as the housewife's friend.

A shopping spree in a supermarket was not what anyone else would have considered a major win, but to Mom it was the answer to our prayers. Our aunt Lucy, a bank teller who lived down the road in Bryan, bought a lot of our weekly groceries, but a freezer filled to capacity would relieve Mom's worries about food for months.

Weeks before the scheduled shopping spree, Mom gathered the family around the dining room table to help plan her assault. Dad had fled the scene, increasingly sullen since "Moneybags," his sarcastic nickname for Dick, had won the Western Auto contest.

"Okay," Mom said, "there are some ironclad rules. First, I've got only ten minutes to grab everything I can."

"That's not very long," I said.

"Just stay in the candy aisle," offered Mike.

"Second," she said, "everything has to fit in one shopping cart."

"One?" Betsy said. "I thought each of us would get a cart."

"Third, everything has to be edible."

"Bruce will eat anything," said Rog.

"Open your mouth, Rog," Bruce said, clenching his fist. "I've got your lunch right here."

As they lunged across the table at each other, Mom yelled, "Knock it off, you two! I'm not finished." They sat back down, trading menacing stares as Mom continued.

"Fourth," she said, "only one of everything. I can get different sizes of the same brand, or same sizes of different brands, but only one of each brand and size."

"The list would have been shorter," said Dick, "if they'd listed the things you *can* have."

"It's still okay," Bub said. "Everything comes in lots of brands and sizes."

"Besides," said Lea Anne, who was home from nursing school for the weekend, "none of the meat packages will weigh exactly the same, so you can at least start there."

"One last thing," Mom said. "I have to fill the cart by myself. No one can help me."

"We don't get to go along?" moaned Barb, expressing the sagging disappoint-

ment we all felt. I wasn't the only one with visions of being let loose for a few minutes in aisles filled with potato chips, jelly beans, cupcakes, and ice cream.

"You can come," said Mom, "but you'll have to stay back with the store clerks and the Seabrook representative. What you *can* help me with is planning how to do it."

We decided that the first step would be mapping out the store, aisle by aisle, so Mom could memorize every inch of the place. The Big Chief Supermarket was huge, about half a football field long. Dad had to join in this time—he was the only one in the family who could drive—taking several of us along to scout it out.

Anybody else in Mom's position might have gone after the usual milk and bread and bologna and ketchup. Not Mom. "Think big," she said. "If I'm going to get a cartload of free food, I'm not going to waste cart space or time going after on-sale chicken parts and fish sticks." (We ate fish sticks almost every Friday night for supper.) "We can ignore the five-pound bags of sugar and gallons of milk, too."

"The Mars bars are on aisle five," said Mike.

"I want you kids to taste chateaubriand, New York steak, lobster, and anything else you've never tried before. Heck, I want to try them too.

"I'll have to grab a token amount of Seabrook's frozen food first," Mom added, ever aware of pleasing the contest sponsors. "But after that I'm heading for the meat department."

The only problem was the shopping cart itself. It looked no bigger than the inside of a large suitcase. Even the bottom rack seemed paltry, barely big enough for a ten-pound sack of potatoes. While we stood over the meat cases at the back of the store, the butcher, Bob Wallen, came out to say hello. Everyone in Defiance, including Bob, had already heard about Mom's upcoming shopping spree.

"If there's any special cut of meat you're interested in, Evelyn," he said, "tell me now, and I'll have it ready ahead of time."

"I'm half afraid I won't have room for everything I want," she said. "The cart is so shallow."

Bob's blue eyes lit up. He came out from around the counter and measured the sides with his knife-scarred hands. "Hey, we can fix that," he said. "I can cut some flat slabs of beef and extra-long sides of bacon. See, you can stand them on end all around the inside edge and make the sides *taller.*"

Now Mom's eyes lit up. "That would double the cart's capacity," she said. "Bob, you're going straight to heaven!"

"This is no ordinary shopping spree, Evelyn," Bob said, a huge grin on his round face. "This is a treasure hunt! You won't have to come back to my counter for a long, long time."

When the day of the shopping spree finally arrived, we were ready. Mom knew exactly what she wanted and where it was in the store. Even so, she was slightly nervous. In the car on the way there, she said, "I wish I had twenty minutes instead of ten. I wish all of you could help me. I wish I had won a station wagon instead of a shopping spree." Then she laughed and said, "Who am I kidding? This is going to be fun."

The shopping spree was scheduled to take place before the store opened for business. Mom had the option of doing it after business hours, but by that time of night Dad would have been too drunk to drive her to the store and too argumentative to be out in public. As our old Chevy pulled into the nearly empty lot on the appointed morning, we could see the store manager, Harvey Ward, the Seabrook executive, who I will call Miles Streeter, and a few clerks waiting just inside the glass door for Mom's arrival. She stepped out of the front passenger seat and into the store, and everybody applauded. Mr. Streeter watched the stream of kids pouring out of the car like clowns out of a Volkswagen.

"How did you all fit in there?" he asked as we trailed into the store after Mom.

"With a shoehorn," Mom laughed, as she pulled a shopping cart from the rack. "They won't get in the way. They're just going to yell out the time every few minutes so I can keep on schedule."

And then an act of kindness occurred, altering the outcome of the day for the Ryan family. Mr. Streeter looked at us and looked again at the rule sheet. He placed his thumb over the line specifying that the shopper couldn't have help. He turned to two of the store clerks, Pauline and Hazel, who had come in early to watch Mom's ten minutes of fame. Both in their sixties, the two women were rooting for her as much as any of us kids were. They also had a better understanding of the store's layout than Mom did, Mr. Streeter knew, and they wore industrial-strength shoes that had run up and down these aisles many times before. "I'm going to turn my back," he told them. "Any help you give Mrs. Ryan in filling the cart won't be seen by me." Everyone's eyes lit up.

Mom tested the cart by rolling it back and forth a

few times, making sure she didn't have to fumble around the store on defective wheels. Harvey adjusted his bow tie and held up a stopwatch. Mom's hands gripped the cart handle. She bent forward slightly, standing like an Olympic sprinter waiting for the starting gun.

"Go!" yelled Harvey as he clicked the watch on.

Down the aisle they all flew, Hazel and Pauline following Mom in a trot toward the meat department, where Bob pointed out the prepackaged sheets of beef ribs and bacon—even extra-long rolls of salami—to use in supporting the sides. Pauline and Hazel held the slabs of meat up in the cart and Mom filled in the center, hauling huge beef and pork roasts, platter-sized steaks, and six-packs of filet mignon out of the case and tossing them into the cart.

"Seven minutes to go!" called Rog from the front of the store.

"I think we should split up," said Mom, her voice a few octaves higher than usual. "I'll take the frozen food aisle. You two hit the European food section."

"What do you want?" Hazel asked, already running toward aisle eight on the heels of Pauline.

"Exotic things!" Mom said. "Expensive things! The *good* stuff! But only one of each!"

At the front of the store, Bub lifted Betsy up onto his shoulders. "Six minutes, Mommy!" she shouted.

Mom shot through the frozen food aisle like a missile, grabbing game hens and emptying the seafood section of lobster thermidor, crab claws, filet of sole, salmon steaks, halibut, everything but fish sticks. "Absolutely no fish sticks!" yelled Mom, as Pauline and Hazel careened around the corner, arms filled with cans of pâté, mushrooms, caviar, artichoke hearts, blanched asparagus, hollandaise sauce, and who knows what else.

"Three minutes!" shouted Bruce.

Mom wrestled with several quarts of gourmet ice cream. Pauline and Hazel loaded up on frozen broccoli in cheese sauce, lasagna with truffles, bourbon-laced ladyfingers, and French chocolate sauce.

At the one-minute mark, Mike yelled from the front of the store. "Candy in aisle five!" And a barrage of Toblerone chocolates, jars of roasted pumpkin seeds, and several six-, eight-, and twelve-packs of Mounds and Almond Joy candy bars landed atop the piles of meat, frozen food, and canned goods already in the cart.

In the final seconds, as Pauline and Hazel jammed the bottom rack with fresh pineapples and coconuts, Mom tried and failed to balance two family-sized bags of potato chips on the pyramid of cans that was now taller than the meat walls.

"Hurry, Mom!" Barb screamed, as Mom and the cart rocketed out of the produce section on the way to the checkout stand. Giving up trying to weigh the bags of chips down with cans of Finnish sardines as she ran, she grabbed a large candy cane from a Christmas display on her way by and stabbed it through the heart of the bags into a box of frozen bonbons below.

A cheer erupted from the assembled spectators as Mom rounded the magazine racks and nearly catapulted her teetering mountain of goods into the checkout aisle. "Time's up!" yelled Harvey, bringing his stopwatch down with a mighty click.

It was over.

In all, Mom netted $411.44 worth of food (the equivalent of $3,000 today), a fortune in our eyes.

Later we would learn to hide the imported food from him, but that night Dad inexplicably threw a dozen cans through the open back door into the yard.

We sat around the kitchen table, which was piled high with the rest of the canned delicacies, in silence. When Dad finally went to bed, Bruce turned to Mom. "What was that all about?"

"I don't know," she sighed. "He's been drinking."

"What exactly is caviar?" asked Barb.

"Fish eggs," said Mom.

A long silence engulfed the room. It was self-explanatory. No one was going to eat the caviar.

"Do you know that U.S. Army research has shown a relationship between intelligence and a willingness to eat unfamiliar foods?" Mom said.

Except for Mom, nobody would eat the lobster either—it was just too different from fish sticks.

 PART TWO

CHAPTER FOUR

The Sleeping
Giant

The supermarket spree filled our new freezer and then some. We couldn't cram in the sides of beef no matter how many people sat on the lid. So Dad put the slabs of meat in the backseat of the car and drove them over to Goldenetz's, a small food market across the river on the east side of town where he and Mom did most of their day-to-day grocery shopping. Mr. Goldenetz knew that Mom had chosen the Big Chief for the shopping spree only because the store was big and carried an extensive stock of expensive foods. Goldenetz's would lose the publicity, but Mom would be back to shop at the smaller, friendlier grocery store closer to home. So Mr. Goldenetz had made Mom a magnanimous offer. "Go load up on all their high-priced meat and bring it over here, Evelyn," he said. "We'll keep it in our freezer for you." Considering our family's daily consumption—twelve quarts of milk lasted two days—the sides of beef would disappear from Gold-enetz's freezer in a few weeks.

Despite our exhilaration after Mom's supermarket spree, Dad's moods seemed to grow darker. Each night after supper, while he held forth in the kitchen to an audience of bottles, the kids did homework or watched television in the living room, while Mom sat on the couch with her contest notebook, perfecting her latest entry:

Joy is so pleasantly habit-forming
(generous suds, cleaner-feeling dishwater, and
* cleaner,*
brighter dishes become dishwashing habits—nice
* ones)*
one bottle calls for another.

In her own way, Mom was grappling with the realization that Dad's "problem drinking," as it was called then, had begun to create a disharmony in the house. Even inanimate objects seemed out of sorts. Despite their newness, major appliances started to break down. Mom had won most of them in contests, but we couldn't afford the maintenance or repairs to keep minor flaws from growing into big ones. No one in the house was handy enough to fix the things that needed fixing. Although he sculpted tools out of metal at his job at the screw machine shop, Dad didn't know how to use them. Usually, he broke more things, thumbs and knuckles included, than he repaired.

Family lore held that Dad, as the youngest of seven children in his family, had grown up with no chores or responsibilities and had never developed the routine skills expected of an adult man. Further, his whole family was known for being distinctly unhandy, particularly his mother, our grandma Ryan, whose idea of tying back a curtain was to nail it to the wall. A thin, spry woman who had learned to fix things quickly and crudely on the family farm just outside of Defiance, Grandma moved through her days full-bore, slamming every door she passed through, breaking plates and cups just by using them. In 1909, she built a fire in the kitchen stove that burned the family's house to the ground; in 1935, she razed a second farmhouse the same way. The trees surrounding the house survived the second fire—you can still see the scorch marks high up on the trunks.

"Grandma is the kindest person you'd ever want to meet," Mom used to say, but the family knew she was often "helpful" in unhelpful ways. One Saturday night, when we lived on Latty Street, Grandma Ryan agreed to baby-sit while Mom and Dad spent a rare night out at the movies. Mom was nervous about leaving her in charge, but she remembered that Grandma had raised seven children and tended countless farm animals, all of whom survived the experience. How much harm could an elderly woman do? Mom thought. So she threw caution (and, as it turned out, the bulk of her living room furniture) to the wind.

When they returned that night, Mom and Dad instantly noticed something amiss. The large wool living room rug had disappeared, and the dilapidated, frayed couch had puffed up considerably. Grandma greeted them with the announcement that she had "redone the davenport." Its squashed springs and flattened stuffing had bothered her, so she got our biggest carving knife from a kitchen drawer and slit open the seat along the front edge. Then she rolled up the rug, stuffed it into the five-foot-long slash, and nailed the seat cover back to the frame. "Now you can sit on the thing without busting your behind," she explained proudly. Dad and Mom were aghast, but the next morning, the rest of us had to admit our behinds rested a little higher.

Mom may not have been handy in the traditional sense, but she was a born inventor. She began thinking up ingenious Rube Goldberg solutions to fix household problems, like the new clothes dryer that ceased to work six months after she won it in the Western Auto bicycle contest. With a little "dickering," as she called it, Mom discovered the problem: a faulty pilot light that needed relighting before each use. This should have been simple to do, but the gas jet located at the back of the dryer was accessible only through a small door at the front, two inches above the floor.

No one had an arm long enough to ignite the pilot light, so Mom invented her own method. Every time she used the dryer (at least once a day), she brought out two matches, a pair of scissors, and a fan: Lying flat on her stomach, she would grasp one unlit match with the tips of the scissors, light the second match, use it to light the first, then stick the scissors through the door as far as she could reach. The fan, brought oh-so-carefully to the door with her other hand, was used to "jump the flame," as Mom explained it. Sure enough, the breeze from the fan blew the flame from the match to the pilot light. Peering over Mom's shoulder through the little door, we could see a drop of blue fire dance across the dark abyss to land with perfect balance on the gas jet. "There," Mom said every day of her life at 801 Washington, "that's a little better."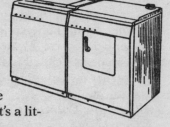

The garbage disposal in the kitchen sink presented another kind of problem, the kind beyond even my mother's imaginative stabs at home repair. Ignoring any attempt on our part to start it with the on/off switch, the disposal's motor leapt into operation only, it seemed, when it wanted to. Throughout the day, we'd pile the garbage in the sink and leave it there, waiting for Old Unfaithful (as Mom called it) or The Sleeping Giant (as Dad called it) or The Monster (as the kids called it) to awaken from its sleep. While most families had leftovers, ours had leftover garbage. At some point in the evening, usually during the most gripping moment of our favorite TV show, a gargantuan rumble would arise from the vicinity of the kitchen, and the disposal would take off with all the velocity of a rocket leaving for the moon. With the first hint of these rumblings we'd fly out of our chairs and hastily begin dumping in the garbage we'd accumulated since its last show of life.

"This infernal thing thinks *it* owns *us!*" Mom said after one noontime eruption that could be heard all the way from the backyard and brought us tumbling through the back door to stuff the disposal before it stopped. Still, what we couldn't repair, we got used to. We had no plans to buy a new garbage disposal, probably ever.

In spite of the failing appliances, life took on an ebullient tone in the Ryan house after the supermarket shopping spree. Mom renewed her efforts to have her poems printed in the Toledo *Blade*, this one based on her own allergic tendencies:

Allergy in a Country Churchyard
Friend, bring few roses to my bier;
Go easy on sweet peas;
And . . . Heavens, friend . . . no goldenrod . . .
Or I'll sit up and sneeze!

She also used our cat, Mammy, for inspiration in a Puss 'N Boots contest promising a $10,000 first prize:

Puss 'n Boots pampers Kittenlittle's fish 'r meat
"druthers,"
proves purrsuasively *appetizing, provides balanced*
nutrition—
making every portion a daily dosin' that purrPET-
tuates purrfect *"shape"!*

What Mammy had "purrfected," in fact, was letting herself into and out of the house whenever she felt like it. Often we looked up from our homework to see the front doorknob turn, expecting a person to walk in, only to see Mammy stroll through the open doorway with a don't-bother-to-get-up-on-my-account attitude. Dad, who was unaware of Mammy's magical powers, was outraged at her frequent presence indoors. "If I ever see one of you kids letting that mangy cat into the house, I'll throw the both of you out."

Dad thought all animals were smelly and dirty and belonged outdoors. Mammy was fastidiously clean. We couldn't understand how a man who abhorred pet odors could love the aroma and taste of Limburger cheese, which he kept, wrapped in paper, in the refrigerator. The stench was so powerfully foul that it traveled easily through walls and floorboards, sending many a kid flying outdoors whenever Dad opened the package. The one occupant of the house who shared Dad's interest in Limburger was Mammy, who more than once attempted to open the refrigerator to get at it. She failed, only because the door handle was gone, broken off in some long-ago kitchen scuffle. Opening the fridge required slipping a screwdriver between the rubber door seals at just the right spot to pop the door loose.

Almost overnight, it seemed, the empty, cavernous house Mom had won for us began to feel as crowded and confining as the single-story rental on Latty Street. Since there weren't enough tables and chairs for eleven or twelve of us to sit down at once, the Ryan kids ate in shifts. The older kids ate in the dining room, the younger kids in the kitchen. Mom stood at the stove and ate while she was cooking. Never in my entire childhood did I see my mother sit down to eat lunch or supper.

No one ever lingered over dessert. While Mom had her notebooks to attend to, the rest of us were united in a common pursuit—staying away from Dad. One night, I took refuge in the living room and found that everyone else had the same idea. Rog sat on the front steps reading his comic books. Dick and Bub played catch in the street. I stepped over Bruce and Mike, who sat on the hardwood floor playing rummy, and propped open my math book on the coffee table. Barb, Betsy, and Dave rocked to and fro on one couch singing their favorite song, the lyrics varying according to the singer. Barb—*My bonnie lies over the ocean;* Betsy—*My body lies over the ocean;* Dave—*My mommy lies over the ocean.* Mom sat on the other couch with her feet up, busy with an entry for a poetry contest:

Hippopotapoem
Behold the hippopotamus
bestowing hippo kisses
Upon a hippopotamiss
Who's not his hippomissus.

Turning to my homework, my fingers froze. Too late I realized that I had left my assignment on the table in the kitchen, where it was no longer safe to be. Ordinarily, Mom, the bravest among us, would retrieve crucial items from the kitchen when Dad was drunk. But seeing her engrossed in her contest, I didn't want to bother her.

Besides, I had an idea. From the living room I could hear the voices coming from Dad's radio, which tonight was tuned to Major League Baseball. I waited to hear how the game was going. In a moment the announcer said, "With three men on base, the Indians hope to break it open here. They already lead three to one."

Dad loved the Cleveland Indians but despised the

announcer, Jimmy Dudley. "Yeah?" he snarled. "What would *you* know about it?"

I crept closer to the kitchen. Standing just outside the kitchen door, I peered in. My homework was sitting under a half-full bottle of Pabst Blue Ribbon beer. Dad stood facing the radio on the counter, his back inches away from the table. He poured himself another shot of whiskey. I hoped Dad couldn't hear my heart pounding over the play-by-play of the game as I waited for the right moment. This was going to be close.

"Fastball on the inside corner for strike two," said Jimmy Dudley, to a roar of disapproval from the fans, including Dad, who growled, "When's the last time you had your eyesight checked, you four-eyed moron!"

My moment was coming. I inhaled deeply, adrenaline filling my veins. "Bases loaded, nobody out," Dudley continued. "Another three-two count. Here comes the pitch."

Now! I thought. I cut around the corner into the kitchen, lifted the beer bottle, and grabbed my homework sheet just as Dudley yelled, "Strike three called!" and my father yelled, "You idiot!" smashing his fist into the countertop and toppling several jars of jam and jelly. I was barely out the kitchen door when Dad turned to the table for his bottle of beer. He hadn't noticed the small breeze left in my wake, and I hadn't even disturbed Mom, who clearly was lost in creative thought.

But he's no hippocrit, is he,
This hippopotamister

> *Because the hippopotamiss*
> *Is his little hipposister.*

We had learned by this time to follow Mom's example and dissociate from the white noise of Dad's outbursts. There was no doubt we were better students for it. It was only when we looked up from our books that we heard any sound at all. Such a studious atmosphere reigned in the living room that Mom had begun rereading her favorite poets—Carl Sandburg and Robert Frost. Her own poetry was influenced by Ogden Nash, whose talent for brevity in humor she had long admired. She often wrote poems for no reason other than her own satisfaction:

> *No woman problem had young Adam,*
> *Being made before they had 'em.*

"Birds of a Feather" not only gave her satisfaction, it earned $25 from the Toledo *Blade:*

> *Birds of a Feather*
> *To public buildings,*
> *Types indigenous*
> *Are litter-ally*
> *Always pigeonous.*

Mom spent the money on a new baseball glove for Dick, whose skill at playing and pitching seemed to improve with every game he played. She had been watching Dick's progress since his first Little League game, and despite breaking his arm in the bicycle accident that lost him his paper route—temporarily, it turned out, after Mom won the new bike—Dick, at fifteen, was turning into "a top-flight pitcher," as Mom put it.

Most of the Ryan kids were inheriting Dad's love of baseball—including his addiction to live broadcasts. Although his worst rages were often triggered by an umpire's calls, the background drone of a baseball game on the radio brought a certain peace of mind to each of us, including my mother. She needed it. When there was no game to hold Dad's attention, he entertained himself with a rant using the F word, the D word, the GD word, and the S word and centering on Mom's family name (Lehman) and the small town where she grew up (Sherwood, Ohio).

The younger kids took it for granted that "Lehman" and "Sherwood" were swear words like the others Dad bellowed into the night. My mother didn't like to hear profanity, and she certainly never spoke it. She had always told us that swearing was the sign of a lackluster vocabulary and, worse, a stunted imagination. "There are so many interesting words to use, alone or in combination," she said, "that I don't know why anyone would fall back on one-syllable obscenities."

The older kids were beginning to think that my mother had a secret. At the least, they suspected that she must have regretted marrying Dad. We all noticed that my parents didn't celebrate their anniversary like other couples we knew. They didn't even acknowledge it. The few pictures Mom kept of their wedding were stuck away in a closet somewhere and rarely mentioned or displayed. None of us knew when they were married, where, or who attended the ceremony.

One of the rare photos of Mom and Dad on their wedding day in 1936.

Still, our life seemed as normal as anybody's. The great difference for us was the part that didn't seem at all normal—Mom's ability to turn the mundane and ordinary into what she called "a little art form." So when *Parents* magazine sponsored a homemaker's "What's the Idea" contest for the best original suggestions on improving the average housewife's daily life, Mom leapt for her notebook. Making money by turning household tips into poetry was right up her alley:

When washing windows come cleaning days
Stroke opposite windows in opposite ways;
Then it's easy to tell which side is OK
'Cause those streaks you missed go "that-a-way."

Mom never washed the windows this way in our house. She didn't have the time. The porch windows—about two hundred seven-inch-square panes—were lucky to be hosed off once a year from the outside. However, she won a set of sleek new carving knives for the suggestion, allowing Dad to toss out the blunt old gas station giveaways we had used as long as I could remember.

Then Mom went on to the next household tip: How to wax wood floors and have a family party at the same time.

In the age of labor-saving devices, this one, she felt, was a beaut: Mom simply applied wax on the hardwood floors and had everyone in the house go foot-skating in three or four pairs of their oldest socks. The more we skated, the slicker and more mirrorlike the floor became, and soon even Dad was laughing at the combined ballroom-dancing and Roller Derby going on in the living room.

The fact that not a single floor wax company had yet sponsored a contest calling for household tips of this nature did not deter our mother. "Why, Johnson's would be fools not to follow up on this idea," she said, folding a letter to the Johnson's floor wax company in which she suggested they do that very thing. "And when they do, I'll have my entry ready." It wouldn't be the first time.

CHAPTER FIVE

Father of

the Year

In 1955, almost a year after moving to Washington Avenue, Mom had collected enough contest cash to give us an Easter bonanza that loaded even Mike down with more candy than he could handle. She received $25 from the American Tobacco Company alone for this Lucky Strike jingle:

Send me laundry, send me dough
Send me Luckies to send my beau
I'm true to him, he's true to me
And we're true to Luckies, eternally.

Usually when Pokey the mailman brought a letter announcing a win, Mom knew without even opening the envelope where it came from and which contest she had won. But when Pokey brought Mom an additional $10 from Nabisco, she couldn't remember what contest it was for, let alone what her entry for it might have been. This was happening more often—a bounty of small checks that kept us almost comfortable. In this case the $10, combined with the Lucky Strike money, bought a hefty Easter ham and about ten pounds of chocolate eggs and bunnies.

During the early morning egg hunt in the back-yard, Betsy, combing the back porch for painted eggs and jelly beans, found an unexpected prize. Mammy had given birth to a litter of kittens in a box of old towels Mom had been saving to rip into rags. The same day, a well-meaning relative brought us an Easter chick about the size and shape of a fuzzy ten-nis ball, whom we named Charley. Our initial fears that Mammy might regard him as food were un-founded. Mammy, sensing that Charley was a moth-erless babe, treated him like one of her own kittens, nudging and purring at him as he settled in to sleep with the rest of the litter. Not long after, Mom looked up from the kitchen sink, dish in hand, and called us to the window to witness a very odd sight: Mammy walking across the yard, followed single file by five black-and-white kittens and one yellow chick.

Mom regarded the Mammy-Charley relationship as more than a brief poem for a newspaper or *Reader's Digest* submission. In her best Life in the Ryan Family style, she sat down one day and began writing the paragraphs that would become "The Chicken Who Thought He Was a Cat." In the piece, she described Mother Cat, as she called Mammy in the story, accepting Charley "as one of her own, even granting him bathing privileges" by licking him clean, "though she discovered that in spite of great persistence, feathers that grow downward just will not lay flat if they are licked upward."

Charley loved it. "He submitted to this grooming as though it were his due, his beady red eyes almost crossing in ecstasy as Mother Cat's abrasive tongue sandpapered his scrawny head; shared the food put out for the cats; and when we finally got around to buying corn for him he eyed it curiously, picked it up, dropped it, and refused it flatly."

Charley began to relate to Mammy's kittens as his brothers and sisters. "He would scrabble among the leaves beneath the shrubbery to find bugs and worms and call the cats frantically. He was absurdly crestfallen when his friends refused these treasures, though he never let their lack of appreciation affect his own conduct at their festive board. Whenever cat smorgasbord was announced he fell over himself and all six cats trying to get his share and theirs, too."

For Charley's story, Mom was awarded an astounding $50 by the Toledo *Blade*, which she put to immediate use by paying part of our dental bill. This and her continuing entries for weekly and monthly contests kept us "turning the corner," as she liked to say. Whenever we fell hopelessly into debt again, she wouldn't wait at the window for news of wins from Pokey's mailbag. She'd walk down the block to meet him halfway.

Dad didn't mind Mammy, Charley, and the kittens as long as they stayed outside. In fact he enjoyed watching them play in the backyard grass, wrestling around in a pile of fur and feathers. At these times, his laughter was sweet and affectionate. On rare occasions, Mom would reminisce about their courtship in the mid-1930s.

When the two of them were "running around together," Mom told us, Dad could be intelligent and entertaining. We marveled at the news that our father sang tenor at St. Mary's Catholic Church and at town and county dances, where he also played the violin with a band. Kelly and Evelyn met at one of those county dances, opposites colliding in an appreciation of differences. He had blue eyes, hers were brown; he was Irish Catholic, she was German Methodist; she loved to read and write; he loved to drink and dance. They wrote each other's names over and over again on a cocktail napkin. "All the women were crazy about him," Mom said. "Women always love a good Irish tenor." He was everything she wasn't. Her family hated him immediately.

Mom came from a Protestant background of European settlers, churchgoing teetotalers whose idea of music was confined to hymns. Even their names were oddly spelled, difficult to pronounce, yet somehow very Midwestern (traditional and hardworking) and very foreign at the same time. The people Mom grew up with in Sherwood were mostly German—Fitzenrider, Ehlinger, Shingledecker, Weisgerber, Weisen-burger, Schlotterbeck, Zuttermeister. Their names sometimes looked like out-and-out typographical errors—Halbgewoks, Schmiedebusch. Virtually all distrusted Catholicism, especially Irish Catholics.

Not long after they were married, Mom said, Dad had a car accident, and a piece of the windshield slit his throat as he was thrown from the car. He was lying on the pavement, blood pumping from his carotid artery, when a passerby applied pressure to the wound to stop the bleeding. He would have been dead in minutes otherwise. The doctors discovered that his vocal cords had been partially severed, and he couldn't sing anymore, at least not the way he wanted to, not the way he used to. So he never did again.

Everyone in town, it seemed, wanted to believe the Ryan family wasn't in peril due to Dad's drinking, and most of the time they were right. Pots and pans might fly from one room to another, plates and glasses might crash about, but as long as Dad stayed in the kitchen, we learned to live relatively undisturbed.

Until the night Mom discovered that the church, especially, wasn't going to be of any help. The Cleveland Indians had just lost another game. Dad was throwing kitchen chairs into the backyard and threatening to kill the neighbors if they objected to the sight of flying furniture. Thinking that the presence of Dad's brothers (with whom he wasn't on speaking terms) might infuriate him even more, Mom called our parish priest.

Father McCague had been in the business of religion a long time, so Mom figured he must have acquired some mediation skills along the way. He was just as Irish as Dad, though his red hair was turning gray and had receded enough to reveal a skull as pink as his face. He was imposing in his brown, button-front cassock, and with the extra-long black-beaded rosary hanging from his belt, he looked as if he had come directly from God. When he stepped onto the porch, we backed away in awe.

Father talked to Dad in private for half an hour or so and then to Mom for a few minutes at most. Dad calmed down, but only because a stranger was in the house. Father's message to Mom was clear. He expected Mom and the rest of us to endure Dad's behavior and "keep the family whole." According to the church, putting up with an alcoholic and abusive husband was considered at best a woman's lot and at worst her fault. I think we stopped listening to Father as soon as he opened his mouth and we detected the familiar aroma of whiskey on his breath.

Father wasn't alone in his stern advice to women like my mother. Lovelorn columnists of the day preached that a wife should quit complaining and learn to love her husband better so he wouldn't feel neglected and turn to drink. Instead of getting mad, Mom chuckled openly at this idea. To her, the world's blind deference to the man of the house was a grand mistake that we should blithely ignore. Besides, this was exactly the kind of idealization she could use for contesting.

In "Flaw," for example, Dad's worst trait is a humorous, benign ignorance that the world at that time found universally charming in husbands. She received $6.75 for it.

Flaw
A husband's a treasure,
A jewel, and a joy;
An in-the-rough diamond;
A gem of a boy;
A pearl of great price,
It has often been said . . .

But mine has one foible
That makes me see red!
It's been a hard day
From the opening gong;
The washing, the cooking
Have all turned out wrong;
The kids have been hellions;
The house is a wreck.
Now, watch how far Hubby can
Stick out his neck:
With hand on the doorknob,
With pause to survey,
With "Mother, what have you
Been doing all day?"

We were often astonished that my mother presented a picture-perfect image of my father in her contest entries and poetry. On entry blanks, he was an ideal dad, in the tradition of Ward Cleaver on *Leave It to Beaver*—responsible, hardworking, fun-loving, a true "master of the house." In a Crisco–Duncan Hines "Father of the Year" contest, she nominated Dad with this entry sent in under my name:

My father should be named "Father of the Year"
because
Who "manned" the helm when Mom was sick?
Who mastered bargain-hunting, QUICK?
Expertly minded lass and lad?
That selfless, self-"maid" Mom, MY DAD!

With that, Mom only won one of five hundred third prizes—a Van Heusen shirt. I thought the judges didn't award Mom the top prize because they some

how knew that Dad was nothing like the man described in the poem.

The one person Dad loved without reservation was his sister Lucy, who, nine years older than Dad, had raised and protected him in their brawling family of seven children. And Lucy, in turn, loved us. Every Thursday, I waited on the curb for her green DeSoto to turn the corner from Arabella onto Washington Avenue on its way to our house. Aunt Lucy was a bank teller who liked to bring canvas bags of pennies or nickels or dimes for the three of us who were coin collectors (Bruce, Mike, and me) to sift through for old coins. On the days she forgot to bring coins, she would give us a $50 bill that was ours to keep for three hours, the precise length of her visit.

Any bills from her purse carried the faint aroma of her sweet lilac perfume, making the money seem all the more valuable to us as we ran the five blocks between home and the First Federal Savings & Loan, taking shortcuts under the railroad trestle, across the flat, black asphalt of St. Mary's playground, and down the rocky alley behind the Presbyterian church. At the bank, we traded the bill for bags of pennies or nickels and ran back home. Unlike the professional collectors we yearned to be, with their numismatic catalogs and magnifying glasses, we dumped the money onto the dining room table and clawed our way meticulously through the pile to find the old, valuable coins. One day I found several Indian head pennies. I was elated, and not just because of their cash value— probably a dollar each. "Touch this, Bruce," I said grandly as I placed a worn 1889 penny into his palm. "You are holding the past in your hand."

Once we removed any collectible coins from the pile, we rebagged the rest, ran back to the bank, and traded the bag for bills, which we returned to Lucy after running home again. She got back anywhere from $49 to $49.50 of her original loan.

I kept vigilant on my lookout for Lucy because she "drove like a Ryan," as those on Mom's side of the family liked to joke—making her arrival something of an event. On a typical Thursday afternoon, Lucy's car would come zooming down Washington at full speed. Just at the moment when I thought she would surely fly past our house, she would slam on the brakes and park abruptly, yet neatly, at the curb.

She walked like a Ryan, too, with speed and determination, pitched slightly forward on the low heels she always wore, looking dangerous in the Grandma Ryan sense: Sooner or later, something in her path was bound to be broken. At her home in Bryan, a floor-to-ceiling display case held at least a hundred collectible ceramic dishes, vases, cups, and jars—every one of them valuable, every one of them chipped, cracked, or held together by strong glue.

Lucy never came to our house empty-handed. She brought a few dozen eggs from a neighbor's chicken coop or bags of homemade noodles. Her visits directly followed her weekly trips to the beauty parlor. Her bright red hair, newly washed and curled, sat on her head in short, foamy waves. At sixty, her figure was slightly rounded, but not what you would call overweight, just Midwestern.

Inside, Lucy would perch nimbly on the edge of a dining room chair, tilted forward in her enthusiasm to greet each of us as we came by. "Hiya, kid! Whatcha been doin'?" She had taken to calling all of us "kid," because otherwise she got tangled up in our names. She usually ran through nine before getting to the right one.

After a half hour or so of socializing with Mom, Lucy would exclaim, as if the thought had just occurred to her, "Say, Evelyn, what do you need from the store?"

"Oh, Lucy," Mom would reply, suddenly self-conscious and shy, "nothing really."

"Well," Lucy would remark, as if she had shopping of her own to do, "let's go pick up a few things."

Mom was reluctant to pick up any package off the shelf, but Lucy always took the lead and piled the shopping cart high with food. The knowledge that Lucy was saving our family from going hungry left Mom grateful but morose. There was no way, she knew, we could ever pay her back. Then one Thursday Mom had a flash of inspiration. Looking at the cart full of food, she saw past the cereal, flour, soup, toothpaste, ketchup, tea, cooking oil, and soft drinks to the brand names on the labels: Kellogg's, Gold Medal, Campbell's, Colgate, Heinz, Tetley, Wesson, Kool-Aid—every one a sponsor of contests Mom already had labels for at home. Mom knew, suddenly, what she could do, or attempt to do, for Lucy. Surreptitiously, she grabbed a few more of every entry blank in the store as she and Lucy continued their ritual down the aisles. "How's the laundry detergent holding out?" Lucy said, a large box of Tide from the aisle display already in hand. "Oh, Lucy," said Mom, as if on cue, "you don't have to do that."

But now there was a sparkle in Mom's eye. She was on a mission. Instead of sending in multiple submissions with variations of the Ryan name, she

filled out the blanks using Lucy's name: Mrs. Lucy
A. Moore, Mrs. Lucy B. Moore, Mrs. Lucy C. Moore.
She submitted her own entries along with Lucy's, ef-
fectively doubling her contest efforts:

I love my cup of Tetley Tea,
Tea-rrific taste consistently.

Dial soap sponsored a weekly contest for which
the grand prize was a producing oil well. Mom
laughed at outlandish prizes like this, but she entered at least once a week, hoping to win the alter-
nate prize of $25,000:

I'm glad I use Dial
It does what it's supposed to.
Gets me clean, keeps me fresh,
Makes me nice to be close to.

All her kids loved these light rhymes so much, we
tried it ourselves. "Here, Mom," I said unselfishly.
"You can have this one:

"I'm glad I use Dial;
Hallelujah.
Now I don't smell
So peculiah."

"If that one wins," Mom laughed, "I'll hang up my
pencils and become your manager."

Dad loved the idea that Mom was trying to win a
contest for Lucy. He seemed barely aware that Mom
was filling up the house with prizes of appliances
and furniture, but now in his daily routine he asked

about Lucy's entries with an optimism that we couldn't help but notice. He even seemed grateful when we took turns bringing him his lunch, which Mom made for him an hour beforehand. The usual fare was two fried-egg or bologna sandwiches, an apple, and a few cookies. When it was my turn, I rode Dick's bike the four blocks across town by the railroad tracks to the shop. Walking through the open loading dock, I had to cover my ears from the assault of a hundred hot and oily, hammering, clanking machines running at once. I wondered how he endured the heat and noise day after day. Verbal communication was impossible. Instead, we used hand signals or wrote notes like, "Dad, can I have a nickel?" He always said yes.

When it came to animals, however, his answer remained a resounding "No!" This went double for dogs, so of course a dog was the one pet we desperately wanted to have. When the youngest kids, Betsy and Dave, kept trying to sneak one particular neighborhood mutt into the house, Dad told them to get the "flea-bitten dog out of here," so it was left to Mom to explain why to the two hopeful faces close to tears.

"But, Mom," said Betsy, "he's not dirty."

"And he's fun," said Dave. "He bit right through the tire on Bub's bike."

"We can't have a dog," Mom told them, "no matter how clean he is or how strong his teeth are."

"But he's so furry," said Betsy, pleading now.

"We currently have six cats and a chicken," Mom said. "Except for Charley, they're furry, too."

"We already have plenty of food for him," Dave said.

It was true. As luck would have it, Mom had just won six cans of Lucky Dog dog food for her poem on the superiority of canned food by showing that dry food was

Vitamined, formulated, cooked and kibbled;
Expensive, tasty, but unnibbled.

Undeterred by the fact that we didn't own a dog, Mom had also sent an entry to Purina Dog Chow with the reverse message, praising the kibbled food she had criticized in her Lucky Dog entry:

The chow that K.O.'s that old K-9 ennui.
Purina Dog Chow—Bow-wow-ee!

Mom opened her notebook to show these rhymed entries to Betsy and Dave. "The words on this page," she said apologetically, "are the closest we're ever going to get to having a dog." Betsy and Dave sadly returned the dog to the yard where they got him. They also left six cans of Lucky Dog dog food on the owner's front porch.

When Betsy and Dave then tried to smuggle a stray tiger cat into the house, Mom warned them against "pushing our luck."

"But, Mom," said Dave, "he's not a dog. He's a cat."

"And he cleans himself," added Betsy, sighing. "We don't have to do *anything*."

With this, Mom relented, telling the kids that they had to make sure Tiger stayed in the yard with Mammy and her brood, so that Dad wouldn't see him. Thus inspired, Mom sent this entry into a contest for Kleen Kitty kitty litter:

My cat likes KLEEN KITTY because:
Tom can answer Nature's call,
Yet leave NO MESS or smell AT ALL;
Instinct cautions: "Tom, BE TIDY!"
Lucky pet! Kleen Kitty's HIDE-Y!

Clearly, Mom thought cats were cleaner, too. She even convinced Dad that Tiger had been part of Mammy's fold for the last several months.

The first time Dad looked out the dining room window to see Tiger shoot across the backyard, he wasn't amused. "Who the Sam Hill is that?" he said gruffly.

"Oh, Dad, that's Butch," Mom answered casually. "You know, the oldest of Mammy's last litter."

"That's Butch?" Dad muttered in disbelief. "Since when did he get stripes?"

Although he was the last to know, Dad's days of "laying down the law," at least as far as cats were concerned, were over.

CHAPTER SIX

Too Damned

Happy

My mother was a great follower of baseball, though never a placid fan. Years of screaming for her sons' success had blown out her vocal cords, permanently altering her voice to a lovely, low crackle, like an old radio in a hardwood cabinet.

At home, Mom was known to play an inning or two with whichever boy needed the practice. She wasn't especially athletic, but the poet in her recast the experience and won $5 from *The Denver Post*:

Fielder's Choice
There are moms who can cook,
And moms who can sew,
And moms who will come
When they're beckoned;
But give me that pearl

Of a mom-type girl . . .
A mom who can slide
Into second.

Baseball had become the one great connector in
our family. When Dick was a ten-year-old Little Lea-
guer, Mom was the first to notice that his pitching
had begun to break league records. By the time Dick
entered high school, the coach had appointed him
the starting pitcher for the Defiance Bulldogs.

Though Dad felt proud of Dick, jealous anger
was never far below the surface. During the day
(when he was sober), Dad, who never embraced his
kids, patted Dick on the back and gave him a few
fatherly pitching tips—ideas he'd been thinking
about, clearly, at every game he'd attended since
Dick, and later Bub, had learned to play. But at
night, Dad's temper got the better of him. What
began with taunting at the supper table got physical
as Dick's debut as a starting pitcher approached.
Dad shook Dick by the shoulders, his red face so
close to Dick's ear that tears streamed down Dick's
face.

By this time, my mother's options—calling the
cops, the neighbors, Dad's brothers, or the parish
priest—had been exhausted. She couldn't pile all ten
of us into the car and leave my father. Mom would
have been horrified at the very suggestion. The concept of "domestic violence" didn't exist in the 1950s,
let alone shelters for women and children. Mom had
no money, no job, no driver's license, and no place
to go.

As a last resort, Mom could have written to a TV
show like *Queen for a Day,* a popular daytime pro-

By the time I was two years old, Bub and Dick (both shirtless), ages eight and ten, were already baseball stars and Mom had ruined her voice cheering and screaming at Little League games. From left to right: Bruce, Bub, Mom, Lea Anne, me, Dick, and Rog.

gram that invited women living in wretched circumstances to compete against one another and determine which of their lives was *more* wretched. The audience voted by means of an "applause meter," bestowing a sense of justice to the lavishing of washer-dryers, vacuum cleaners, and furs upon the weeping winner. When in doubt, this show seemed to say, trust in democracy: Prove your worth (or lack of it) and the American Dream is yours.

Of course, after being Queen for a Day, the housewife would return to her wretched life, presumably to use her newfound wealth in support of her husband.

My mother got the message of the show loud and clear. A husband and father like my dad was never going to change. The only hope for our family depended on the way *she* could change and raise happy and healthy kids to boot.

Despite the many times we saw *Queen for a Day,* we never pictured our mother as a candidate. We felt sorry for those poor crying women, even though their home lives may have been better than ours. We knew our mother would never describe her life or ours as wretched. Her delight in living, reflected in her poetry and contest entries, rose out of bed with her every day. It was the one thing Dad couldn't drink away.

Not that he didn't try. One night he walked into the living room, his red Irish face almost purple with Kessler's whiskey and rage, and said, "You know what your problem is, Mother? You're too damned happy." She and the kids erupted in laughter at this ridiculous comment, and after a few minutes, even Dad began to laugh.

These days, Mom was even more grateful for Lucy's generosity and redoubled her efforts to win our aunt a prize of some kind. Thus far, she hadn't won the producing oil well in the Dial soap contests, and she hadn't won a lifetime supply of tea from Tetley, so Mom turned her attention elsewhere. *The Big Payoff*, hosted by former Miss America Bess Myerson and Bert Parks, appeared on daytime TV right after *Queen for a Day*. Here again, ordinary women were feted with extraordinary prizes—furs and the latest fashions—but in a game-show format without competing against each other as victims. Mom wrote a letter under Dad's name, in honor of Lucy. Mom wanted the appeal to sound authentically working-class and male, so she altered her writing style:

Dear Bess Myerson:

I'm writing for my sister, Mrs. Lucy Moore, who I would like to have some of your very high-style Big Pay Off fashions.

Lucy has been my guardian angel for longer than I remember. During school days it was she who made violin lessons possible for me, bought my new suit for eighth grade graduation, conferred other favors without number.

During the early years of my marriage, old man Depression saw to it that my work was extremely irregular, and when my 13-month-old son Dick was hospitalized for a serious operation, I hadn't a cent in the bank. But Lucy was there to pay the bills.

My wife and I are now the proud parents of ten children, and all through the years similar incidents have arisen.

But no one ever needed to tell Lucy, who has no children of her own, that Barby had outgrown her last winter's coat, or that Bubby needed dental work done. She had a sort of sixth sense about such matters and one day the child in question would go for a ride in Aunt Lou's car, and return with whatever it was he needed.

Her generosity does not stop with me and my family. She has likewise helped her own parents, the families of brothers and sisters, and many friends.

My sister is by no means wealthy, or even well-off. There are many of the newer things she does not have for her own home, yet she's spent her entire wage-earning life helping others. It's always made us unhappy that we can do so little to repay one who has done so much for us. I surely covet a Big Pay Off for her.

Just in case the Big Payoff didn't come through, Mom also supplied the last two lines of this jingle to Gold Medal Flour's "Twin Star" Silverware contest:

I like to use Gold Medal—
the 'flower' of the wheat,
It helps to make my baking
a 'flower' of a treat!
I'd like to set my table
with lovely new 'Twin Star',
With such 'good taste' this maid in haste
Would snare her Lochinvar!

No matter how little money we had, Mom always had enough change to mail her contest submissions.

In Mom's case, considering what a stamp was capable of generating in return, postage was more of a staple than bread or milk in our house.

Both the *Big Payoff* letter and Gold Medal entry were mailed on the way to Dick's pitching debut for the Defiance Bulldogs. Dad dropped the envelopes off at the post office before driving Dick and Bub across the river to Kingsbury Park for the first high school game of the season. Dick, sitting in the front seat wearing his crisp blue-and-white pinstripe uniform with a capital D on the chest, was nervous, but not about Dad, who, after all, was in his daytime mode; that is, not drinking. When they arrived at the ballpark, the wooden bleachers were already jammed with fans of both the Bulldogs and the Bryan Bears, the opposing team, whose players looked fierce and older than the Defiance boys. The three Ryans split up. Dick met up with his teammates, Bub climbed high up into the stands, and Dad took his usual position behind the batter's box, standing silently and still, his fingers laced through the high chain-link fence above the waist-high backstop.

Mom, who loved baseball as much as her sons did, had to stay home that night because Mike had the mumps—or, as Mom put it, "the mump," since only one side of his face was swollen. She waited until he was asleep to work on her contest entries. She still hadn't given up on trying to win that oil well:

I'm glad I use Dial
Summer, fall, winter, spring
Its unusual protection's
The usual thing.

Mom had said good-bye to Dick at the door, giving him a four-leaf clover she found in the yard that afternoon. She had flattened it out and slipped it into a small plastic sleeve. Dick probably had enough of these to last his life through. Mom had an eye for four-leaf clovers, and she gave them to all of us on special occasions that might require a little luck in addition to ability. Dick slid the plastic sleeve into his back pocket. "Thanks, Mom," he said. "I need all the help I can get."

"Oh," she said, "that's not why I gave it to you. I just thought a four-leaf clover might enjoy being in the pocket of the winning pitcher."

Sure enough, Dick's pitching was almost perfect. By the bottom of the third inning, he had allowed only a single hit by the opposing team. The game was well pitched on both sides, and as the scoreless innings played on, large black zeroes were hung, one by one, on the wooden scoreboard behind left field. In the bottom of the fifth inning, with Defiance batting and the game still tied at zero, Dick sat in the dugout with his warm-up jacket covering his right arm. Dad, for all the shouting he did at home, never said a word. Clouds of moths hovered like halos around the field lights as the Bryan pitcher went into his windup. The opposing team droned the usual chant: "Hey batter, hey batter, hey batter batter batter." When the ball swept across the plate, the batter clipped an inside pitch and fouled a line drive back into the chain-link fence, directly in front of my father's face. The *clang!* of the baseball hitting metal sounded like a rifle shot.

On instinct, Dad jerked his head away, even

though the fence prevented the collision. Then, suddenly, his body seemed to cave in on itself and he collapsed in the dirt behind the wooden back-stop.

None of the players or officials were aware of what had happened at first. Dad had landed behind the backstop, invisible to anyone on the field. Neither Dick nor Bub saw him fall. In the dugout, Dick had turned away to get some water. Bub sat in the top row of the bleachers, eating a bag of popcorn and swatting the bugs away. But people nearby swarmed over to the fallen figure of our father, who by now was clearly unconscious.

By the time an ambulance arrived, siren blaring and lights swirling, Bub had climbed down from the bleachers and pushed through the crowd to find out what all the commotion was about. Watching the paramedics lift the stretcher off the ground, he was so surprised to see Dad that he didn't think to ask to ride along to the hospital. He came to his senses as the ambulance's taillights receded into the distance, and he ran to the dugout to get Dick. "That was Dad in that ambulance, Dick! We have to go!" They sprinted home, Dick's steel baseball cleats clattering down the dimly lit streets, but Mom, alerted by a phone call, had already been driven to the hospital by a neighbor. The rest of us gathered in shock around Dick and Bub on the front porch. We sat in the dark, watching the breeze lift the window curtains, listening to the creak of the porch swing, feeling like orphans.

"What if Dad dies?" whispered Betsy, tears visible in the eye not covered by a patch.

"He can't die," said Mike, one cheek twice the size of the other. "He's not old enough."

"He *could* die," said Bruce. "Uncle Bill died last year, remember?"

"Yeah, but he was Dad's *oldest* brother," said Barb.

Finally Mom phoned to say that Dad was alive but very sick. There was nothing we could do. "Now behave yourselves and go to bed," she said. So we did. Lying under the covers, each of us wide awake, we listened to the rasping song of crickets through the window screens, waiting for the sound of Mom's first footfall on the porch.

By midnight, Mom still wasn't home, and we were still nowhere near sleep. Suddenly a deep, grinding growl like the sound track of a horror movie erupted from downstairs. "Oh no!" someone yelled from a bed down the hall.

"It's Garbage Time!" yelled someone else. "Let's go!"

One of the little kids voiced encouragement: "Mom would *want* us to!"

We threw off our covers and rushed downstairs like a militia called to arms. "Quick!" yelled Dick. "Get the scraps off the counters."

"How about the Limburger?" Mike asked seriously. "It smells worse than the garbage." As the motor roared and ground away, we were too busy to notice Mom standing in the doorway watching a kitchenful of children in pajamas feeding mounds of orange peels, apple cores, coffee grounds, and eggshells into the hungry maw of The Monster of 801 Washington Avenue.

Overcome with laughter, Mom sagged against the kitchen counter. In spite of everything—Dad in the hospital, finances stretched to the limit, everyone's exhaustion, the disposal kicking to life in the dead of night—every kid in the kitchen burst out laughing with her. We didn't stop until the last celery stub was put to rest.

CHAPTER SEVEN

Defiance

*I*n the history of much of Middle America, farming is a far more prominent motif than violence, but Defiance, as its name might imply, is an exception. In 1794, General "Mad" Anthony Wayne built a fort at the confluence of the Maumee and Auglaize rivers, christened it Fort Defiance, and said, "I defy the Indians, the English, and all the devils in hell to take it." They didn't, but a thousand Shawnee, Miami, Ottawa, Potawatomi, Chippewa, Sauk, Fox, and Iroquois people died in one day trying.

Prior to the Anglo invasion of the Maumee Valley, miles of connecting Shawnee, Miami, and Ottawa Indian villages lined the rivers on both sides, along with a thousand acres of corn and bean crops. Pontiac, great chief of the Ottawa people, was born about 1712 on the banks of the Maumee just across from the river from the spot where the general would eventually build his fort.

The general's view of the two wide muddy rivers, their banks secluded by lush overhangs of beech, cottonwood, ash, and oak trees, their waters meeting in slow-moving eddies, must have inspired a little greed in his heart. Almost overnight, the tribes who had lived here for centuries were gone, their villages and crops burned to the ground.

Growing up in a small town like ours, history continually came to life in the most unexpected ways. All we had to do was step out the back door and walk three minutes down to the Auglaize River, just one street and a cornfield away from the house. Following a tractor at plowing time was a sure way of finding churned-up Indian arrowheads and tools. Backyard vegetable gardens turned up flint or pottery shards last touched two hundred years before. One summer some kids became the envy of the neighborhood when they found a deerskin bag tied to a branch high in a river oak tree, its sinew seams bulging with stone arrowheads and tools.

Prior to 1794 and the building of the fort, the area was called Au Glaize, referring to the clay-filled rivers. We felt the presence of the Ottawas, Shawnees, and Miamis as we retraced the steps—slipping silently through the woods along the riverbanks—they must have traveled, carrying messages of victory and defeat. Even in history class, we found ourselves rooting for them, though the war had been lost long before, our town named in triumph by a madman.

A few weeks before school ended, Bruce and I

walked four blocks down Washington Avenue to the Defiance Public Library. The red sandstone library, adjacent to the original site of Fort Defiance, was built at the turn of the century with money from Andrew Carnegie. Wide windows provided as good an escape as any book inside library walls. Kids spied out at old cannons and stacks of cannonballs; adults admired the sweeping river vistas.

With so much to see and do at the library, it was easy to get distracted. But we were here for another reason. We wanted to get a book for Dad. He had been in the hospital for four days, and the doctors still didn't know what was wrong with him. Dad had regained consciousness in the ambulance, but remained, Mom said, nervous, listless, and very weak. He could barely walk by himself. Kids weren't allowed in the hospital except as patients, so we relied on Mom for daily news bulletins.

"The doctor said it wasn't a heart attack," she reported.

"What then?" we asked.

"Maybe a nervous collapse," she answered. "But he's not sure."

We could picture a heart attack—Dad in pain, grabbing his chest, falling down—but not anyone collapsing from "nervousness." If that was possible, the whole family would have met the same fate many times over.

The only benefit of Dad's continuing stay in the hospital was that he couldn't drink there. We saw this as a step in the right direction. The drawback was that he didn't go to work and, of course, didn't make any money. Mom's constant worry about this made her write even more furiously in her contest notebooks. One entry sounded like it was written with Dad in mind:

➤━━━▶

I'm glad I use Dial
It's the one "bar" in town
With a "chaser" for "troubles"
Plain water can't drown.

Every day that Dad was in the hospital, Mom walked the two miles out to visit him and the two miles back home again. On the fifth day, as she started out the door in her Sunday dress, good shoes, best hat, and whitest gloves, Bub said, "Why can't we come, too?" "Yeah, Mom," the rest of us said, "why not?" We were beginning to think we'd never see Dad again. "You'll just make him more nervous than he already is," Mom said. "He'll be coming home one of these days, and you'll see him then."

An hour after Mom left, Bub had an inspired thought. "Hey, Dick!" he shouted up the stairs. "Mom never got anybody to drive the Chevy home from Kingsbury Park. Let's go get it and surprise her at the hospital!"

"Great idea!" Dick yelled down. "We can perk Dad up, too." They rifled through every drawer in the house until Bub found the spare set of car keys in the kitchen cupboard, hidden among Mom's Dial soap labels.

"I'm coming, too," said Rog.

"Let's all go," yelled Bruce.

"No," Bub said. "Just Dick and me. Mom would kill us. The rest of you are too little."

Somehow it didn't register that Mom would kill

them as Dick (age fifteen) and Bub (fourteen) flew out the front door on their errand of mercy.

Neither boy was old enough to have a learner's permit, let alone a driver's license, and neither of them had driven a car before. Oh, they had sat in the driver's seat with the motor off in the driveway, pushing on pedals and turning imaginary corners with the steering wheel, but never when the car was moving. Their inexperience only added to their enthusiasm. After running on foot to the park for the old blue Chevy, they climbed in, Bub in the driver's seat, both of them glistening with sweat and excitement.

The steering column was marked R-1-2-3, which Bub felt fairly certain referred to gears, but his legs were too short to shift and step on the clutch at the same time. "I'll shift," said Dick, "You take the clutch." With that, Bub started the engine and they sputtered off, lurching with each clumsy gear shift, gradually learning when to press the clutch and when to press the gas pedal. For the most part, they ignored the brake pedal, except for the few times Bub mistook it for the clutch and sent Dick thudding into the dashboard. "Forget the brakes," said Dick, rubbing his head. "We're not stopping till we see Dad anyway." They stopped shifting, too, after a while. There was no need, since they never stopped or slowed down on their way to the hospital, clipping bits of lawn here and there as they rounded corners at full speed.

By the time the car screeched into the hospital parking lot, they had switched places and Dick was driving. "Which room is Dad in?" he asked as he careened between cars, still not slowing down. "I'm

"See the U.S.A. in your Chevrolet"

not sure," said Bub. "Keep circling and honk the horn. Maybe he'll come to the window." After several trips around the lot with the horn blaring, Bub looked up to see Mom's face appear at a second-floor window. "Mom!" he shouted and waved happily. "It's *us*. Tell Dad to come to the window." Instead of the pleasant surprise Dick and Bub expected to see on Mom's face, she looked stunned, then horrified and frantically waved them away with her hands, all the while mouthing, "GO! NOW!"

"I don't think she's happy to see us," Bub said.

"Doesn't she recognize the car?" asked Dick as he tried the brake pedal gingerly with his toe. "Tell her we picked up Dad's car."

Bub leaned out and pointed to the hood. "Mom, look! We . . ." But Mom only waved them away more vehemently until they gave up. Dick aimed the car out of the lot toward home. "I have a feeling we're in trouble," he said, and he was right. "If Dad had seen you kids in that car," Mom told them later, "he *would* have had a heart attack."

"We thought a visit from us would cheer him up," said Bub.

"You could have killed him and every pedestrian in your path. Good grief, you could have been arrested! Didn't you think of that?"

They hadn't. In all of her future visits to Dad, Mom took the car keys with her. Beyond the fear that the boys may have damaged Dad's old car, she had to face the larger picture. Her kids were edging out of control. With Dad in the hospital, she realized more than ever that the burden of the family's survival—and sanity—rested entirely on her shoulders. She needed to get Dad home so that *she* could be home.

From her spot at the ironing board, Mom attempted to win a new Chevrolet. At the very least, it would eliminate Dad's nervousness about the old car, and it might give him something to look forward to when he came home. Contestants were asked to supply the last line to a tune Dinah Shore sang on television, "See the USA in Your Chevrolet." Mom outdid herself. Never before had we seen such a wide range of subjects—from pop singer Eddie Fisher to autobody-maker Fisher; from cinch to clinch—or so many rhyming "oo" sounds:

See the U.S.A. in your Chevrolet
America is asking you to call
Drive your Chevrolet through the U.S.A.

America's the greatest land of all.
Get that big car feel—get behind the wheel
Thrill to beauty, power, safe performance,
too
When your drive is done, you'll want to order
one

That's how thousands end their Chevrolet preview.

> Mrs. L. Ryan

Chevrolet beats any ride you've had hereto.

> Mrs. Evalyn Lenore Ryan

Chevy ride's a cinch to clinch the deal for you.

> Mrs. Evelyn Lenore Ryan

In a Chevrolet there's style, and "room" with view.

> Mrs. Evelyn L. Ryan

You can pick and choose style, price, shade best
for you.

> Mrs. E. L. Ryan

Service, sleekness, safety's built-in Chevy-through.

> Mrs. Evelyn Ryan

Hairpin curve or straightaway, this car comes
through.

> Mrs. Leo L. Ryan

Any Chevrolet you choose is news: it's new.

> Mrs. Leo Joseph Ryan

Chevy "drives" 'em into buying PDQ.

> Mrs. Eve Ryan

A Fisher jewel, the Chev's a G.M. all through.

> Mrs. Evalyn L. Ryan

"On the level" Chevy wins climb-trials too.

> Mrs. Evalyn Ryan

Chev's another "Fisher" "hit"—makes records too.

> Mrs. Kelly Ryan

"Drive" a bargain if your Chev is overdue.

> Evelyn L. Ryan

Totin' tots? Six Chevy "wagons" wait your cue.
Mrs. K. J. Ryan

None of these entries won Mom a new Chevy, but she considered losing entries good mental exercise. "It's like using a rowing machine," she said. Mom had won one of these "infernal contraptions" and used it until she pulled too many muscles. "You row for miles, never moving an inch, but your body feels like it's been around the world."

After two weeks in the hospital, Dad was scheduled for release. On a Saturday morning, Aunt Lucy drove her dark green DeSoto the eighteen miles from Bryan to pick up Mom so the two of them could bring him home. The day was stifling, heavy with humidity and the damp smell of river, with not even the suggestion of a breeze to lift the flimsy white curtains hanging over the porch windows. Mammy led Charley and her offspring to the darkest area of the yard for relief from the ninety-five-degree heat. Our house had no air conditioning, but it was big and old enough to have cool corners. Mom used these corners well, setting fans in strategic places to even out the hot spots. Now for the first time, she shut all the windows on the south side and closed the blinds. Mom wanted the bedroom to be as cool as possible by the time Dad came home.

"He's still not himself," Mom said to her assembled children before leaving for the hospital in Lucy's car, "so when we come back, you have to be very quiet. I mean *very* quiet—no running around, no shouting, no fighting, no loud TV. His nerves just can't take it."

After they drove away, everyone practiced being

quiet, speaking in whispers and tiptoeing our way around the house. There was no chance we could keep this up for more than a few minutes, and Dad hadn't stepped in the door yet. When the DeSoto finally pulled into the driveway, we stayed in-doors so as not to overwhelm Dad with welcomes. Whole minutes passed before the front door opened, and when it did it moved slowly, delicately, as if the force behind it was fragile.

We barely recognized our father as he shuffled into the house, Mom on one arm, Lucy on the other. He had gone to the baseball game two weeks before a powerfully built man with a full head of red hair. Now he was thin and stooped, his hair streaked with white. Each of us said hello as he passed us on the way to the bedroom. "Hi, kids," he said, without looking up. "Just gonna lie down a minute." The minute turned into days. He didn't get up to eat— Mom brought him his meals— and he didn't get up to drink. "He must be really sick," said Bub.

After a few days, Dad complained to Mom that he couldn't sleep very well. "Mother," he said, "this mattress is killing me." His back bothered him, and he spent his nights tossing and turning. The mattress they'd been sleeping on was at least twenty years old, one Aunt Lucy had given them secondhand, so Mom blitzed the Sealy Posturepedic company with entries for their new contest:

Once you sleep on a Sealy, you'll say:
"What a mattress! It's strictly Okay!"
Neither too soft nor hard
With its new comfort-gard,
Built just right to sleep tight Nature's way.
                    Mrs. Evelyn L. Ryan
Made to make rued a-w-ache-nings passe!
                    Mrs. Evelyn Ryan
Sealy sleep brings a wide-awake day.
                    Evalyn Ryan
You'll feel rested, not "bested," next day.
                    Mrs. Evelyn Lenore Ryan
Will arrest sleep-slump strain right away.
                    Evelyn Lenore Ryan
Sans buttons or bumps stowed away.
                    Evelyn Ryan
Sealy says, "Twenty years—or we pay!"
                    Mrs. E. L. Ryan
And for flying-cloud ease—bumps away!
                    E. L. Ryan

Feeling bushed after writing and mailing all those submissions, Mom retired for the night. As she stepped around the foot of the bed, she saw the streetlight reflected on something shiny sticking out from beneath Dad's side of the mattress. "Oh my Scot," said Mom, "Is that what I think it is?" Sure enough, she pulled out a full bottle of Kessler's whiskey that Dad must have hidden before his collapse. "Wake up, Dad," she said. "I think I've found your bad back."

She told us later she should have sent in one last entry to Sealy:

Once you sleep on a Sealy, you'll say:
"What a mattress! It's strictly Okay!"
Neither too soft nor hard
With its new comfort-gard,
Keeps those fat whiskey bottles at bay.

CHAPTER EIGHT

Tickle Hills

Mom's worries about money worsened as Dad remained in bed. Dinners and lunches—mostly plates of white rice with milk, sugar, and cinnamon—got skimpy and monotonous. One lunchtime we sat down to bowls of noodle soup Mom made from an envelope of dry ingredients that was clearly the last bit of food in the house. Just as we lifted our spoons over the bowls, Bruce and I noticed a new ingredient—little black spots floating on top. "Mom!" I yelled from the dining room. "There are bugs in the soup." All the kids suddenly dropped their spoons and stared into their lunch bowls.

"Those aren't bugs!" Mom said when she looked at them. "Those are *spices*."

Betsy lifted her eye patch for a better view. "Do spices have little legs?" We looked more closely at our soup. The spots had definite appendages, spaced at regular intervals.

"There are no legs on the spices. Spices don't have legs!" insisted Mom. Maybe her eyesight wasn't as good as ours, or maybe she figured the bugs were boiled and therefore a safe source of protein.

After a short silence during which no one picked up a spoon to eat, Bruce said, "Do we have any soup *without* spices?"

"This is the soup we have," Mom said, with an air of finality. "And it is *bug-free!*"

We looked from Mom's face to the bowls. It came down to this: Were we going to believe our mother or our own eyes?

We ate the soup.

Mom's fiery insistence that the soup was perfectly pure sparked this submission to a Lipton soup contest:

✏️

Seasoned right for season-round zest,
Cents and minutes are all you invest.

She took it well when we kidded her about the entry, reciting en masse:

✏️

Seasoned right for season-round zest,
***Bugs** and minutes are all you invest.*

Our milk supply was about to run out, too. The milkman hadn't been paid in weeks and threatened to stop deliveries. At night, Mr. Goldenetz called Mom to remind her about our growing grocery bill. Without Dad's weekly paycheck, even Aunt Lucy's benevolence couldn't save us.

Our family income had dwindled to the prizes and few dollars coming in from Mom's jingles and poems. Once again, our dire straits served as inspiration:

Toothache Headache
I took his word on cavities.
It merely confirmed my fears;
But when I got the fellow's bill
I could hardly believe my arrears!

About this time, Sister Joan Marie, one of the nuns at St. Mary's, took Mom aside after Sunday Mass. "I imagine Mr. Ryan's illness has put a financial strain on the family," Sister said. "Wouldn't taking in laundry be less risky than entering those contests?" Mom thanked Sister for her good intentions but couldn't help laughing all the same. She believed the only risk in contesting was not trying. "Don't you believe in miracles, Sister?" Mom said.

Because the bigger contests drew hundreds of thousands of entries, some people thought the chances of winning *anything* were too remote to bother. In Sister's mind, doing laundry would at least establish a dependable source of income.

Mom barely kept up with laundering our own clothes, let alone anyone else's. The very phrase "taking in laundry" didn't sit well with my mother. Perhaps it was the stereotype of desperate Irish housewives hauling in tons of other people's dirty clothes—or the knowledge that she had ruined more than one load of our own clothes by hiding a dozen doughnuts in the dryer and forgetting them until the cycle had welded the chocolate frosting to the fiber. Or perhaps it was my mother's insistence that her kids have normal childhoods and never feel trapped by poverty in any way.

Right or wrong, Mom felt an inner certainty that her "knack for words," as she called it, would surpass a hundred thousand other entries and hit the right note with judges. And she knew the difference it made to us: Instead of seeing Mom take in laundry week after week, we watched her systematically pursue contests as if she were born to win. Every time Pokey the mailman ambled his way up the front walk to deliver news of another prize, no matter how small, a thrill shot through our household. At that moment we knew that as long as we used our brains, we were not victims. By striking out to write our own ticket, we would grow up to be like our mother, winners.

This is not to say that Mom didn't enjoy—in fact, revel in—her life as a "contester." My mother loved writing and was often torn between that love and household responsibilities. This poem, for which she received $7 from *Pen Magazine*, cheerfully reflected her dilemma:

✏️

Writer's Resolution

Enough's enough! No more shall I
Pursue the Muse and scorch the pie;
Or dream of authoring a book
When I (unhappy soul) must cook;
Or burn the steak while I wool-gather,
And stir my spouse into a lather
Invoking words like "Darn!" and such
And others that are worse (Oh, much!)
Concerning culinary knack
Which I (he says) completely lack.

I'll keep my mind upon my work;
I'll learn each boresome cooking quirk;
This day shall mark a new leaf's turning . . .
That sm--l! Oh H--l! The beans are burning!

After Dad had been in bed for four days, he seemed stronger physically, but the thought of returning to his workaday life left him sagging. "Kelly," I heard Mom say one morning when she thought none of the kids were up yet, "you've just got to get up today. You've *got* to go back to work."

"Mother," he said, his voice shaking, "I can't handle it yet."

"Get hold of yourself, Dad," she said. "We have no money for the mortgage payment or the milkman. We have no money *period*."

"I'll try some other day. Not today." He sounded on the verge of tears. We had never seen any man cry, let alone our father.

After a few minutes of silence, Mom tried another approach. "You know what your problem is, Kelly? You're too damned *unhappy*." At this, Dad burst out laughing, for the first time in weeks. Mom laughed too, loud enough to wake up the kids who were still asleep. It was the first indication that his illness, whatever it was, might not be permanent.

Later that afternoon, Dad got out of bed, dressed himself, and slipped out to the living room to watch a baseball game on television. When the Indians lost, he took it well. He hadn't had a drink for weeks. Dad went back to bed after the game, and when Mom cracked the bedroom door open later to see how he was doing, she found Mammy nestled in beside him. "Did you know, Mother," Dad said with a note of awe in his voice, "that this cat can open doors all by herself?"

Two days after getting up for the first time, Dad seemed like his old self, the good one. He went back to work, and when he came home at four o'clock after the first day, he seemed almost content. "Who wants to go for a ride and find some tickle hills?" he said happily to Barb, Betsy, and Dave. A "tickle hill" was Dad's answer to Disneyland—a low rise in the road, which, when properly traversed, could give passengers the illusion of being on a carnival ride. Dad would step on the gas just before hitting the rise, and the tires would leave the pavement for a second, making us feel that the car was flying and sending our stomachs into euphoric flips.

We began for the first time to enjoy the company of our father. Softhearted and shy, witty and fun, lovable and loving, he took us for long drives in the country, bought us bushels of apples and tomatoes, and even cooked for us. He was a better cook than Mom was. When he made caramel popcorn, he filled every pot and pan in the house—twenty or thirty of them—much to Mom's dismay. She was the one left with the daunting task of scraping off the dried caramel.

At the same time, Dad seemed so weak and fragile that we worried about him whenever he was out of sight. Sometimes he told us to go play in the woods while he sat in the car, breathing heavily. On weekends, he slept far too late, causing Mom to check on him every hour. Often he didn't seem to hear us when we spoke to him. Worst of all, to us, he stopped going to church. We never spoke our fears aloud, but we suspected our father was waiting to die. Dad must have felt himself reach a low point. He began to drink again, and soon his stamina increased. Just one or two shots of whiskey at first, or a few beers. Within a week, he was back to his old routine. Seeing Dad succumb to his demons was devastating for all of us, yet strangely heartening. The more he drank, the stronger he got, at least physically.

Each morning we awoke again to Dad's sweet side. "J'know the capital of Alaska?" he asked Barb and Betsy one morning as they came sleepily down the stairs. "No," Barb said. "What is it?" "I just *told* you," he laughed; "I said '*Juneau* the capital of Alaska.' " Barb and Betsy loved that joke so much they told it to everyone coming down the stairs to breakfast.

As much as Dad endeared himself to his family, he was useless as the "man of the house." Now that he had started drinking again, he resumed his old habit of hiding things from the rest of us—his whiskey, the keys to the car—never remembering afterward where he had stashed them.

One Saturday morning, several kids and Mom were helping him search the house for his wallet. "The last time he hid the car keys, we didn't find them for nine days," Mom muttered as we searched through dresser drawers in my parents' bedroom.

"Mother!" Dad called from the living room window. "Here comes the milkman."

Mom stepped into the living room and spotted the milk truck at the front curb. "Just what we need," she said to Dad. "How am I supposed to pay him?"

"Just tell him we'll pay next time," said Dad lamely.

Mom told the milkman the truth—that Dad had hidden his wallet and couldn't find it—and promised to pay him Tuesday. The milkman took the news well. We weren't going anywhere; he stopped here three times a week. He set the usual order—twelve quarts of milk and two quarts of cottage cheese—down on the porch floor and left. Mom picked up both wire milk carriers and wedged the cottage cheese cartons between her chest and her arms. The balance was precarious, but she was used to it. When she stepped into the living room, though, she slipped on the welcome mat and fell heavily on the hardwood floor, shattering every one of the milk bottles.

In a house as crowded as ours, there were lots of crashes. As Mom balanced gingerly on her bleeding hands and knees, she called out, "Would someone please help me?" Dad snapped to, rushed out from the kitchen, and took one look at Mom, the milk, and the blood. "Oh, Mother, what have you done?" he choked out and collapsed in a chair. Betsy ran down the stairs and stared at Mom with similar disbelief. "Oh, Mom," she said, and ran back upstairs, crying. Dave passed Betsy on the stairs, sat down hard, and began sobbing softly. Now the pink river of blood and milk had reached the corner and began spilling down into the heat register. Mom pleaded again, only louder this time, "WOULD SOMEONE PLEASE HELP ME?" That knocked Dad out of his stupor long enough to get two paper towels from the kitchen and hand them to her before collapsing again into the chair, weeping. I stood frozen in the dining room, listening. Exasperated with us all,

Mom groaned aloud as she hauled herself up off the floor.

"You know what the worst part of this is?" she announced to the nearly empty room. Incapable of speech, Dad shook his head. "At least a quart of milk has been sucked up inside my girdle. That means that I'm going to have to walk into the hospital with milk dripping from every pore."

The emergency room staff spent hours picking chunks and bits of glass out of her knees. "That was a close one, Evelyn," the doctor said. "You barely missed severing a ligament." Yet for months afterward, Mom could be found sitting in the light of the dining room window, using her tweezers to remove slivers the doctors had left behind. It didn't seem to depress her that she couldn't rely on anyone, including medical experts. In fact, she laughed about her fall and turned the story into a family classic. The ten-second accident became a ten-minute Keystone Kops routine. "If more of you had been home," she joked, "it would have taken me a lot longer to realize I was going to have to get up by myself. I probably would have bled to death in the meantime." Later, Mom turned even this bloody disaster into light-hearted verse:

✏️➤

Complaint
Forgive me if I mutter, Lord,
Against my bitter cup;
But why can't bread 'n' butter
Ever land with the butter up?

Dad could laugh along with Mom, but he was shaken by the accident. It was the first time our mother showed any kind of fallibility. The prospect of raising ten kids on his own was unfathomable, though he enjoyed taking his children with him to the bars.

In the early days of our family, Dad never drank at home, and he was never mean or belligerent. From the time I was three years old, he would take me with him on his rounds. We stopped first at Woolworth's to buy a bag of bridge mix for Mom, then moved on to Tom's Bar, just off Clinton, the main street, and around the corner from the court-house. As Dad ordered a beer and joked with the bartender, I sat at the bar picking out the chocolate-covered nuts and eating them as slowly as I could. The regulars at Tom's came to know me and bought all the root beer I could drink.

Now that I was eleven and too old to go with him, he took Betsy along when he drove to the liquor store for whiskey. They both enjoyed these pleasant little outings. "Betsy-tetsy, get in the car; we'll go rid-ing wide and far," Dad would offer playfully. When he was happy like this, the genes of a thousand Irish ancestors shone lovingly out at her through his water-blue eyes. Along the way, he would tell her how proud he was of her and of Mom, and how lucky we were to have such a great family. But when they arrived home, all that good nature evaporated as soon as he walked into the kitchen and poured himself a drink.

The older boys spent a lot of evenings out of the house just to steer clear of Dad. Mom was growing especially worried about the "wayward tendencies," as one nun put it, of Rog, who had begun "running with the wrong crowd." At fifteen, he and some

older friends had been arrested in a
neighboring town for drag racing. When
Dad read the police report in the *Defiance Crescent News,* he got so angry he
ripped the door off the kitchen stove.

After that, baking required more of
Mom's home-repair ingenuity. She would
set the door in place, slide two yardsticks down
through the handle of the broken door and the handle of the still-attached broiler door below, and prop
a hardwood chair against the front of the stove to
keep a close fit. This worked fine for potatoes or fish
sticks, but cakes required a seamless seal. To keep
the cake from falling, she had to sit in the chair
pressed against the door for forty-five minutes until
the cake was done. She used the time to work on
contest entries, once for a product many of her children loathed:

✏️⟶

**I serve my children school-day breakfasts of
good hot Quaker Oats or
Mother's Oats because:**
*Tots and Teens savor
its hot, oat-y flavor;
for breakfasting youngsters or prep-school gay
blades—
what goes in the tummy shows in the grades.*

In fact, Mom didn't feed us hot oatmeal. As a
group we couldn't stand its mushy consistency—too
much like the rice-sugar-cinnamon concoction we
had to eat when money was running low. But Mom
loved oatmeal and pretended for Quaker's sake that
we did too.

Rog's run-ins with the police department didn't end with drag racing. One lunchtime, he phoned from the station. The police had arrested him for riding spread-eagle on the hood of a car going sixty miles an hour down the highway.

Dad was at work when Mom trudged on foot to retrieve Rog. The two of them walked solemnly home. "I don't know what gets into you, Rog," she said. "You could have killed yourself."

"It was a bet, Mom. I made five dollars."

She sighed. "It's pretty discouraging, Rog. I've spent most of my life trying to raise a bunch of kids under some pretty trying circumstances, only to see you do something as stupid as this." After a heavy pause, she added, "Whatever you do, don't tell Dad about it."

"He's going to find out," Rog said. "He always does."

"This time," Mom replied as they turned up the sidewalk to the house, "we can only hope the paperboy throws the newspaper into the bushes where Dad can't find it."

The next day, the afternoon paper landed as usual on the front steps. Mom brought it into the house and poured a cup of greasy chili over the "Police News" column. Dad wasn't happy that the paper was ruined, but nothing so minor bothered him early in the day. We were spared.

The following Thursday when Lucy paid her weekly visit, she took Rog home with her for the summer, much to Mom's relief. Lucy lived on a farm outside Bryan with her husband, our uncle Dinny— a huge man about the height and width of a doorway. Rog could burn up his energy tending the acres of popcorn that Dinny grew on the farm, far from town and its attractions, legal or otherwise.

Early that same evening, the phone rang just as Mom was cooking supper. "Evelyn!" laughed Lucy over the phone. "Do you have any idea how I could have won a fifty-piece set of silverware from Gold Medal flour? I know you had something to do with it."

"You won a set of silverware?" said Mom excitedly. "It must have been that Lochinvar jingle! I *knew* they'd like the romantic angle."

"I'm so surprised, Evelyn," Lucy said, her voice unexpectedly serious. "No one has ever given me anything like this in my life."

Mom sighed. "Well, finally!" she said. "I've been trying to win you something for months."

"And you know the best thing about it?" Lucy asked.

"Yes, I do," said Mom. "It's unbreakable."

Rog seemed to thrive at Aunt Lucy's farm. "I get everything I want here," he told us on the phone, "comic books, doughnuts, 7-Up, and all the grapefruit juice I can drink at breakfast." More than material things, even more than learning how to drive Uncle Dinny's tractor, Rog loved being the lone kid in the house of a childless couple.

The rest of us were happy for him, and envious, too. It was a fact of life in a house with ten kids that no one would ever get enough of food, privacy, clothes, or attention. Most especially, no one would ever get enough of Mom.

PART THREE

CHAPTER NINE

Poet Laureate

Until now, Mom brought a conservative approach to contesting. Like the "producing oil well" that drenched Dial soap entry blanks with rich black droplets, sensational grand prizes had not attracted her as much as cash or practical household items.

Of course, all contestants found themselves imagining what they would *do* with a prize like an oil well, and the Ryan kids helped Mom out in that regard.

"Can we visit our producing oil well if you win it?" Mike had wanted to know. "Can we work on it and get black and greasy every time we hit a big gusher and walk around yelling when it starts raining black oil?" The movie *Giant* had just come through town, and Mike had obviously been impressed by the thought of owning his own source of "black gold."

"Mike, if we were to win the grand prize, it's hard to know what we'd get for it," Mom said. "I always go for the cash equivalent so we can get some of these bills paid. Think about it for a minute—it would be kind of hard to deposit buckets of oil in the bank."

"If everyone helped," said Mike, "we could form a bucket brigade."

"Too messy," said Mom. "I prefer clean cash."

Mom needed a new cash equivalent, it turned out, because Lea Anne, now twenty-one, announced that she wanted to get married. Fresh out of nursing school and hard at work at a Toledo hospital, she had brought Bob home for weekend lunches (never for dinner or overnight), where he had endeared himself to the family. Still, Mom was not happy about Lea Anne's news.

"You know we all love Bob," she said to Lea Anne. "Even Dad likes him. But you've just begun your career. You have so much in front of you—"

"But, Mom," Lea Anne laughed. "When you and Dad got married, you were only slightly older than I am now."

"Well, yes," Mom said after a pause. "And looking back, I think I was too young—"

"Mom, you didn't have a skill like I have. I'm a registered nurse."

"No, but I had plans, and I—"

"But if your family had asked you to wait, would you have?"

Mom stared at her oldest child for a long moment. "Well, as long as you're sure," she said finally. "So tell me when and where, and let's start planning."

Mom felt a lump rising in her throat, as much from pride as from loss. Lea Anne, who had helped raise many of us when we were little, had always been strong and independent. She was certainly capable of starting a family of her own, Mom knew. The only question was how the bride's parents would pay for the ceremony and reception. As of this moment, Mom's contest wins hadn't resulted in one saved cent.

So when Dial soap announced a new contest, offering the winner a chance to "Win Your Weight in Gold," we found Mom peering closely at the entry blank, from which the winning housewife waved from one side of a scale, balanced by stacks of gold on the other.

This was the kind of grandiose prize that ordinarily wouldn't appeal to her, but now for the first time, Mom, who weighed about 150 pounds, wondered how it would feel to win something as valuable as that much gold. "At last," she laughed, "the upside of all this avoirdupois. If we win *my* weight in gold, we'll be very rich indeed."

Since every entry had to be accompanied by a Dial wrapper, our two bathrooms were soon stacked high with old JCPenney shoeboxes jammed with slippery, naked bars of soap. Not that Mom had to purchase the product for every contest. She wasn't above pawing through the contents of neighbors' garbage cans for box tops and soap wrappers.

And so she started in, returning to the romantic theme that won Aunt Lucy the silverware from Gold Medal flour and that seemed appropriate to Lea Anne's immediate future.

Dial is wonderful
Sweet young things
Declare that Dialing
Gets those rings.

Meanwhile, the rest of her kids took pains to assure Mom that as far as we were concerned, she was the perfect weight and shape. I walked down to the library to copy the Metropolitan Life Insurance chart "Ideal Weights for Men and Women." It showed that Mom was only five pounds above their 145-pound maximum for a woman of five feet six inches. I took it into the dining room, where she was sweating over the ironing board, both from the steam and the damp heat rising off the surface of the Auglaize River a block away.

Dial is wonderful
Come high humidity,
Friends needn't sniff,
"Tain't the heat—just stupidity!"

"I don't think I'm on the right track yet," she was muttering to herself as I brought out the Metropolitan chart. Her eyes widened. "Why, Tuff," she said, holding the chart at arm's length, "this is just what I need for the Toledo *Blade* poetry contest." And before I knew it, Mom had turned to a different page in her notebook, newly inspired.

Fitting Advice
Of all sad words,
Give these the prize:
"My dear,
You'll need
Our larger size."

Mom's ability to work on many chores at once reminded me of the plate-spinning acrobat on *The Ed Sullivan Show.* With jars and labels soaking in the sink, box tops and labels alphabetized in the kitchen cabinets, half-completed entry blanks in the typewriter, and notebook at the ready by her iron, Mom also kept her eye on each one of us as we moved through school and life. She still somehow had time to clean the house and our clothes, keep us fed, and wonder how she was going to pay for Lea Anne's wedding.

In the summertime, Mom labored hard and long at her backyard flower garden, where she grew purple iris, tall white hollyhocks, and orange daylilies. Much to her chagrin, poison ivy prospered too. Mere proximity to the plant caused her body to erupt in a bubbly red rash. "If a breeze blows by a patch of that godforsaken weed in the neighbor's yard on its way to ours," she said, "I'll be laid up for a month."

Once again, Mom was able to wring humor out of life's little setbacks:

Poison Ivy
Victims share a symptom,

"WIN YOUR WEIGHT IN GOLD" CONTEST

OFFICIAL ENTRY BLANK

GRAND PRIZE
Cash equivalent of your weight in gold—no matter how much you weigh—figured at $246.50 per pound!

SECOND PRIZE . . . . . . $5,000.00 CASH
5 THIRD PRIZES . . . EACH $500.00 CASH
200 FOURTH PRIZES . . EACH $50.00 CASH

Just finish a 2-line jingle in space below, starting

"Dial is wonderful—the ounce of pre-
ventiontion, the pound of cure
That saves, through Life's crises, your fresh young allure! ."

Make the last word in both lines rhyme. ➔

Fill in your name and address on reverse side.

Which is:
Everyone who has it
Itches.

In all, Mom wrote ten poems for *The Blade's* poetry contest and asked Mike and me to walk down to
the post office to mail them, along with her many
Dial soap "Win Your Weight in Gold" submissions.
She could have handed them all to Pokey as he
made his daily mail rounds but thought better of it.
"If he's as slow getting *to* the post office as he is getting *from* it, Dial and *The Blade* won't see my entries
until sometime in the next century."

There was only one catch. We had to get past
Charley.

Now a full-fledged rooster, Charley's tolerance for
human beings other than my mother had dwindled
to nothing. He still loved Mammy and his cat "siblings," and he would wrap his yellow-feathered body
around my mother's legs in adoration whenever she
appeared in the yard. He attacked the rest of us on
sight.

On this particular day, Mike and I stood at the
porch screen door, each of us holding at least a
dozen stamped envelopes apiece. "I don't know,
Mike," I said. "It's awfully quiet out there. I can feel
Charley waiting for one of us to step out the door."

"Yeah," said Mike, his eyes wide. "Yesterday he
knocked off my baseball cap and bit holes in my
best socks."

It didn't make any difference if Charley happened
to be at the back door when we went out the front.
In speedy chicken fashion, he was able to half-run,
half-fly around the house and mow us down anyway.

"Give me all the letters, Mike," I said, formulating a plan. "You go open the back door—slowly and quietly so Charley won't know—and then slam it as hard as you can and run back here. I'll make sure he takes the bait."

Right on schedule, the *wham!* of the back door propelled Charley out of the front bushes like a heat-seeking missile. As he tore around the corner of the front yard headed for the back door, we shot out of the house and narrowly made our escape.

All the kids used this method of escaping the house for weeks before Charley caught on to the opposite-door trick. We resorted to slamming both doors at the same time to ensure at least a fifty-fifty chance of getting out safely.

At the post office, Mike and I separated Mom's entries into two piles. They seemed to run the gamut of contesting opportunities, from wild and fanciful ("Win Your Weight in Gold") to contemplative and Midwestern (poetry for the Toledo *Blade*).

"Which one do you think Mom has the best chance of winning?" I asked Mike.

"I'm going for the hundred and fifty pounds of gold," he said brightly.

"Well," I said, holding up the pile of Dial entries, "some of these are going to win at least ten dollars. That's what happened last time." Indeed, during the oil well contest, Mom had won $10 twice. Now with Lea Anne's wedding coming up, she hoped this blitz of entries would bring in enough $10 bills to at least pay for the rental of the church.

Dial is wonderful, *colorful stuff!*
For amplest protection, Dial's always enough.

Mrs. L. J. Ryan

Dial is wonderful—*'s fact, gals, absorb it!*
Your satellite can cling closely in orbit.

Evelyn Ryan

Dial is wonderful, *makes a clean sweep*
Of odors (offensive) I'd otherwise keep.

E. Lenore Ryan

Dial is wonderful, *sees you through*
When you're "sweating it out" in the check-out
queue.

Evelyn Lenore Ryan

Dial is wonderful *in crowded places,*
Saves a lot of reddened faces.

Mrs. Evelyn Lenore Ryan

Dial is wonderful. *Of all beauty buys,*
The one that cuts odor down to "bath size."

Evalyn Lenore Ryan

Dial is wonderful, *gently repealing*
What most fresheners just succeed in concealing.

Mrs. Evalyn L. Ryan

Dial is wonderful—*freshness to spare*
Attends the bather who gets Dial "care."

Mrs. Evalyn Ryan

Dial is wonderful. *After the shower*
It reigns on for hours in germ-killing power.

Mrs. Leo J. Ryan

Mom spent the rest of the month waiting for
Pokey's arrival each day, but not a single dollar from
her Dial soap entries appeared. This was a surprise,
even to Mom, who thought her jingles at least
equaled the quality of previous $10 winners. She did,

however, hit paydirt with the "blind-judged" poetry contest sponsored by the Toledo *Blade*.

The paper's editors had deleted the authors' names before submitting the poems for judging by a team of English professors from the University of Toledo and Bowling Green State University. The professors pored over the fifteen hundred entries received in the humor category and eventually whittled the number of winners down to the twelve best. Then they matched the authors' names to the twelve finalists.

My mother, they discovered, had written ten of the twelve.

Mom took a Greyhound bus sixty miles to the awards luncheon in Toledo, where she received a $50 first prize and the title "Poet Laureate of the Toledo *Blade.*"

The judges wanted to award Mom all the prizes, including runner-up, but were overruled by *The Blade*'s editors, who thought she should share the wealth with other entrants. Mom was seated between two other winners—a Roman Catholic nun named Sister Schnapp (her real name) and a man who had written a poem about a poolroom in which he used the word "bastard." His poem won a prize but wouldn't be printed in *The Blade* with the other winning entries because of what the paper deemed its obscene language. This brought out some good-natured griping from Mom and Sister Schnapp. It was a story Mom told many times afterward:

"What's wrong with 'bastard'?" Sister said. "A perfectly good Anglo-Saxon word. In fact it's one of my favorites."

"Wow," said *The Blade* editor. "Are nuns allowed to say words like that?"

"My pupils hear worse than that every day of the week," said Sister.

"How are you going to acknowledge my win if you don't print the poem in the paper?" the poet complained to the editor.

Mom turned to the editor. "You could put an empty square with a black border in the middle of the page," she joked.

"You might deliver all the papers in plain brown wrappers that day," added Sister, winking at Mom.

"I can see the headlines in tomorrow's paper," Mom said. *"Brawl Erupts at Poetry Awards—Nun and Bastard Arrested."*

"Don't you mean . . . ?" said Sister, handing Mom a napkin on which was written, *"Nun and @#!*%@."*

"I thought 'bastard' was spelled with *two* asterisks," said Mom.

"I think we should stop serving alcohol at the annual poetry awards," said the editor.

The last Mom saw of Sister Schnapp, she was still haranguing the editor as they walked down the street together. " 'Bastard,' no. But ads for porny movies, you bet!"

My mother admired Sister Schnapp, who fit Mom's idea of a well-rounded person (nun or layman)—witty, intelligent, and spiritual. Mom began life as a Methodist and converted to Catholicism when she married Dad. She had all the zeal one expects of a convert, none of the lackadaisical languor to be found in the lifelong believer. While Mom's belief in Catholicism grew, Dad's receded, as if the care of his soul had become his wife's responsibility. He stopped going to church completely after his collapse at the baseball game, when any ordinary

Catholic would have been frightened into going more often.

Mom continued to attend services and follow most church precepts. The rituals of the Catholic church seemed to provide an incense-laced backdrop for the brand of religion she concocted for herself over the years, a brew of equal parts Nature, Catholicism, and Spiritualism: All living things, including weeds, have value; prayers to St. Jude, patron saint of lost causes, can work miracles; the dead sometimes walk among us.

In the early days of her conversion, Mom considered the priests to be God's earthly representatives and the nuns earthbound angels. Overall, her opinion remained high, despite several surprising baptisms.

In 1937, Mom missed her first baby's christening because she was too sick to leave the house. Instead she entrusted baby Sally to Dad and Aunt Lucy for the baptism. An hour later, they were back home, Dad and Lucy looking a little sheepish. "What's the matter?" Mom asked. "Well," Lucy said, her new Easter hat slightly askew, "Father McCague refuses to baptize any baby who doesn't have a saint's name."

Mom couldn't imagine where this conversation was going. "And?" she said.

"And so," Dad said, "Sally's new name is Lea Anne."

Mom gave birth every two years or so, not that there was any system to it—birth control wasn't even discussed in Catholic households in the 1940s and 1950s. I'm sure if asked, my mother would have joked that having a child every two years was her body's version of adhering to the rhythm method.

So the baptismal-renaming scene was repeated often. Betsy and I returned from the church as Elizabeth and Teresa, respectively, names my mother had never considered, but none fared as badly as Bruce. He arrived at the church as Barry Bruce and left as Finbar Bryce. By that time, Mom figured out that baptismal names had no relation to legal names and could be happily ignored.

What Mom liked most about the church was the discipline and love of learning she believed the nuns and priests at St. Mary's school instilled in our elementary education. True, Catholic teaching methods seemed stern and rigid compared to the way our public school friends learned their ABC's. But "for language skills alone," Mom said, "you can't beat a good Catholic school education."

She didn't like to hear about corporal punishment, however, and winced when we came home with stories about small knuckles getting rapped with "Sister's ruler."

We didn't mind physical enforcement all that much until one day in 1953, when, as I marched through the halls with my second-grade classmates, I was startled to see a nun slap my five-year-old brother Mike across the face. Mike, hunched over in the hallway, put a hand to his cheek and began to cry. At recess, I passed the story along to Bruce, who was in the fourth grade; Bruce told Rog, who was in sixth grade; Rog told Bub, who was in the eighth grade. Bub ran the half block home to tell Mom, who was standing over the ironing board as usual, scribbling pertinent contest rhymes into her spiral notebook:

For chewy, toothsome, wholesome goodness
Tootsie Rolls are right—
Lots of nibbling for a nickel
And they show me where to bite.

"Gosh," she said, lost in thought, "is school out for the day already?"

"Not yet," he gasped. "Tuff saw Sister Angelus smack Mike. He was crying." Mom calmly closed her notebook, unplugged the iron, and left Bub to baby-sit Barb, Betsy, and Dave while she walked over to the school. By the time she arrived, the bell had rung and she had to wade through the sea of kids flowing the other way. Sister Angelus watched her arrival from the hallway outside the kindergarten classroom.

"Hello, Sister," Mom said, out of breath. "I rushed over because I've heard there's been some kind of trouble with Mike."

"I was just about to call you on the phone, Mrs. Ryan. Mike's all right. I think I hurt his feelings more than anything else."

"What happened?" said Mom.

"I found him with matches in his hand. When I asked him about it, he actually pulled *a bullet* from his other pocket. Now, Mrs. Ryan—"

"Oh, don't worry, Sister. He's done that before," Mom said gaily.

"That's exactly what I was afraid of," said Sister. "I grabbed the matches and lunged for the bullet when Mike stepped back abruptly. In the midst of this melee, I did indeed slap his face to bring some order . . ."

"What I mean, Sister," Mom said firmly, "is that Mike has made a deal with me. He once found a bullet in the street and tried to conduct his own experiment." (Mom omitted the part about the bullet blowing a hole through the basement door.) "Now whenever he finds anything of this nature, even arrowheads, he brings them back to the house so we can investigate them together."

"But the matches—" said Sister.

"He probably found those, too," Mom sighed. "Sister, let me make *you* a deal. If you find reason to punish Mike or any of my kids again, please call me first. You know we live just four houses away. I can be here in less than a minute."

"Well," said Sister, "that's true . . ." She paused, waiting to hear the rest of Mom's "deal."

"And in return, I'll add you to my Sunday prayer list," said Mom.

A smile crept across Sister's face. "Thank you, Mrs. Ryan. If you have any more children like Mike at home, I'm sure we're all going to need those prayers."

Mom returned the smile. "Not to worry, Sister. All of my children are one of a kind."

With the $50 Mom won from *The Blade* contest, she paid off the older textbook bills from St. Mary's and lit a ten-cent vigil candle in the church for Sister Angelus the next Sunday. She stashed the rest of the money in a hiding place in her closet.

This was a new tactic. For as long as we could remember, Mom had given her cash winnings over to Dad, who handled most of the bill paying. But since he'd gone back to work after his collapse, she suspected he was spending more of his pay on himself and less on the family. We heard them arguing over money all the time, but Mom got nowhere. Determined to prevent her winnings from disappearing down the same hole as his paychecks, she decided to manage the family finances her own way. Wouldn't the nun who suggested she take in laundry be proud: Now Mom was hiding money from her own husband.

With Lea Anne's wedding approaching, Mom planned to hide even more of her winnings from Dad, but then something unexpected happened. "Mom, has Aunt Lucy called you yet?" Lea Anne said breathlessly on the phone one day. "She wants to pay for the whole wedding—the ceremony, the reception, everything. Isn't that great?"

Mom found herself unable to reply before Lea Anne hung up abruptly to call Bob. The phone rang in Mom's hand. It was Lucy. "Evelyn, I don't want you to worry about this. It just so happens I have the money to do it, and I *want* to do it."

When Dad heard the news later, he was elated. "Well, that's it, isn't it, Mother? Lucy's come through, and we don't have to pay a dime."

Finally Mom sighed deeply to keep her voice steady. "Don't you *want* to pay for your own daughter's wedding?" she asked. But Dad had already left the room.

Lucy's gesture was a gift from heaven, as my mother well knew. The $27 Mom had hidden in the closet wouldn't pay for the cake, let alone the remaining wedding expenses. Mom couldn't have been happier for Lea Anne, but after that, something changed in my mother. For one thing, Dad never saw a penny of her winnings again. For another, she seemed to have vowed that whatever life threw at our family in the future, financial or otherwise, she would be, above all, ready.

CHAPTER TEN

Giant Steps

Six years had passed since my mother had won the Western Auto contest. By 1960, Mom was shooting for sensational grand prizes right and left, the latest being a three-day weekend in Los Angeles to attend the opening of the movie *Gypsy*. If her entry won, Mom planned to sell the prize for several hundred dollars. This would be a mighty contribution to her hidden cache in the closet, although one that would disappear quickly with so many kids still left at home.

Nevertheless, just the thought of attending a splashy Hollywood premiere triggered Mom's imagination. When she saw that contestants were required to fill in the last line of a jingle, Mom wrote out a dozen entries under different names within an hour:

I'd like to be an honored guest.
I'd like to have a date
With movie stars and chauffeured cars,
This fan would oscillate!
>   Evelyn Lenore Ryan
Where "big busts" reely rate!
>   Evelyn Ryan
Where show folk s(c)in-til-late!
>   Evelyn L. Ryan, Washington Ave.
Sans Cinderella's fate!
>   Evelyn L. Ryan, Washington St.
Midnight won't liquidate!
>   Mrs. E. L. Ryan, Washington St.
Where actors "operate"!
>   Mrs. E. L. Ryan, Washington Ave.
And clearance from my mate!
>   Mrs. Evalyn Ryan
"Beau ties" I'd renovate!
>   Mrs. Leo J. Ryan
What "Golden" prospects wait!
>   Mrs. Leo J. Ryan, Washington Ave.
Where falsie-fying's straight!
>   Mrs. Leo J. Ryan, Washington St.
And minds conglamourate!
>   Eve L. Ryan
Whose "lines" I'll cultivate!
>   L. J. Ryan

"There," Mom said, turning back to her ironing, "that's a start."

Each of us seemed on the verge of a giant step in life that year. I had just graduated from the eighth grade and became the sixth Ryan kid to pass through

St. Mary's brick hallways on the way to Defiance High, the local public secondary school. Four more still attended St. Mary's. Every day that summer, I waited at the mailbox for news of my fall class assignments at the high school. Compared to dreary spelling, general science, and math, the freshman subjects sounded exotic and exciting to me—biology, algebra, physiology. For once, Mom had company as she stood impatiently at the living room window, waiting for news of contest wins from Pokey the mailman.

The winter before, Dick had been signed by a scout for the Detroit Tigers to pitch minor league ball. Bub, recently graduated from high school, had just returned from a two-week Tigers tryout camp in Toledo. The family was thrilled to learn that in his first six innings, Bub struck out fifteen batters and gave up only one hit. In fifteen total innings, he struck out thirty-two batters, walked five, and gave up only three hits. Of 160 hopefuls, he was one of three players signed. So he and Dick were both preparing to leave for Tiger Town, the Detroit Tigers spring training facility in Lakeland, Florida.

Dick's and Bub's success was a Ryan team effort. When they wanted to practice pitching, we took turns catching for them on the front sidewalk—fastballs, curve balls, sliders, each delivered at a speed that could break the bones in your hand if you caught it, every other bone you had if you missed. We became adept at standing out of the line of fire and using the web of the glove to catch the ninety-five-mile-per-hour ball as it went by. Even with these adjustments, it was a painful experience, leaving

*O*ur local newspaper ran a story with this photo of *Dick and Bub packing for Tiger Town, the Detroit Tiger training facility in Lakeland, Florida. Mom won the suitcases they packed, the baseball outfit Davey is wearing, and the stuffed tiger in Betsy's lap. From left: Davey, Mom, me, Dad, Mike, Betsy, Bruce, Barb, Dick, and Bub.*

your hand red, swollen, and useless for an hour or so. In self-defense, I asked Dick once, "Just for my sake, could you throw the fastballs a little slower and the curve balls a little straighter?" Despite the pain, I loved catching for them. We all did. And if they played well in real games, we felt a little bit responsible.

Playing ball with Dick and Bub quickly catapulted our own baseball skills into the stratosphere. Girls weren't allowed in Little League, but I had just pitched a no-hitter in the championship game of the city parks league, an otherwise all-boy group that wasn't organized enough at the time to exclude girls. Everything I knew I learned from my older brothers.

My mother was ecstatic about both boys going to Tiger Town. She saw this as an opportunity for Dick and Bub to get out from under Dad's influence and to create promising new lives for themselves. As it was, they spent most of their evenings racking balls and collecting the twenty-cent hourly card fees for a few dollars a night at Max's Card and Pool Room, owned and operated by Max Sheik, a slender, dapper man, who, according to rumor, wore his fedora even to bed. Max served as a second father to Dick and Bub (and my four other brothers when their time came), who worked at the pool hall during high school. It was the best of all possible worlds for teenage boys—they played pool, ate their fill of Max's concessions, and felt honored to while the nights away in that smoke-filled home away from home.

Besides, the pool hall was the one place in town Dad would never be found. Legend had it that Dad had once been kicked out of Max's, either because of drinking or the boisterous way the Ryan family played poker. Out of respect for Max, who never tolerated any kind of shenanigans, the boys didn't ask why.

Mom never minded that gambling occurred at Max's poolroom. She felt her sons had grown up appreciating the value of a dollar, and hoped that her own goal of winning by her wits without risking more than the price of postage might be an example. Newly inspired by the *Gypsy* contest, she began composing entries faster than Mike and I could run to the post office.

I'd like to be an honored guest.
I'd like to have a date
With movie stars and chauffeured cars,
While "curves" we navigate!
    Mrs. Eve Ryan, Washington St.
Plus plush premier slate!
    Mrs. Eve L. Ryan, Washington Ave.
Unchecked by my "checked" mate!
    Eve Ryan
Start walkin', Dream, we're late!
    Mrs. Leo Ryan, Washington Ave.
Come, Gypsy, state my Fate!
    Mrs. Leo Ryan, Washington St.

"The thing I like most about this contest," said Mike as we trudged home from the post office, "is that Mom has to send a Baby Ruth or Butterfinger wrapper with every envelope. And *we* get to eat the candy bars."

"Even better," I said, "is that if she wins, we might all get to go to California."

*T*he Detroit Tigers signed both Dick and Bub as pitching prospects, in 1959 and 1960 respectively, right after high school graduation. For our small town, this was a major event.

"Just think!" he said. "We could meet movie stars!" We knew Mom would sell the prize if she won, but we loved imagining the trip anyway. It was an encouragement to Mom.

Help of a more substantial kind arrived when Dick signed with the Tigers and received a $3,000 signing bonus, which he used to buy a slightly used 1959 Ford Fairlane. Since 1948, the biggest employer in Defiance, Ohio, had been the giant General Motors foundry at the edge of town, and residents felt strongly about supporting GM products. In Defiance, if you were driving a Ford, you were driving a foreign car. For Dick to purchase a car that wasn't a Chevrolet, a Pontiac, or a Cadillac took some courage. Then again, he *was* leaving town. The best news for us was that Dick gave his old 1954 Chevy Bel Air to Dad, so Dad could retire the expiring 1946 Chevy he had been coaxing around town for the last decade.

Mom's contribution to the boys' trip to Tiger Town arrived in the mail one day—a set of five suitcases she won in a Bostonian luggage travel contest for her 25-word entry, which couldn't have been more appropriate to her situation as a mother of ten:

"Confined" to bi-ennial "vacations" in hospital
  these twenty years,
getting another little son and heir,
I need another vacation for a little sun and air!

Now the Tiger Town Twins, as we called them, had a car and two suitcases between them. The only problem was that Dick had spent every cent of his bonus to buy the car, with nothing left for auto insurance. This didn't bother Dick a bit. He was happy to drive to Florida uninsured. "Don't worry, Mom. You know I'm a good driver."

"I don't doubt that," Mom said. "It's the other drivers I worry about. You could have an accident that wasn't even your fault." She paused to let her message sink in. "And then what would you do? No car, no medical coverage, no nothing." Dick shrugged. Getting in a car wreck on the way to Tiger Town was out of his ken. In his mind, he was already *at* Tiger Town.

Mom knew that asking Dad—who stubbornly persisted in calling Dick "Moneybags" from the big contest won years ago—for the insurance money was out of the question. In her unswerving wisdom, Mom saw Dick for what he was: a kid in a man's body. She knew he'd never get the insurance on his own, so instead of keeping the money she had hidden in her closet for upcoming book bills and dental payments, she used every cent to pay for the first three months of coverage.

Still in their teens, Bub and Dick were young to be journeying so far from home. No one thought it strange when Mom told the two boys to send their laundry home. She knew they'd wear dirty clothes before going to a Laundromat, and, like a lot of women, she believed boys and men were incapable of cooking and cleaning for themselves. So she sent them on their way with a few strings attached, just in case.

We could hardly blame her. Piling out of bed and into the yard at 6:00 A.M. to wave good-bye to Dick and Bub, the remaining Ryans were a sad bunch. The car was so loaded down with food, clothes, and baseball gear that the back end rode a foot lower than the front. The green-and-white Ford disappeared down the street with Dick's and Bub's arms sticking out from either side waving a last farewell. "Pull your arms in!" yelled Mom. "They aren't insured!"

Two weeks later, the laundry started pouring in from Tiger Town. "How could anyone get this filthy?" Mom said as she dumped out the first box. "There couldn't be this much dirt between the pitcher's mound and home plate."

How Mom got it all done and still found time to crank out more *Gypsy* entries was a thing of wonder:

I'd like to be an honored guest.
I'd like to have a date
With movie stars and chauffeured cars,
Where "know-who" carries weight.
     Mrs. Evalyn Ryan, Washington St.
In which we'd <u>palpitate</u>!
     Evelyn A. Ryan
While minked from knee to pate.
     Evelyn B. Ryan
Those "little extras" rate!
     Evelyn C. Ryan
I'd do the Golden "gait"!
     Evelyn D. Ryan

On the same day the luggage was delivered by a mail truck, my high school class schedule arrived. At the time, it was the nuns' responsibility to register their graduates in the public high school. To my shock, the nuns at St. Mary's had not signed me up for biology, algebra, or physiology as my mother and I had requested. Instead, I was registered to take every special-education course possible—remedial English, remedial math, remedial science.

I was more than depressed; I was *thirteen* and depressed. "They think I'm dumb, Mom."

"You know who's dumb, Tuff? *They* are. They equate poverty with stupidity. And they're mean, to boot. I'm sure they did it out of spite for all the years I've badgered them about the way they've treated you kids." She shuddered. "To think I used to picture them as God's angelic helpers."

"Will you talk to them?" I asked.

"Forget them," she said. "They're out of your life forever. I'll work it out with the high school when classes start in the fall."

But before she could do that, Mom was faced with another challenge. In fact, the whole Ryan family's elation at Bub and Dick's good news flattened when seventeen-year-old Rog got arrested again. This time he was charged with breaking into cars and stealing the valuables inside, his most serious offense yet. "I just needed some money, Mom," he said, when the police brought him home. "All my friends have spending money."

"Well, that's no way to get it," Mom said. "How could you steal, especially from people who are your friends and neighbors?"

"I always put the purses and wallets back in the car so the owners would get their belongings back," Rog said. He wasn't lacking in sympathy for his victims. In that unrehearsed comment, Mom saw a glimmer of hope. Rog had been caught only because he stuck around to replace the empty billfolds and bags.

Mom stopped in the street to face him. "If you want money, I don't know why you can't caddy at the golf course like Bruce does. He makes a couple of dollars a day there on the weekend."

"Oh, Mom," Rog said, shaking his head. "That's not for me. I can't even stand to work at the poolroom."

"You're going to have to work someday, Rog," Mom said. "You can't steal your way through life." Turning for home, they walked the rest of the way in silence, saddened for separate reasons.

Mom turned to her *Gypsy* entries, as much for solace and distraction as excitement at the prospect of winning:

I'd like to be an honored guest.
I'd like to have a date
With movie stars and chauffeured cars,
Might Benny pay the freight?
> Evelyn F. Ryan
To Taylor-make a mate!
> Evelyn G. Ryan
Edwards can't duplicate!
> Evelyn H. Ryan
Where "reel" docs hamputate!
> Mrs. Eve Ryan, Washington Ave.
Where "first exclusives" rate!
> Evelyn I. Ryan
Whose "weigh" defrays the "freight"!
> Evelyn J. Ryan

Barb stood by the ironing board to read Mom's latest entries. "Mom," she said, "who's 'Benny'?"

"You know—Jack Benny," Mom said. "He's famous for being stingy."

"Oh, I get it," said Barb. "So 'Taylor' stands for Elizabeth Taylor?"

"Right. You have to picture all these movie stars at the premiere, see—"

"I can see all right, but who's 'Edwards'?" asked Barb.

"That's Ralph Edwards. It means that even on his TV show, *This Is Your Life*, he couldn't duplicate the star-studded excitement of the premiere."

By the time Mom was explaining about "reel" doctors being "ham" actors performing amputations in Hollywood, Barb was concentrating so hard her eyes were nearly shut. "Well, let's just send them off," Mom said, still worried about Rog's upcoming court date.

When Dad found out about Rog's arrest, he went off like a bomb. As the rest of us stumbled and fell over one another in our haste to get out the back door, he chased Rog through the house, bellowing all the way, with Mom following close behind to stop him from killing Rog if he caught him. As they flew through the dining room and onto the front porch, Rog threw open the glass-paneled door and leapt to freedom, unaware that the spring door slammed shut just as Dad arrived at the threshold.

We were so happy that Rog escaped down the street that it took us a moment to notice that something was awry. Dad's white T-shirt bloomed with bright red polka dots, growing larger before our eyes. "Mother," he called, pointing to his protruding belly, stuck through with shards of broken glass.

A collective gasp rose up from those of us in the yard. Everyone scrambled to help, offering Dad towels, finding the car keys, as he and Mom set off for the emergency room. We stood in the street, watching the Chevy disappear under a canopy of maples, knowing that despite everything, we wanted him back again. When he did return, his stomach was patched with stitches, Band-Aids, and gauze, like a battered basketball. Betsy, a precocious seven-year-old, gently placed the palm of her hand on the biggest bandaged area and said, "Why didn't your tummy deflate?"

In court a few weeks later, the juvenile judge had mercy on Rog, giving him the choice of going to jail or joining the armed service of his choice. Quite conveniently, a recruiting office had set up operations a block away from the courthouse. Rog signed up for the air force immediately, taking with him the third suitcase from Mom's set of five.

"Sorry, Buster, you don't pass muster with Birds Eye!"

Just the snappy, stringless beans are for Birds Eye. The tall, tender ones. Young with flavor. The rest are mustered out!

Birds Eye not only selects the best beans, but packs and freezes them in a scant few hours from the time they leave their native soil.

So when you serve Birds Eye Green Beans, you serve the freshest flavor you can find, unless you have your own bean-patch nearby.

Birds Eye Green Beans come two ways, too: Cut and French Style. Either way, like all other Birds Eye Frozen Foods, these are the best buy!

STRAWBERRIES   CHOPPED STEAK DINNER   CRINKLE CUTS

SEE OTHER SIDE FOR CONTEST RULES AND ENTRY BLANK

Mom stored the two remaining suitcases in her bedroom closet, hoping they wouldn't be needed soon. We all hated to see a sibling leave, even though it meant more room for those left behind. We feared each departure was permanent.

That hollow feeling we felt with Rog gone seemed to grow larger when the winners of the *Gypsy* contest were announced and not a single one of Mom's entries won even a mention. "I don't know which is worse," Mike said, "knowing Mom lost or getting sick of Baby Ruths."

Mom took the *Gypsy* loss in stride, as she always did, but I felt the loss much more deeply. I thought back to when I was younger and compared Mom to a baseball catcher diving for a foul ball—she might miss one, but that didn't keep her from going after the next one and the next with equal fervor. Now with the *Gypsy* contest, all I saw was the futility. I began to feel the judges were far too arbitrary in selecting winners.

Mom was not only unfazed by the *Gypsy* loss, she felt renewed by it; once more she lifted the family's spirits by her own determination. Besides, with the four oldest kids out of the house, she had more time to write, and her appetite as financial manager had been whetted by collecting and directing small wins and poetry payments toward buying things we needed, like shoes and jackets, not to mention Dick's car insurance.

Mom returned to the business of contesting like a house afire. She named a new musical group sponsored by Rolo candy ("The Toffeebreaks"), knocked off one liners—

General Mills Variety Pack: Best sellers in cereal form and created simple jingles—

Kool-Aid season's ANYTIME, For more "good" reasons than I've rhyme.

—with a rapidity acquired from her years of experience. She used her own surroundings for inspiration, especially as she watched us troop off to school in the morning:

Colgate Toothpaste:
School yourself for oral ease;
Learn your dental ABC's:
<u>A</u>lways <u>B</u>rush <u>C</u>arefully.

And she turned out more entries of the slack-jawed variety than there were jaws to slacken:

I'd like to win SweetHeart's "Dream Home" because:
"Dream College" could materialize; with dollars diverted—
back rent to backlog—siblings needn't mature
SHORT on FUNDAMENTALS
because Father's SHORT on FUNDS!

All these entries won something, even the mind-numbing one. The prizes started pouring in again in the summer of 1960, much to Mom's delight, and she tucked them away in her closet without even unpacking them. "Are you going to sell the prizes this time, Mom?" I asked, watching her carry in a box labeled "Guitar" (from the Rolo candy contest), one stamped "Gilbert Microscope and Lab" (from General Mills), another announcing a "Fishing Kit" (from SweetHeart soap), and yet another marked "Sleeping Bag" (from Kool-Aid). I knew we still didn't have much money since the older boys left.

"We'll see," she said, her brown eyes bright with mystery. "I may have another idea."

To start a new cash supply, Mom began writing more Charley-type articles for the Toledo *Blade* for $5 each. She wrote about her uncle Frank, "my nasally talented relative, the All-Time Snorer of the First Magnitude." She wrote about a field mouse she called Mortimer, the "mental supermouse," who daily visited Mom at the ironing board, tapping on her toe each time to announce his presence and resting on her shoe as she ironed.

Mom loved these mini essays because they gave her the luxury of drawing from family source material. She wasn't limited to 25 words or less, and they didn't have to rhyme. She outdid herself with a piece about being the "light sleeper" in a family of twelve, which the editors of *The Blade*, usually so strict about space limitations, published without a single trim. The editors phoned Mom after it ran, asking for more. If ever there was a chronicle reflecting the chaos of a big, growing family, this was it—and it didn't even include the daylight hours:

Solved—The Case of Another Homemaker's Lost Sleep

For months now my children have been asking why Mommy always drops off to sleep the minute she sits down to watch television. "Don't tire your mother, children," their father replies. "She's getting on in years now and she doesn't rest well nights. Insomnia, you know."

So in my own defense let me submit the journal of a fairly average night-watch at Rancho Ryan:

11:15—Decide to forego Jack Paar show and get a good night's sleep for once. Hubby already snoring.

11:35—Twenty-year-old arrives home from ball game, bangs car door, bangs porch door, sits on squeaky porch glider to remove spikes, stands (judging by the sound) on glider to drop spikes, bangs house door, proclaims "We won!" to darkened house, bangs refrigerator door, clumps upstairs. (Hubby snoring.)

12:15—Six-year-old, roused by commotion, complains noisily that tooth fairy has not arrived as yet and unless he comes she will be short a dime to go swimming come morning.

12:15½—Sibilant shush from teen-ager admonishes her to be quiet for heaven's sake or she'll wake Mom and Dad.

12:20—Dive-bombing mosquito breaks formation to embroider erratic needlepoint on exposed ankle (mine).

12:25—Phone rings. Thoughtful message informs me that second teen-ager is watching late TV at John's house. Will be home before we've missed him. (Hubby still snoring.)

12:35—Second teen-ager comes sprinting up sidewalk as though Frankenstein were breathing on his flat-top, bangs porch door, trips over spikes, falls over work shoes, bangs house door, assumes refrigerator empty and hot water gone besides which he "ain't dirty yet, anyhow," climbs stairs.

1:20—Four-year-old who ate ham for supper develops prodigious thirst, about which he continues to issue periodical vocal bulletins the rest of the night.

1:55—Marauding cats become involved in melodious argument beneath bedroom window.

2:00—Arise to bang on window screen at cats (Hubby snores on.)

2:01—Cats resume auditions beneath neighbor's window.

2:02—Bird in tree outside window, awakened by cats, complains loudly of cramped quarters in his domicile. There follows prolonged rustling, wing-flapping, squawking, as feathered family rearranges itself.

2:03—Locust, disturbed by bird "rhubarb," sings ill-tempered solo. (Still snoring.)

2:10—Owl, attracted by locust, wants to know who-o-o-o the dickens is responsible for all the ruckus.

4:00—Alarm clock rings. Investigation reveals that fourteen-year-old who plans to go fishing at 5 set alarm early so he could go back to sleep for an hour.

4:50—Ike Walton turns off alarm and decides to forgo fishing.

5:01—Loud-mouthed robin takes it upon himself to rouse every other leather-lunged bird in surrounding four counties.

5:35—Six-year-old shrieks loudly that tooth fairy came and Goody-Goody-Goody she can go swimming after all.

6:00—Angelus rings out from St. Mary's Church bells.

6:10—Fiendishly happy milkman makes delivery

next door. Sings to outdo squeaky brakes and truck radio.

6:30—My alarm. Up and off to the salt mines, chest out, shoulders back!

7:15—Hubby chokes off snore. Yawns. Mumbles he wishes HE had a soft job and could sleep half the day. Arises reluctantly.

7:16—(One of these mornings): WHAM!

The defense rests. But at night, not without ear plugs!

We were always excited to see our mother's name in one of the largest papers in the state, and it didn't matter to Mom that her payments disappeared so quickly. People stopped her on the street to compliment her on her writing, and this appreciation was as welcome to her as any amount of money.

CHAPTER ELEVEN

Name That

Sandwich

I missed my brothers Dick, Bub, and Rog fiercely, but it was my big sister Lea Anne that I longed for most of all. Until the age of four, I slept in a cot next to Lea Anne, who was nine years older. One night I woke up mid-nightmare, sweating and frightened. "Lea Anne!" I cried. "There are worms crawling on my blanket!"

Her calm voice came out of the darkness. "I know for a fact there are no worms on your blanket, but I'll get up and turn on the light to show you."

She was right. There were no worms . . . *until* she turned off the light and crawled back into bed. She got up a dozen times to turn the lights on and off that night, and I always remembered that she never refused or even hesitated to do it.

I missed my tall, capable oldest sibling for many reasons, not the least of which was her willingness to help Mom around the house. For a long time, Lea Anne was the only girl in a sea of boys. By the time I was born, my family was very happy to see me. It had been nine years and four boys since a baby girl came home from the hospital. However, if they were expecting me to inject a shot of femininity into the mostly masculine household, they were mistaken. New kids on our side of town always assumed that, as a girl, I was a pushover. As I grew older, in fact, I stood up to more neighborhood bullies than any of my brothers. I only had to beat them up once to convince them. I had grown "Tuff" in a family of tough boys.

Lea Anne, my exact opposite, helped Mom with a lot of the household chores—laundry, ironing, cleaning—gamely setting an example I was intended to follow at age nine, when she left for nursing school at age 18. Since my brothers had no such expectations placed on them, I saw no reason to work that hard. My mother deserved some help, but I wasn't willing to be the sole source of household support. Instead of cleaning the house on Saturday morning, I watched TV—*My Friend Flicka, Roy Rogers, Sky King*—vacuuming only during the commercials. When my programs were over at eleven, I was done working.

The one place Mom designated as off-limits—even for cleaning—was the spot that attracted me most, her legendary bedroom closet. If our house were the universe, that walk-in closet would be its black hole; its gravitational pull attracted more than clothes. I had never set foot in it. None of us had, as far as I knew, because that's where Mom stored all the minor prizes she won—toasters, cameras, watches, school supplies, tools, radios, toys. She even kept a three-foot-wide "portable" record player in there for a while. If an appliance died, Mom would root around in the darkness and eventually emerge with a new one. We would stand patiently in a semicircle around the closet door, listening to the sounds of her rummaging.

In the fall of my freshman year, my mother did straighten out my class schedule for me, but not until after the first grading period. The teachers wanted to make sure I performed in the remedial courses as well as Mom assured them I would. When I got A's in all of them, I raced home to tell Mom and found her watching *American Bandstand*, of all things. She hated rock 'n' roll music, though she thought Dick Clark was handsome.

"Wait, Tuff. Listen to this." At first all I saw on the screen was a giant hero sandwich, the kind that's several feet long and a half-foot high. Then Freddy Cannon, a popular singer at the time, trotted out to sing a short little tune without words:

✐━━➤

My
dum-de-dum-de-dum
dum-de-dum-de-dum
Sandwich

Mom's interest in the show dawned on me. "It's a contest called 'The Tune Without a Title,' and it's sponsored by Beech-Nut Gum," she said. "You're supposed to name the tune by describing the sandwich, fitting the words to the beat of the song."

"But it's just a hero sandwich," I said, not getting it.

"Yes," said Mom, "but what *kind* is the question— you know, *'full-of-meat-and-cheese, fills-you-to-your-knees'* or something like that."

"Gee, Mom, not bad. What's Beech-Nut got to do with sandwiches?" I said.

"I'm not sure," she said, "but it doesn't matter. The idea, see, is that the sandwich is too big for anybody to eat." Then she flipped a page in her ever-present notebook. "What do you think of this one?"

My
Made-from-odds-and-ends,
Gives-a-guy-the-bends
Sandwich

"Oh, Mom," I laughed. "I don't think so."
"How about this one?"

My
One's-a-plenty-for,
Up-to-twenty-four
Sandwich

"That's a little better," I said.
"I'll send that one in under your name," she said.

By the end of the week, Mom had made up so many new names for that sandwich she almost ran out of aliases. Each new name grew more graphic. One morning while six of us were eating breakfast and watching her move laundry from the washer to the dryer, Mom paused to scribble a line in her note-book. "Okay, kids," she said, "how's this?"

My
Stuff-it-into-mouth,
Chomp-and-swallow-south
Sandwich

Everybody laughed. "That's gross, Mom," Betsy said, "but funny gross."

"Well, if you think that one's funny, I have an-other one I wasn't even going to send," she said, pulling a slip of paper out of the pocket of her dress. "See what you think of this:"

My
Back-the-deli-truck
To-the-lips-and-suck
Sandwich

The kitchen erupted in laughter and cheers. "That's *perfect*," said Bruce.

"Oh heck," Mom said, "I'll send them all in. You never know what's going to do the trick, and a stamp costs a measly four cents." She always thought postage was a bargain, a practically free and poten-tially thrilling form of communication. You never knew what surprise might come back to you be-cause of your efforts and your willingness to part with a few pennies. "What else can you do for under a nickel that's as much fun?" she said.

By October, I had adjusted to my new classes and had started working one night a week at the small bakery that our neighbor Mr. Druhot ran behind his house across the street. He baked and delivered cookies, pastries, and bread to small grocery stores around the county. My job was to clean the encrusted metal sheets and pans. I loved making $3 a night but could never entirely erase the smell of burned crumbs from my hands and hair. It put me off cookies for a long time.

Mom's earnings from the Toledo *Blade* articles and a few poem sales evaporated like a puddle on a hot day when Betsy got knocked off the swing at school. She broke her glasses, including the plastic eye patch, and cut her temple, requiring emergency visits to the doctor and the optometrist. They didn't insist on immediate payment—knowing the family circumstances, they never did—but Mom didn't like owing money if she had any to pay.

Even worse, Mom's recent wins didn't translate to cash in hand, like the basketball she won from the Colgate toothpaste contest, which she slipped into her bedroom closet when she thought no one was looking. Everyone in the family felt our money woes grow worse, not better, even with Lea Anne, Dick, Bub, and Rog now living elsewhere.

Still worse, Dad seemed to be keeping more of his pay for himself. He was probably drinking more than usual, but there was no way to tell, since he drank constantly when he wasn't working at the shop. Mom was furious at him for what she saw as his financial irresponsibility. She argued, sometimes following Dad around the house for hours, to get him to part with dollars for school supplies, dental bills, and other deepening debts.

"We don't *have* any extra money, Mother," I overheard him say once as he poured himself a shot of whiskey.

"Of course we do, Kelly," she said, her nose about an inch from his. "You're drinking it right now."

This took him by surprise. Mom had rarely mentioned his drinking before, at least not within earshot of the rest of us. His anger flared. "It's *my* money," he said, "and I'll spend it any way I want to."

"You might have thought of that before you had ten kids," Mom said, her volume rising to match his own. "You can't expect them to live on nothing." Dad had no answer for that. Usually itching for a fight this time of night, he was defiantly silent as he emptied his glass and poured himself another shot.

As Christmas loomed, Mom grew increasingly desperate. Not that a lack of cash at Christmas wasn't a familiar condition in our house. She had been penniless often enough to write about it in her usual lighthearted way:

In the Red
An old Christmas custom
    too strong to resist:
You run out of money
    but not out of list.

One night in mid-December I counted out the money I'd made working at Druhot's Bakery over the past few months. My "safe" was the pocket of an abandoned coat that had been hanging under eight or ten jackets on the dining room coat rack for years. None of us had our own bedroom, closet, or dresser to keep our valuables safe, so we had to invent hiding places. In a way, the coat was a better hiding place than a vault. Everyone knows that a vault contains money, but no one would dream of finding dollar bills in a worthless old coat hanging at the bottom of a pile.

Thirty-six dollars altogether; I was rich. Leaning to thoughts of largesse, I contemplated sharing it with Mom. Once again the family was so deeply in debt that I was afraid even she couldn't bail us out in time.

Feeling very wealthy indeed, I took $24, returned $12 to the pocket, and walked into the living room, where my mother sat on the couch, sound asleep with her head back and her contest notebook in her lap:

My
Frisk-the-Frigidaire
Clean-the-Cupboards-Bare
Sandwich

"Mom," I whispered. It took her a moment to open her eyes. "Do you need more money for Christmas presents?"

At that, she sat straight up and blinked herself awake, eyeballing the bills I had brought with me. "Yes," she said, smiling at me. She seemed almost giddy. "I'm a little short this year. Thank you, Tuff."

As she got up to put the $24 away, I felt a surge of holiday goodwill. "Wait, Mom, I've got some more," I said, and retrieved the last $12 from the pocket of the old coat. I expected her to resist, but she took the money gratefully, grasping my hands in hers. Clearly, this was all she had for Christmas. Still, I couldn't imagine how she could buy enough gifts for everyone in the family with a mere $36.

But on Christmas morning, Bruce, Mike, Barb, Betsy, Dave, and I stumbled downstairs to discover a living room full of presents, more than enough to make everyone believe anew in St. Nicholas. Scattered around the tall but spindliest of trees were packages of the usual scarves, socks, and underwear for all, but much more, too:

* two four-foot-long stuffed tigers and a guitar for Barb and Betsy
* a pair of roller skates, a baseball bat, and a set of bongo drums for Dave
* a Gilbert microscope/laboratory set and a basketball for Mike
* a sleeping bag and fishing kit for Bruce
* a record player and an ink pen for me
* an electric shaver for Dad
* an Admiral clock radio, a new notebook, and a roll of postage stamps for Mom.

In the living room, dining room, and kitchen, Mom had piled the tables with bowls of oranges, nuts, Christmas candy, and iced cookies. I began to wonder if she had robbed a bank.

Of course we were used to Mom winning some of the gifts we received, but not *this* bounty, and not this Christmas. Later that day, as Mom sliced the Christmas ham in the kitchen, I slipped into her bedroom and cracked open the door to her closet.

With the exception of the two suitcases, it was empty. She had stored away enough prizes over the year to host a Christmas for eight.

But then, as though the contest gods declared a moratorium on Evelyn Ryan, the prizes stopped. She won nothing. Neither did she sell any new poems or stories to pump up her cash reserves dollar by dollar. This caused more blowups between Mom and Dad than ever.

"The contest wins can't *replace* the money you make from working, Dad." Mom stood, with her hands on the back of a kitchen chair, facing him as he drank at the kitchen counter. "They're just not as reliable or as profitable as your job."

Dad's face grew red, whether in anger or embarrassment, Mom wasn't sure. "Do you know what it's like, Mother, to work all day in that greasy sweatshop? Your life is so easy. You get up when you want to, lie around all day writing in those stupid notebooks. Why don't you try *working* for a change?"

Mom fired back. "For God's sake, Dad, those 'stupid notebooks' are the only reason we're not living in debtor's prison." Reflexively, Dad reached out with the palm of his hand and pushed her away.

My father was a burly man, and drunk enough not to realize he had shoved her hard enough to knock her out of the kitchen, where she tripped and fell onto the dining room floor, her head slamming hard against the wooden baseboard.

All six kids in the living room vaulted out of our chairs and came running to help her. "Get away from her!" I shouted at Dad. "Get away!"

Barb, Betsy, and Dave, crying openly, sat down surrounding Mom, who wasn't moving. She lay flat on the floor, unconscious, bleeding from one ear. "Oh God!" I said, looking up at Bruce. "What should we do?" But he was already on his way out the back door. "I'm going to tell Mrs. Bidlack," he called back. "You stay with Mom!" Dad backed into the kitchen counter and stood there as if his feet were planted in cement.

Mrs. Bidlack, our neighbor three houses down the back alley, rushed to the phone when she heard the news. Another neighbor was using the party line. "Mrs. Ordway!" Mrs. Bidlack shouted, "would you hang up please? I've got an emergency!" Already distraught, Bruce paled when he heard that someone was on the line. Party lines were notorious for spreading the news of events like Mom's "accident." Bruce felt a bit better knowing it was Mrs. Ordway. All the kids liked her, chiefly because she didn't mind that her daughter Vicki could sing and belch at the same time.

Bruce raced back to the house as soon as Mrs. Bidlack got a clear line. We waited impatiently for the ambulance, and when it arrived in the driveway, flattening one of Barb's metal roller skates to the thickness of aluminum foil, no one said a thing. By this time, Mom was groggy but alert enough to calm each of us in turn. She locked her gaze on Bruce. "I'm all right, see?" And she grabbed Barb's hand and Betsy's, then Dave's arm. "I'll be back soon, Tuffy," she said to me, and ran her hand through Mike's hair.

Still wearing nothing but work pants and an undershirt, Dad followed the ambulance to the hospital in his car, tears streaming down his stubbly cheeks.

An hour later, as Bruce, Mike, Dave, and I sat in the living room listening for the car to pull up or the phone to ring, we heard a rhythmic mumbling coming from the bedroom. I traced the muffled rising and falling of small voices to Mom's closet. "Hailmaryfullofgracethelordiswiththeeblessedartthouamongst women." I couldn't believe anyone was in there. We had been forbidden to enter this closet for so long that I felt guilty just opening the door. Inside, Betsy and Barb were kneeling among Mom's shoes, hands folded in prayer, squinting their eyes at the sudden influx of light. I leaned down to their two small faces. "Hi," I said. "What's going on?"

"We're praying to St. Jude that Mom won't die!" said Barb, her brow creased with a single worry line. "Yeah," said Betsy, patch over the correct eye for once. "A lot of Hail Marys."

I nodded. "That's good." We stared at each other in silence for a minute. These two little girls seemed to be dealing with the crisis better than anyone. "Okay then," I said, and closed the door. They had chosen their "church" well, I thought, returning to the living room. The hanging clothes held Mom's fragrance, the vestiges of stored prizes her spirit. And praying to St. Jude, hero of lost causes and Mom's MVP (most valuable patron saint), seemed more than appropriate.

True to her word, Mom was back in a few hours, alert but exhausted. Dad followed her into the bedroom, apologizing all the way. He closed the door, but we could hear him anyway, even as we sat a room away on the front porch. "I'm sorry, Mother. It was an accident. I was trying to push you away, not knock you down."

"We'll talk about it later, Dad. I'm too bushed right now." As she climbed into bed, Mom started the conversation anyway. "To tell you the truth, I think your comment about my contesting still hurts worse than my head."

Dad pulled up a chair and sat down. "It does? Well, there's a reason I said that. Every time you win something new, the guys down at the shop give me a hard time about it for weeks."

"About what?" she said, sitting up now in bed. "What do you mean?"

"Like when you won the five thousand dollars and the bike from Western Auto," Dad said. "You know Hayden Krutsch and Vern Allspeier? They got everybody laughing about it. 'We know who the *real* breadwinner in the Ryan family is,' they said. 'And it ain't *you,* Kelly!' "

Mom stared at him in disbelief. "Why, Dad, they're just jealous. Green with envy! Don't pay any attention."

"Well," Dad said, "it's not that easy. I have to work with these men all day long." He hesitated, then blurted out the rest of his story. "Then when you won the freezer, they said you must have known the judges or rigged the contests some way. Same thing after the shopping spree. They spread the word there was no way you could win so much without cheating."

Mom shook her head. Dad was behaving like one of her children. "Tell them that cheating your way to a first prize in a national contest is about as easy as lying your way into heaven. It can't be done. You know it, they know it. They're just trying to get your goat."

And then a thought struck her. "Is that why you've been acting so odd every time I win something?"

"No," he said, meaning yes. Then, eyes filled with tears, he pulled his weathered black wallet out of his back pocket and gave Mom his last ten dollars.

Afterward, seven-year-old Betsy tiptoed up to Dad as he sat at the kitchen table, flipping sadly but soberly through the Toledo *Blade*. Her tiny body barely came up to his elbow when he was sitting down. "Dad, why did you do that to Mom? She would never knock *you* over." He looked pained, and he folded up the newspaper slowly and said, "I would never hurt your mother, Bets. Not on purpose. You know me better than that, don't you?" Betsy wasn't sure. "Well, don't do it again!" she said. Without ever saying it aloud, the kids who witnessed Mom's fall resolved that we'd never let him hurt her again.

For quite a while after that, the closet remained as empty as it had been after the Great Christmas Clean-Out. Mom seemed resigned to not winning anything, though she was in perfect health again. One lunch period, we came home to find her at the dining room table, writing a note to the doctor explaining why she couldn't pay the emergency room bill. The phone rang, and Mom, inhaling deeply at the thought of another creditor calling, answered it. The man on the other end of the line introduced himself as Tom Hall from the Burns Detective Agency in Detroit. Her first thought, Mom told us later, was "Oh Lord, what has Rog done now?" Then she remembered he was in air force training in Texas and couldn't have done anything wrong, at least not in Michigan.

Mr. Hall then asked to speak to Bruce. Mom, her eyebrows raised in surprise, called Bruce over and handed him the receiver.

"Hello?" Bruce, a junior in high school, spoke shyly and briefly into the phone. None of us over-hearing his conversation could figure out by his answers what was being asked: "Yeah. Yeah. Really? Yeah. Okay." He handed the phone back to Mom, the grin on his face so wide you could count his teeth. "He needs directions to get here. He says maybe I won something in the Beech-Nut sand-wich contest, and he wants to ask me some ques-tions."

Mom stopped breathing for a minute as she stared into Bruce's eyes. Then she grabbed the phone to tell Mr. Hall how to get to our house once he was in Defiance. Her voice trembled just enough for us to know how extraordinary this call might be.

Hanging up, Mom rushed over to her notebooks to look up the prizes. She read aloud: "First prize is a 1961 Triumph TR3 sports car, a full-size Seeburg jukebox, and a trip to New York to appear on the Merv Griffin *Saturday Prom* show. Second prize is a Seeburg jukebox." Six children exclaimed in unison until Mom raised her hands for quiet. "Remember," she said, "they interview *all* the potential winners.

There's no way of knowing which prize we're up for, or whether we'll pass the interview." Then she looked up the entry she submitted in Bruce's name: *My Frisk-the-Frigidaire, Clean-the-Cupboards-Bare Sandwich*. "Oh," she said, smiling broadly, "I just had a feeling about that one."

"Why wouldn't we pass the interview?" Bruce said, suddenly a little nervous.

"Don't worry," Mom said, collecting herself. "Just be yourself. We want to make a good impression, so be as nice as possible. He's probably coming to make sure you exist and that you submitted the entry."

"But I didn't," said Bruce. *"You* did."

"Oh, the judges encourage parents to help kids write their entries. Of course, there's no sense shooting ourselves in the foot, so take credit for it if he asks you."

The detective, Mr. Hall, wouldn't make it to Defiance until late in the afternoon, so we went back to school. Bruce, who had a midterm exam in geometry, had been getting straight A's all year, but he was so flustered that he couldn't concentrate and left several answers blank.

Mr. Hall arrived at the front door promptly at four-thirty that afternoon. We had never seen a real detective before and were hoping he might be packing a gun, but it was hard to tell from his buttoned-up gray wool suit. Mike bumped into him intentionally to see if he could feel any gun-shaped metal objects, but Mom ushered Mike out of the way before he could tell for sure.

Mr. Hall—a short, balding man in a polka-dotted

tie—didn't look a thing like Joe Friday or other TV detectives. But he seemed very official as he approached the only empty chair in the room, the upholstered one with an old issue of *The Saturday Evening Post* resting in the center of the seat. The magazine had been there for years, covering an exposed spring. As he moved closer to the chair, our eyes flashed in alarm. Was he going to sit *there*? To Mr. Hall, it must have seemed that one of us had just put the magazine down to answer the door. Before Mom could stop him, he picked up the magazine so he could sit down and the loose spring shot up like a jack-in-the-box through a large hole in the fabric. Now *he* looked alarmed. "Here, Mr. Hall," Mom said, rushing over. "You take this chair," indicating the rocker I was sitting in. "Tuffy can sit in that one." I took the magazine out of his hands, put it over the spring, and sat down. From then on, we sat completely still in the living room as the detective asked his questions:

"Bruce, do you subscribe to contest publications that write the contest entries for you?"

"Nope."

"Did you have help from any such contesting company?"

"Nope."

"Do you like Beech-Nut chewing gum?"

"Yep."

I could tell by looking at Mom that she wished Bruce would be a little more elaborate in his responses. If she were the one being interviewed, she would have gone on for several minutes for each answer, in an attempt to convince Mr. Hall that our family deserved to win first prize. As it was, she couldn't stop herself from leaping into the conversation occasionally.

"Oh, *all* my kids love Beech-Nut gum—isn't that right, kids?"

We stared at Mr. Hall as if hypnotized. "Uh-huh."

"Bruce"—she looked at him pleadingly—"isn't spearmint your favorite?"

"Yep."

For days after the interview, Mom waited for Pokey the mailman less patiently than usual, but still very respectfully. She even took the time to make sure our crazy rooster, Charley, wasn't hiding in the bushes to bite at Pokey's ankles as they made their way up the sidewalk to our mailbox. But nothing came from Beech-Nut. Very little else came either.

Then, about a week after Mr. Hall drove back to Detroit, Bruce received another telephone call. Mom answered the phone as usual, then handed the receiver to Bruce, knowing what the news must be. Tears flooded her eyes. She could barely speak.

"Bruce," said the representative from the Young & Rubicam advertising agency in New York City, "I'm happy to announce that you've won first prize in the Beech-Nut contest! Your award consists of a Triumph TR3 sports car, a Seeburg jukebox, a weekend trip to New York for yourself and your mother, and an appearance on Merv Griffin's *Saturday Prom* TV show on NBC."

Bruce, a dazed look on his face, passed the phone to Mom. "Mom," his voice cracked, "I think we *won.*"

Mom held up her hand to stop us from erupting until she confirmed the details with Young & Rubicam. But as she hung up the phone, eyes gleaming, every kid in the house began yelling and leaping in the air. We estimated out loud how many other entries must have been submitted. "Fifty thousand . . . seventy-five thousand?" No, the number had to be over a hundred thousand—the contest had been promoted on *American Bandstand*, after all, one of the most popular shows on television. Every time we forgot for an instant that Mom had won, we remembered and began celebrating all over again. We let our imaginations soar. We tried to picture how ten kids and two parents would fit into a two-door sports car, and we wondered where we would put the jukebox—knowing all along that Mom would have to sell both prizes for needed cash. Mom called Aunt Lucy at the Citizens National Bank in Bryan, where she worked, and asked her to look up the value of a Triumph TR3 in the Kelley Blue Book.

Over the telephone line, Mom could hear Lucy flipping through the pages of the book until she got to the right one. "Why, Evelyn," Lucy gushed, "you appear to be twenty-seven hundred dollars richer." Lucy's coworkers at the bank hooted their congratulations in the background.

If $36 of Christmas money made Mom giddy, $2,700 brought her to her knees with joy. We danced around the house for another hour, filling the rooms, the yard, and the block with our cheers: "We won! We won! We won!"

On Friday morning that week, using some of the spending money Beech-Nut had mailed to Bruce for the New York trip, Mom dragged him down to JCPenney and bought him a new suit and a pair of dress shoes. "It wouldn't do for you to show up at the studio in pegged jeans and saddle shoes, now would it?" At the same time, she bought herself a new outfit, the first store-bought clothes she'd had in years.

Early that evening, Mom dug out from her closet the two suitcases remaining from the set of five she'd won the previous fall. She packed one for Bruce and one for herself. The next day Dad drove them to the Toledo airport, two hours away. They flew directly to New York—the first time either of them had flown in an airplane—just beating the blizzard that would paralyze our corner of Ohio for a few days.

Once in New York, they found themselves "awash in luxury!" as Bruce liked to say. The limousine that met them at the airport and ferried them into the city was, as Mom described it, about as long and black as one of the Baltimore & Ohio locomotives that pulled freight trains past our house thirty times a day. Their accommodations at the Waldorf-Astoria left her speechless. "Nothing in Defiance compares to it," she told us later. For the first time, Bruce got his own room—a huge, elegant suite, completely empty except for him. He could barely sleep for all the quiet.

We knew that Mom would feel at home in the Big Apple. She had told us that as a young woman she had dreamed of living by her wits, writing a newspaper column on a big city paper, selling clever verse to national magazines. Now, here she was, in the most prestigious city in the country, if not the world, rewarded for her skill with words. In her original dream, I'm sure she imagined staying longer than forty-eight hours.

Mom and Bruce counted themselves among the very rich during their two days in New York. They spent most of Saturday morning in the back of the limo, sightseeing their way through the city. "Is there anywhere in particular you'd like to go?" asked the driver. Without a thought, Bruce said, "The best pool hall in New York City." The driver turned to stare at Bruce, hoping he was kidding, when Mom broke in. "We are *not* spending a minute of our time in any poolroom," and that was the end of that. Later in the afternoon, the driver took them to see a matinee of *The Music Man* starring Bert Parks. For dinner, they stopped at Sardi's and were escorted to a table next to Milton Berle.

Bruce was ecstatic—with the hotel, the limo, *The Music Man,* Milton Berle. "You can win another contest in my name anytime you feel like it, Mom. It's almost worth having to wear this suit."

Mom ordered prime rib and a glass of wine; Bruce, a cheeseburger and a milk shake. "Oh, Bruce," Mom said, "don't you want to try something you've never eaten before?"

"Please, Mom," he said, "don't give me that speech on the U.S. Army saying smart people eat weird food."

"But it's true," she said. "Intelligent people are more likely to try new things."

"I've never eaten a cheeseburger and a milk shake at *Sardi's* before," said Bruce. "Will that do?"

"Well," she laughed, "at least fish sticks aren't on the menu."

Later that night, they sat backstage at the NBC studio—with Gene Pitney and the Shirelles, who were going to appear on the show—and waited for Merv to call Bruce onstage. The last strains of the Marvellettes' "Please Mr. Postman"—the one Motown hit Mom could identify with—drifted through the studio walls:

Please, Mr. Postman, look and see
Is there a lett-er in your bag for me?

Mom had one last message for Bruce as she brushed a speck of lint from the lapel of his new suit. "Now, remember, take credit for naming the sandwich and don't let on that I had anything to do with it."

Mom stood just a few feet offstage where Bruce could see her. Merv Griffin, ever the affable and expansive host, introduced Bruce as the winner of the sandwich-naming contest and asked him a few questions.

"How'd you come up with the *Frisk-the-Frigidaire, Clean-the-Cupboards-Bare* entry, Bruce?" Merv asked.

"Well," said Bruce, "I come from a large family—ten kids in all—and food doesn't last very long with so many hungry hands searching the fridge and the cupboards for it." He could almost hear Mom's sigh of relief from backstage. Then he pointed in her direction and said, "Of course, my mom—Evelyn Ryan—who is right here, helped me with the entry."

Mom's jaw dropped. "No!" she mouthed. But Merv was already on to the next question. Bruce was happy—he wanted to give Mom *some* credit.

Then the music started. "Pick a partner, Bruce!"

said Merv. Bruce looked at all the girls his age standing around waiting to slow dance, then reached offstage and grabbed Mom's arm, pulling her out in front of the cameras. She was flustered for a moment, and then, looking spiffy in their JCPenney finery, they danced to "Moon River." He stepped on her toes only once.

Back in Defiance, the rest of the Ryan family, gathered around the TV to watch Bruce on national television, saw nothing of the show. The blizzard ruined the reception, and "snow" was all we were able to pick up. We sat inches in front of the TV for the entire hour anyway, unable to hear or see a thing. Not even the Shirelles singing their tribute to mothers everywhere, "Mama Said."

PART FOUR

CHAPTER TWELVE

The Affadaisies

The Beech-Nut win gave us some breathing room, although there was no evidence of the money for months. Just the idea that we had won a $2,700 car and a $1,000 jukebox was enough to make us feel, if not wealthy, almost well-to-do. Mom arranged for the Seeburg jukebox to be delivered directly to Augie Van Brackel, Dad's old drinking buddy, who ran the vending machine business in town. Augie bought it for half its value, but Mom thought losing $500 was worth not having to hear rock 'n' roll blaring nonstop in the house.

The Triumph took longer to sell, so it sat for three months in the driveway. It was small, low to the ground, and shaped like a rocket with wheels. Painted buttercup yellow, it looked more like a shiny Tonka toy than a functioning automobile. Mom put an ad in the "For Sale" section of the *Defiance*

Crescent-News that sounded like one of her 25-words-or-less contest entries: "Brand-new, never-driven, yellow convertible Triumph TR3 sportscar, black leather interior. Family of 12 loves—but can't fit into—2-seater. Call 2-2325 today!"

Scores of people telephoned about the car, most of them almost as poor as we were. They couldn't buy it, but they wanted to see it and sit in it. Defiance with its GM factory was, after all, Chevrolet country, and the Triumph was the foreignest of foreign cars. The wealthiest man in town also stopped by and offered Mom $900 to take the TR3 off her hands. She declined, and as we watched him walk across the street to his Cadillac DeVille, she said, "Now we know why he's got so much money. He probably never has to pay the right price for anything."

My brothers and sisters and I were allowed to take turns sitting in the black bucket seats, but Mom wouldn't let any of us drive the car, not even Dick and Bub when they came home from the Detroit Tiger minor leagues for the winter. We got around this rule by never turning on the engine, so from the house Mom couldn't hear what her children were up to outside. Each of us took a turn behind the wheel as the others pushed the car out of the driveway—the crunching of rubber tires on gravel the only sound to be heard—and silently up and down Washington Avenue. Our driving days came to an abrupt end one day when Dad sat on the edge of the bed, his back to the window overlooking the street, putting on his socks. Mom came in to ask him a question, and just as Dad raised his head to answer, a streak of pale yellow flew past on the street behind

Bruce, formally accepting delivery of the Triumph TR3 sports car, first prize in the Beech-Nut sandwich-naming contest. Since Mom wanted to sell it, no one in the family was allowed to drive it. We pushed it silently up and down the street when she wasn't looking.

him. From Mom's viewpoint, it seemed to travel into one of Dad's ears and out the other. "I could swear I just saw the Triumph go by the front window," she said, "but unless I'm going deaf, the engine wasn't running."

"Those kids don't have a whole brain among 'em!" Dad yelled as he ran shoeless for the front door.

Eventually Mom sold the TR3 to a Triumph dealer from Detroit for $2,100. It was now understood that she was in charge of all the money from her wins. So the family was flush for a while. Mom paid off all the doctor and dental bills, schoolbook bills, bought everyone in the family new clothes and shoes, had Dad's Chevy tuned and re-tired, sent us all to the movies twice a week, and still had enough to pay additional installments of Dick's car insurance until he made enough money to cover the cost himself.

The one extravagance she allowed was for Bruce, who had been caddying at Kettenring Country Club for over a year. He liked making money as a caddy, but he loved playing golf more, so Mom spent $70 to buy him a junior membership in the club and a pair of golf shoes.

Mom thought Bruce deserved a present, and not just because she used his name to win the Beech-Nut contest. It was probably Bruce's interest in golf that prompted Mom to write and sell this poem to *Golf* magazine:

Clubhouse
Where, soon or late,
Each genial foursome
Stops to chat;
Perchance to pour some.

Mom was almost as pleased with the acceptance note written by *Golf*'s contributions editor as she was with the $5 payment:

Your verse,
We thought,
Was good.
We bought.

Bruce had grown several inches in the past six months, and his appetite showed it. On his first day as a junior member of the country club, Mom packed him his usual lunch—two apples, an orange, a banana, four ham sandwiches, eight cookies, and half a bag of potato chips. That day, Bruce played sixty-seven holes of golf, seven and a half trips around the nine-hole course. When he arrived home, he said, "That wasn't nearly enough food, Mom. I ran out on the twenty-third hole." Mom wrote this poem with Bruce in mind:

A bottomless pit too deep to sound
Is what growing boys are wrapped around.
By the pile of bones left on the plate
Off which my teenage son just ate
I'd say if I hadn't seen it fried
A chicken walked up there and died.

With the new year came a third Dial soap contest that excited Mom even more than the last two. She hadn't won the producing oil well; she hadn't won her weight in gold. But she was positive she could win the next sensational headline-grabbing prize, "A Trip for 12 Anywhere in the World!" Mom felt a victory was fated, since her family consisted of precisely twelve people, so she began composing jingles to go with the new opening phrase, "People who like people":

People who like people, *for their favors, vying,*
make pleasing impressions when they Dial, trying.
Mrs. Leo Ryan

"Gee, Mom," I said, reading her entries over her shoulder, "that one's pretty sophisticated."

Sophisticated was my new euphemism for "Huh?" Mom was never fooled by this attempt to spare her feelings. "Well, I hope the judges don't think it's 'sophisticated.' 'Dial, trying' is a play on the words 'Die, trying.'"

"Oh! I get it," I said. And I did. I hoped the judges were as smart as Mom was, or at least smarter than I was. Then I read the next entry:

People who like people *learn in life's school:*
Make "Dial unto others" a "Beholden" Rule.
Eve Ryan

I wasn't sure about that entry either. "Don't you think 'a Golden Rule' would be better than 'a Beholden Rule'?" I asked. The word "beholden" seemed flat and colorless compared to "Golden."

"'Golden Rule' will probably be duplicated by a hundred other contesters," Mom said. "And the judges automatically throw out duplications. 'Beholden Rule' is better anyway. It's a double entendre. It means if you want someone to *be holdin'* you, you'd better wash with Dial."

"Oh! I get it," I said. Those judges better be alert, I thought.

Of course Mom had many of the more straightforward type:

People who like people *sometimes fail,*
   wooing—
They fail to use Dial before billing and cooing.
                                    Mrs. Kelly Ryan
People who like people *make close friends*
But not without Dial, or friendship ends.
                                    Mrs. Kelly J. Ryan
People who like people *chorus aloud:*
"Less Dial's company, two's a crowd!"
                                    Mrs. Kelly Joseph Ryan
People who like people *dine tete-a-tete.*
With Dial's timely aid, the hour's never too late.
                                    Mrs. Leo Joseph Ryan
People who like people *seldom have "words"—*
When their Dial-logue's right, discord's for the
   birds.
                                    Mrs. Leo J. Ryan
People who like people *for Dial are emphatic—*
Tempers flare, tempus fugits, but freshness is static.
                                    Eve L. Ryan

"Wait, Mom," I said, feeling proud of my expertise in freshman Latin, "you made a mistake in the last one. That should be 'tempus fugit,' not 'tempus fugits.' "

"Tuff, Tuff, Tuff," she said patiently. "It's a joke. 'Time flies.' 'Tempus fugits.' Get it?"

"Really, Mom," I said, a little worried. "I hope those judges live up to your standards."

Mom seemed confident. "This is their bread and

butter. They *expect* entrants to play with words and make plays on words. It's what contesting is all about." I needn't have worried. Proof of Mom's wisdom was soon to show up at our door.

After we sold the Triumph, Bruce received a letter in the mail from a woman named Dortha Schaefer, who lived 25 miles away, just outside of Payne, Ohio. "I saw your name on the Beech-Nut win list. My daughter, Mary Kay, won a jukebox in the same contest. As you probably know, the sponsoring companies never publish the winning entries, so I would very much like to know the sandwich name that won for you. Mary Kay's was: *My Stack-It-Thick-and-Quick Snack-It-'Til-I'm-Sick Sandwich.*"

Her letter continued: "We have a club in Payne called the Affadaisies, composed of women who contest as a hobby. If you don't care to write to a mother, perhaps your mother would write to me."

That last sentence was telling. It was Dortha's way of saying, "I wrote my daughter's entry. Did your mother write yours? If so, have her write to me. We have lots to talk about."

"She wants me to join the Affadaisies, Mom," Bruce said. "What kind of name is 'Affadaisies'?"

"It must refer to the affidavits that come in the mail sometimes when you're in the running for a big prize. I guess they added the 'daisies' to cuten up the name," said Mom.

Bruce—at six feet two inches, closer in size to a young tree than a flower—seemed to wilt. "I don't think I'd make a good 'daisy,'" he said, handing Dortha's letter to Mom, "but I know *you* would."

Of course, my mother was elated to discover other women out in the world who shared her love

of contesting. Not that she felt alone in her efforts.
She had subscribed for years to the two publications
no contester worth her weight in gold would be
without: semimonthly *Contest Magazine* and bi-
monthly *Contest Worksheet*, both of which announced
upcoming contests, rules, and deadlines, and offered
helpful hints and essays from consistent winners.

But Dortha was a living, breathing contester, and
Mom responded to her letter immediately with the
name of the winning entry: *My Frisk-the-Frigidaire,
Clean-the-Cupboards-Bare Sandwich*.

"Well, no wonder I came in second," Dortha wrote
in her next letter. "But I'm proud to say I also came
in fourth." (This was true. Dortha had won two of
the top four prizes in a single contest.) "My fourth
place winner was *My Gastro-Comical, Tummy-
Yummysome Sandwich*," Dortha wrote. "And my absolute favorite entry—*My Ding-Dong-Double-Decked,
Left-the-Kitchen-Wrecked Sandwich*—didn't win a thing.

"By the way, Evelyn, what did you do with the
jukebox? Seeburg has offered me $400 or a color TV
instead, but $400 doesn't seem like enough money,
and I've already won eleven televisions, so I sure
don't need another one."

"Call up Augie Van Brackel," was Mom's advice.
"He gave me $500 for my jukebox."

Mom had found a soulmate. In addition to the
eleven TVs, Dortha had won thirty-nine radios. And
between the two of them, they had seventeen children, hundreds of product labels and box tops
(called "qualifiers," or "quallies," in the contesting
biz), and a single approach to life: "No matter how
many kids you might have," wrote Dortha, "I'm
firmly convinced that a person can find time to do

the things they want to do, and you and I must *want* to contest.

"Come to the Affadaisies meeting at my house the first Tuesday of every month," she wrote. "We trade entry blanks, 'quallies,' and fish stories about the 'won' that got away. You'll love it, and besides, I'd love to meet you."

My mother never had any time off, unless you counted Sunday Mass—at five forty-five in the morning, she was guaranteed to be alone—or the family's annual one-day "vacation" at the Toledo Zoo. The zoo trip, ten hours door-to-door, was never much fun for her anyway. She had to fill the car trunk with lunch for ten people, get everyone dressed to go, mediate fights over who got the prized window seats and for how long, and count heads every hour or so to make sure Bruce wouldn't be left behind at the elephant cage again.

"Much as I'd love to come, Dortha," Mom replied, "I can't get away. Too many little kids at home. No driver's license, anyway. Do you ever come to Defiance?" It so happened that Dortha did occasionally have a reason to come to town. For one thing, Defiance had the only JCPenney for a hundred miles, and everyone stuck in the shopping wasteland between Toledo and Fort Wayne, Indiana, drove to the store in town at least twice a year. Dortha decided to make a special trip, just to meet the woman who came in first in the Beech-Nut contest.

On the day that Dortha was scheduled to arrive, I came home from the library and found Mom working at the ironing board. Not on contest entries, I knew, the moment I opened the porch door. The familiar odor of scorched rubber and latex in the air could mean only one thing. It was **Girdle Day** in the Ryan house. She was always apologetic about it, especially in the winter when the windows had to be kept closed. "What else can I do?" Mom said, the first time it happened. "When Playtex discontinued my favorite girdle, they left me no choice but to cut up the old ones and melt the pieces together."

Years before, just after the "Mold 'n Hold" model had been discontinued, Mom wrote a letter to the Playtex company—the International Latex Corporation in Playtex Park, Dover, Delaware—pleading with them to reconsider their decision. Playtex didn't sponsor contests as often as Maidenform did, but she wrote to them anyway. Playtex ignored her first letter, so she wrote more—about one a week— usually including a humorous poem to explain why she loved her girdles:

The fashion model's slim and sleek points
coincide with all my weak points.

When Playtex ignored the poem, she sent another to entice the company into responding:

Growing old gracefully's
Less of a hurdle
Since science perfected
The three-way stretch girdle.

This time, Playtex surrendered, at least in part. The Mold 'n Hold model would not be resurrected, the communications director wrote, but he sent her the five girdles of that type that Playtex had left in storage. Mom was elated.

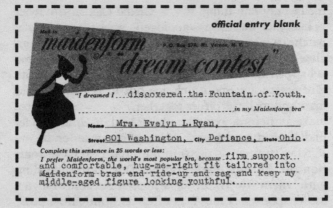

official entry blank

maidenform P.O. Box 576, Mt. Vernon, N.Y.

dream contest

"I dreamed I....discovered..the..Fountain..of..Youth..
....in my Maidenform bra"

Name Mrs. Evelyn L. Ryan,

Street 801 Washington, City Defiance, State Ohio.

Complete this sentence in 25 words or less:
I prefer Maidenform, the world's most popular bra, because firm.support...
and comfortable, hug-me-right fit tailored into
Maidenform bras end ride-up and sag and keep my
middle-aged figure looking youthful.

Now, years later, the five girdles had fallen into various states of disrepair and decomposition. Mom used four of them for parts. That is, she cut them up as needed to fix the fifth. Anytime a split developed in the good girdle, she would cut a small section from one of the four others and iron it onto the split until the material melted together.

The process was similar to repairing tires, and with the same risks. Mom always worried that if the patch wasn't seamless, she could suffer a blowout when she least expected it. Wanting to look her best for Dortha's visit, she waited until the last moment to make her repairs.

Mom also took the rare step of capturing Charley and enclosing him in the back porch. That way, she wouldn't have to run after him if he flew out of the front bushes as Dortha approached the door. "It wouldn't make a very good first impression if I tried to introduce myself at full speed from ten yards back," she said.

The girdle was still warm against Mom's skin when a knock came at the door. Mom—a head shorter and ten years older than Dortha—greeted her new pen pal like a long-lost sister. Dortha started smiling as soon as she saw Mom's face, and Mom grinned in return. They were already having a good time, and they had barely said hello. With her green eyes and light red hair, Dortha looked like a true Celt. "You must be Irish," Mom said. "You look as Irish as any Ryan."

"I've got a drop of Irish blood in me," said Dortha, "but it's diluted pretty well by French, German, and Dutch. The hair fools everyone. My mother says it isn't red. She calls it 'sky-blue pink.' That must be French for 'red.'"

The two of them spent the afternoon in the dining room over cups of coffee, sharing contest lore and discussing the principles every contester must know to win even a single prize. For the first time, Mom had a friend who spoke the same language she did. "Jingles like naming the sandwich come easy for me," said Dortha, "but those prosy 25-words-or-less entries stop me in my tracks."

"Let's face it, Dortha," said Mom. "The jingles are *fun*, while the 25-words-or-less submissions can be dreary, especially if the judges aren't looking for humor."

I sat on the front porch, reading *An American Tragedy* for extra credit in English, but found that Theodore Dreiser paled in comparison to the conversation going on in the dining room. I had learned from Mom long ago that the most important consideration in entering a contest was not the sponsor or even the product. It was the advertising agency hired to judge the contest. "Peanut butter or laundry soap,"

Mom had often said, "Tootsie Rolls or motor oil—it makes no difference. You won't win anything if you don't know who's judging."

Both Mom and Dortha knew, for example, that D. L. Blair, the judges for the Beech-Nut sandwich naming contest, preferred humorous, witty entries. Other agencies went for serious, almost convoluted prose.

"What did you send in for Heinz?" Dortha asked. She was referring to the Heinz contest requiring entrants to complete this statement in 25 words or less: *"Red Magic" Describes Heinz Ketchup Because* . . . "That's being judged by Chicago Donnelley this year."

Donnelley had offices in all the major U.S. cities, but the Chicago office was known to prefer honest-sounding, straightforward entries, leaning to trite.

"I think I blew that one," said Mom, shaking her head. She recited her entry from memory: " *'Red Magic' Describes Heinz Ketchup Because: Like the cardinals' flight over winter-drab landscape, the scarlet flash of piquant Heinz ketchup is an abra-cadabra red accent that brightens interest, appetites, table!"*

"Well *I* like it," laughed Dortha, giving Mom a sympathetic look. "It's colorful. It's . . . it's *red!"*

"Oh, Dortha, I could just kick myself!" said Mom, sounding dejected. "I was trying for something different, and I violated at least two of the four unspoken rules. It was two days before the deadline, and I used my last Heinz label on it."

Even I knew the "four unofficial rules" for 25-words-or-less entries that contesters lived by. It was true—Mom had violated the first two:

1. Make your statement.
2. Use a conjunction like "yet," "while," or "so."
3. Use a series of three nouns ("the mystic three").
4. Include an unusual word or turn of phrase, preferably at the end.

"If I'd been smart," said Mom, "I would have stuck to the formula and cut out the cardinals. I should have tightened it up to something like: *Piquant Heinz ketchup is an abracadabra-red accent that brightens interest, appetites, and table—yet my color-blind hubby loves the true-blue tomato taste!*"

"Oh yeah, Evelyn," said Dortha, "Donnelley would have given a second look at 'true-blue tomato taste.' It's got inner rhyme and alliteration. And they just might consider 'abracadabra-red' to be a Red Mitten. They're smitten with Red Mittens—I know that's the reason I won fourth prize in the Beech-Nut contest."

I had to smile at that. The one linguistic mechanism that *all* the judging companies loved to see in entries was word-coinage, or—as it was known in contesting circles—the "Red Mitten." The purpose of the Red Mitten was almost self-explanatory—it made an entry stand out from the rest. In a basket of mittens, a red one will be noticed. Mom's sandwich name won first prize using only rhyme and alliteration *(Frisk-the-Frigidaire, Clean-the-Cupboards-Bare)*, but Dortha's fourth prize win used inner rhyme and coined words *(Gastro-Comical, Tummy-Yummysome)*.

"You're right, Dortha," Mom said. "And I'm sure the judges gave you extra points for using *two* Red Mittens in a six-word entry."

In the middle of the afternoon, Bruce and Mike tumbled through the porch door shoving and kidding one another. Mom called out from the dining room, "Hey, boys, keep it down, will you? I've got company, and I don't want to scare her away." Dortha laughed, as my brothers continued their shoving match up the stairs to the second floor. "Believe me, Evelyn," she said, "I'm used to it. My kids are probably tearing the house apart because I'm not there." She stood up. "I should probably go back soon, but I'm going to drive to all the supermarkets in Defiance to refresh my supply of entry blanks. Why don't you come along?"

Mom leapt at the chance, and grabbed for her coat. "Doesn't Payne have food markets?"

"Payne has twelve hundred people in it," said Dortha, "so the grocery stores are small. They throw all the entry blanks away, even though I've asked them not to."

"Tuffy," Mom said as she and Dortha passed me on the porch, "you watch the kids, okay?"

"But, Mom . . . ," I began, remembering the fiasco that ensued when Mom and Dad left me in charge of the house a few years back. As if on cue, a loud crash of shattered glass came from upstairs, followed by complete silence. "See?" I said. "You're not even gone, and it's already starting." Bruce and Mike raced down the stairs, each trying to get to Mom first. "It was an accident!" puffed Mike. "We were wrestling, and my shoe kicked through the bedroom window."

Mom rolled her eyes in Dortha's direction, then turned to the boys. "Go up with a broom and sweep up the glass, so you don't track splinters all over the house. Then get Dad to board up the window so the house doesn't freeze." The temperature outside was about thirty degrees.

On any other day, Mom would have dealt with the problem herself, but once she put on her coat to take a drive with Dortha, there was no stopping her. Mom ventured away from home so infrequently that if she had looked in the rearview mirror to see the house exploding, she would have told Dortha to step on the gas.

Dortha and Mom traveled all over Defiance that day, hitting the biggest grocery stores in each part of town—the A & P on the west side, the Big Chief on the south side, Kroger on the far east side, and Goldenetz's on the near east. When Mom got home two hours later, it had begun to snow lightly. She put two full grocery bags on the porch floor—one clean, new bag brimming with contest entry blanks, and the other bag stained and greasy from the residue of empty cans and bottles inside.

"Do a little shopping at the town dump?" I joked.

Mom seemed surprised. "How did you know?"

My eyes widened. "You really *did* go to the dump?"

"Well," Mom said, peering into the bag of garbage, "it's amazing how many empty cereal boxes and soup cans people throw away without even bothering to remove the box tops and labels. These are the quallies I need to send in more entries. If I had known about this earlier, our bathrooms wouldn't be brimming over with bars of Dial soap."

I was shocked. Rooting around in the top layer of a neighbor's garbage can for an elusive cat food label was one thing. Making a special trip to the municipal repository for all the trash in town was another. "Was that your idea?"

"Dortha's," she said. "There's even a name for it that sounds fairly respectable. It's called a 'qualifier search.' All the Affadaisies do it," she said happily, and dumped the empty cans and bottles into the kitchen sink to soak off the labels. Of the four sinks in the house, at least one was usually full of soaking future "quallies."

Even with the hundreds of qualifer labels in her kitchen cupboards, Mom sometimes found herself without the one she needed for a particular contest. True, we had enough Tang labels to underwrite a rocket to the moon, but not a single Skippy peanut butter when the time came. The glue on the Skippy jars could survive a forty-eight-hour bath, but the paper dissolved into mush. Frustrated in her attempts to enter a Best Foods' Skippy contest before the deadline (*I'll have nuttin' but "Best" for my kin*), Mom finally inserted her typewritten entry in an emptied jar (sodden label still attached), screwed the top back on, and mailed the whole thing off to Best Foods, knowing she would never win for breaking the rules in such a way. "At least," she said, "they'll get the message about the glue."

Dortha heard about the Skippy jar entry later that evening when she called Mom to thank her for her hospitality. "Evelyn, old girl," she said admiringly, "that is an entry worthy of your town's name."

The next morning Mom climbed the stairs to wake her children for school. Standing in front of Bruce and Mike's bedroom door, she was still thinking about her adventures with Dortha the day before when she felt a chill against her slippered feet. She opened the door a crack then drew back in surprise as flurries of snow fluttered out into the hall. "Oh my Scot!" she said. "Didn't anyone board up the broken window?"

Mike and Bruce, beginning to stir under a mound of blankets about a foot thick, seemed undisturbed by the drifting snow that spread halfway across the floor. Their crude attempt at keeping out the snowflakes— a pillowcase Scotch-taped across the open gap— flapped crisply in the morning breeze. Mom stood ankle-deep in the icy pile and pulled the collar of her robe tightly around her neck. "For God's sake, kids," she said. "There's enough snow in here to open an icehouse! Didn't Dad fix the window?"

"Are you kidding?" said Mike.

Mom sighed. "Sometimes it feels like I live in a circus, and all the animals are loose."

"Besides," added Bruce, "we knew you'd fix the window eventually—you're much better at things like this than Dad."

Mom seemed to snap. "Am I the *only* one who can do anything around here?" she said, exasperated. "Doesn't anyone else feel even a glimmer of responsibility? Can't I go away for a single afternoon without worrying whether the house will still be standing when I get back?" Then she sat on the edge of the freezing bed as if resigned. "At this rate, I will never get to an Affadaisies meeting in Payne."

Hearing the anger and frustration in Mom's voice, Mike and Bruce vaulted out of bed and began yanking on their clothes. "Don't worry, Mom," Bruce said, shivering as he pulled on his frigid socks, "we'll clean it up."

"Get the snow shovel and the buckets off the back porch before Dad wakes up," she said. "And be quick about it before we're all as frozen as those socks."

But Dad was already up. He sat in the dark living room, sipping a cup of coffee and watching snowflakes melt against the warmth of the front window-pane as the two boys filed down the stairs and quietly past him on their way to the porch. He turned to look at them only briefly, and without interest. He wasn't fully awake, unaware of the gathering snow-drift directly overhead. A minute later, they filed past him again on their way back upstairs. Dad watched them go, this time noting their cargo of snow shovel and four clanging metal buckets. A look of confusion crossed his face. "Boys," he said, pointing out the window, "the snow is that way."

Back upstairs, Bruce and Mike found Mom still sitting on the edge of the bed in the icy room with a sad look in her eyes. In an effort to cheer her up, Bruce said, "It's not that bad, Mom. After we get rid of the snow, we'll wipe up the floor with towels."

"Yeah, Mom," said Mike. "When we're done, there won't be a single snowflake indoors."

Mom smiled at her two sons. "It's not the snow, boys, but thank you. I'd just like to be as free as everyone else is to go where I want when I want."

Mom couldn't drive, but she wasn't about to learn, either, as Lea Anne, Dick, Bub, and Rog discovered in turn when they offered to teach her after passing their own driver's tests. She didn't want to become the family chauffeur, but more than that, she regarded her refusal to drive as an act of independence. Mom walked everywhere—the library, the Penney's store, the hospital, the post office—powered by more than mere muscle and bone. Her stride reflected a sense of expectancy, as if anything were possible "on this path called life" (as she once put it in a leaning-to-trite Chicago Donnelley entry for Cat-Tex shoe leather: *Good for the sole on this path called life*). She walked out the door with her head back, shoulders square, and feet flying—a woman of purpose, even if that purpose was nothing more grandiose than the purchase of a few four-cent postage stamps.

So throughout the winter of 1961, Mom had to be content hearing the Affadaisy contest news from Dortha through the mail and occasional phone calls. With each new tidbit on the Affadaisies, Mom grew increasingly frustrated that she couldn't be present for the meetings herself. "You've got to meet the cofounder of the group, Betty White," Dortha said in one telephone call. "Smart as a whip. She's the reason I started contesting in the first place."

"What did she do?" asked Mom, intrigued.

"Oh nothing," Dortha laughed, "except win a car! She made it look so easy, I decided to try contesting myself."

Mom wanted more. "What car?" she said. "What contest?"

"It was a few years ago," said Dortha. "The 'Big M Dream Car' contest on *The Ed Sullivan Show*. She won the first prize—a 1957 Mercury."

Mom voice rose in excitement. "*She* won that first prize? I won our first television set in the same contest! I'd love to meet her."

"She'd like to meet you, too, Evelyn. All the girls would. You know, three of our group were Pillsbury Bake-Off winners—Betty Yearling, Gladys Tierney, and Christine Shamanoff."

Mom was thrilled. It was rare to meet a Pillsbury winner, since hundreds of thousands of women sent in recipes. Pillsbury was one of the few contests in which Mom had failed entirely (not even an honorable mention), and the prospect of talking to an actual Pillsbury winner consumed her. It wasn't that she admired women who could bake well; she admired anyone who could *win*. "Oh, I wish I were half as good at cooking as I am at eating," said Mom. "I don't seem to do well in bake-offs."

"Aren't you a good cook?" asked Dortha.

"In a word, no." She laughed. "Do you think that's necessary? I always start with a name I think the judges will like, then make up a recipe around it. Probably not smart. 'Cheesy-Pleasy Pie' was one. I threw everything I had in there, even Jell-O. My kids took one look at it and ran. Another one was 'Tropicranberry Bars,' which I thought had a nice sound to it even though no one in my family can stand cranberries. Pillsbury apparently couldn't stand them either."

"Hey," Dortha said, "'Cheesy-Pleasy Pie' and 'Tropicranberry Bars' sound a heck of a lot more tasty than 'Cupcakes with Gum,' which is what another Affadaisy sent in."

Mom laughed in disbelief. "Now I don't feel so bad," she said. "That one is beyond even *my* inabilities in the kitchen."

Mom's attempts at creative cooking left most of her children breathless with surprise. The Cheesy-Pleasy Pie was essentially cooked vegetables in a crust, which looked deliciously edible until we discovered the cream cheese and lemon Jell-O inside holding the ingredients together. But our disappointment in the pie was nothing compared to the shock generated by her first Pillsbury entry—mashed fish rolled into balls and coated in crushed cornflakes—a dish she optimistically called "Sardine Puffs." Only Dad and his brothers would eat this so-called food. It pushed some of us over the edge, away from cornflakes for life.

Dortha talked about other contesters, too. "There's a woman living in Goshen, Indiana, who I go see a couple of times a year. Her name is Emma Hartzler. Emma's won the usual assortment of TVs, radios, blenders, and carving sets. She also won a rifle she's been trying to hide from her teenaged sons since it arrived. Why don't you come with me when I go in a few months? I think the two of you will hit it off."

"Oh, Dortha, I think our trip to the dump is the only outing I'll have for another year. Does Emma ever come to our neck of the woods?"

Dortha sighed. "I wish she could, but Emma can't even get out in her *own* neck of the woods. She's had polio for about fifteen years now. She spends all night in an iron lung, and all day in an automatic rocker bed so she can breathe."

Mom was taken aback. It took a moment for the full meaning of Dortha's remark to register. "I'm so sorry," she said. In the 1950s, polio had been brutally unpredictable in its choice of victims, like a viral sniper. No one felt safe. "How does she write contest entries if she's paralyzed?"

"Believe it or not, Evelyn, she gave birth in that iron lung three days after being stricken. Now she can move only her arms, and only from the elbow down, but there's nothing wrong with that head of hers. She does all her contesting flat on her back."

"What an inspiring use of time!" Mom exclaimed.

It was exactly what Mom would have done in the same situation. Now she couldn't wait to meet Emma. "Let me think about this, Dortha. Even if I can't get to an Affadaisies meeting, there's got to be some way I can get away from Defiance for a day to meet Emma."

Dortha had a sudden inspiration. "Evelyn! I think you might not have to come to the contest meetings. I think the meetings could come to *you!*"

Mom almost choked. "Oh my," she said, wondering how she would ever fit that many people into her already bulging house, with Dad in the kitchen to boot. "I don't think—" Mom said.

Dortha interrupted, "It's not what you think, Evelyn. Leave it to me!"

CHAPTER THIRTEEN

Round Robin

*M*om's backyard garden bloomed that spring with an abundance of perfumed surprises. Not just the usual crowd of daylilies and white hollyhocks hugging the south side of the house, but a huge thatch of wild dame's rocket, a patch of pink peonies that she swore she never planted, and violet clematis climbing up past the windowsills. Groups of delicate lilac impatiens colored the base of the arborvitae bushes, as if each tall, narrow shrub had donned purple anklets.

As kids, we loved to stand as still as possible in this uproar of color and fragrance. The scent of one plant mingled with another until the backyard smelled like nature's bakery. Bees droned overhead, intoxicated. The tall stands of purple iris smelled almost edible, like sugared ginger. We breathed it all in, as if it were vapor from a candy store.

The only intrusion into this bucolic tableau was the weekly run of the Defiance mosquito truck down the back alley. The liquid toxins were the city's defense against the army of summer insects that rose up from the Maumee and Auglaize rivers at dusk in search of exposed flesh. Residents couldn't decide which was worse, the bugs or the cure. The truck emerged from an overhang of trees in the alley, a slow-moving, gunmetal hulk with a giant accordion hose that spewed clouds of yellow-gray pesticide over lawns and houses like a poisonous weather front, or what we liked to call "the yellow fog of death."

Despite the threat of officially sanctioned toxins in the air, spring shone in all its glory. Nothing was so abundant in the yard this fine May day as Mom's precious tulips, planted two months before and now standing at attention everywhere, even at the base of the laundry poles in the yard, where she now hung the day's wash. The clothes dryer had expired earlier in the morning, in the middle of drying a heavy load of sheets, towels, and six bananas that she had hidden inside and once again neglected to remove before baking them into the weave of the linens.

Mom's dismay at the banana'd sheets had long since dissipated. Here was another catastrophe she could use as inspiration for contesting—in this case, adding a rhyme about laundry to a Sta-Flo starch/Sta-Puf rinse jingle, for which she would win three pairs of Enchantress nylon hose:

✏️▬▬▬

For laundry magic at its best,
Make the Sta-Flo/Sta-Puf test,

Just one trial and you'll agree
"These <u>stand</u>-bys save <u>work</u>, washing, <u>me</u>!"

Mom was hanging the second basket of laundry
when she noticed an odd movement in the tulips
clumped beneath a large black walnut tree at the
edge of the alley. Mammy, having given birth to another litter a few weeks before, emerged from the
forest of spring-green stems and peach-colored blossoms with what appeared to be a kitten in her
mouth. But on closer inspection, the "kitten" in
Mammy's mouth seemed to be feathered.

"What do you have there, Mammy?" Mom said as
the cat strolled toward her. The black-and-white kittens followed their mother in clumsy baby steps
through blades of grass as high as their heads. Mom
bent down just as Mammy gently laid a half-bald
but healthy baby sparrow at her feet. Since the day
Mammy had adopted our Easter chick, Charley, her
maternal instincts had ceased to separate furry ba-
bies from feathered.

Mom lifted her gaze toward the dense branches
of the black walnut tree. Even if she could make the
climb, returning the foundling to its nest would be
next to impossible. Mom and Mammy stared gravely
at one another. Between them, these two veteran
mothers knew all there was to know about infant
care. Mom cupped the helpless sparrow in her
hands and carried it into the house.

Once inside, she lined an empty shoebox with
cotton batting and set the trembling little body inside. Careful not to jostle the box, she carried it
down to the cellar and nestled it between two pipes
on top of the water heater.

We all trooped down the basement steps to watch Mom feed the tiny orphan. "He looks like a ball of dryer lint," said Mike.

"He must be tired," said Dave, who had to stand on a chair to look into the box. "He's always yawning."

"He's not yawning," said Mom as she dropped small bits of bread soaked in warm milk into the bird's gaping beak. "He's hungry. Who knows how long it's been since he fell out of his nest." The bird gulped down five mouthfuls and wanted more.

"What should we call him?" asked Barb, joyful at this latest addition to the family. "He should have a name."

Dad was there, too, looking over Mom's shoulder as she continued offering bits of wet bread to the bird with her thumb and index finger. "That mouth is as wide as an open barn door," he said.

"That's a pretty accurate description." Mom laughed. "Go to sleep, Barney. We'll be back with more food later."

"Good night, Barney!" we chimed in. It felt as though Mom had come home from the hospital with another little Ryan.

A few feet away, just outside the ground-high basement windows, Mammy sat with her kittens, staring through the screen at Barney in the box. "Good work, Mammy," said Mom as we trooped back upstairs. "You saved that bird's life."

It was to be a day of birds. When the mail arrived at 801 Washington, my mother was so happy she could have kissed Pokey on his postal forehead. First there was a letter from Dick, who sent news that he was pitching for the Decatur Commodores, a

Detroit Tigers' minor-league team in Illinois. Ordinarily, this would have been more than enough to brighten my mother's day. But Mom put Dick's letter aside to give her full attention to a fat packet from Dortha Schaefer. "It's my first Round Robin!" she exclaimed, slitting the envelope open with her scissors.

"A round what?" I asked.

"A Round Robin," she said, "is a series of letters you get from a circle of friends—hence the term 'round.'" Mom pulled four letters out of the packet, and several Skippy peanut butter labels floated to the porch floor.

"Oh, someone in the group has read my mind," she said gleefully. "I've been soaking Skippy jars for three days trying to get a clean label for my peanut butter poem." I had read this one—a sly takeoff on "Ali Baba and the Forty Thieves," which she'd seen Mike reading for school—fresh off the ironing board several days before:

Survival Kit:
Such simple things young sons require
To keep life's flame aflutter:
A loaf, a jar, and forty knives
to smear with peanut butter.

"Who sent the labels?" I said.

"One of the women in the Round Robin," Mom said. "There are four others—I'll be the fifth 'Bird.' This envelope contains a letter from each one of them. The letters go around in the circle, see, from one member to the next. They write to each other about contests and show the entries they've submitted in the last month so everyone can comment on everyone else's submissions. And if someone has extra entry blanks or qualifier labels, they throw those in, too. When I finish reading these letters, I'll write my own and add it to theirs. Then I'll send the whole bunch on to the next woman on the list."

So this is what Dortha meant when she promised to bring the Affadaisies to Mom. The Round Robin letters revealed all there was to know about contesting. Because the women critiqued each others' entries, the letters served as a slow-motion brainstorming session. "When I get the packet back in a few weeks," Mom said, "my last letter will be in there with handwritten comments from the other Birds. Help like that is invaluable." Short of winning a major contest, I had rarely seen Mom this excited.

Mom held one of the letters in her hand, and I unfolded the other three out of curiosity. The salutations made me laugh. "Look at this, Mom. These three start out 'Dear Birdies,' 'Dear Lady Birds,' and 'Tweet Things.' "

"Talk about a runaway metaphor," she said. "First, Barney falls out of a tree, then this Robin falls out of the sky!" With that, she was deep into the first letter, like a thirsty woman at the water well.

Reading the four letters, Mom got to know the other Robins a little better. Betty White, winner of the 1957 Mercury, had four children and a no-

nonsense attitude about her wins. "Let's face it, girls," she wrote. "We don't do this for the glory. We do it for the mental stimulation . . . and, oh yes, the *money!*"

Mary Ann Kooker, an art teacher with three children, had just won a clothes washer and a watch. Of all the Robins, Mary Ann seemed to be the "lucky" one, a contester who could enter a "no-frills, no-skills-required" sweepstakes and have her name pulled for a prize.

Much to Mom's delight, Emma Hartzler wrote poetry in addition to contest entries. Her recent wins were impressive: three clothes washers and dryers, and a portable iron lung (which, according to Emma, sounded more promising than it turned out to be).

Later that day, Mom sat down at the dining room table to compose her response. For the occasion, she had taken the time to thread a new ribbon onto the old black Underwood she had used for decades.

Hi Nestmates: Just finished your wonderful group of letters. I never wanted them to end. I plan to benefit tremendously from listening to you other birds chatter!

And I couldn't agree with you more, Betty, on contesting for the stimulation and the MONEY! May our aims be high and our earnings higher.

All five women were in the midst of submitting entries to the annual Real-Kill insect spray contest. First prize was a five-day trip to Paris, but everyone had a chance to win one of the hundreds of other prizes, including a color television, an air conditioner, cameras, and transistor radios. If she didn't win the trip to Paris, Mom was hoping for the TV. The GE television she had won seven years earlier was on its last legs. The only way to keep the picture from wildly flipping up and down was to have Betsy sit on the floor in front of it and exactly one foot to the right side. No one knew why. It had something to do with the metal in her eyeglass frames, or perhaps a certain purity of spirit.

To win the bug spray contest, contestants had to invent a name for the spray, then write a one-line description of it. Mom, who had entered the contest two years in a row on her own, brought new enthusiasm to her submissions because her Round Robin friends were in the wings, so to speak:

Here are my entries for naming the bug spray. I anxiously await your comments:

BR-R-OOM	*It clean-sweeps bugs from every room!*
COUP	*Halts BUGaboo; hails bug adieu!*
BLAST	*The breath of death, from ffftt-to-"last!"*
HAN'T	*That STAYS and SLAYS, tho SOME SPRAYS CAN'T!*
POX	*For bugs, each can's Pandora's box!*
MICKEY	*For "flooring" bugs, a REAL-gone quickie!*
CAPER	*That haunts bug-haunts with lethal vapor!*

| BARRAGE | SURE, like running your motor inside the garage! |

Those seem to me to be about the best, and none of 'em look especially bright, now that they're cold. Ran out of entry blanks, so I sent some of them on plain paper, in which I never put much faith.

P.S. I'm also enclosing a couple of extra d-Con blanks, in case someone needs one. Can't afford to buy a package just to get a label. Gee, wish I had rats!

Mom wrote her critiques of the other women's entries in longhand on their letters. She thought one of Dortha's could win the whole thing:

| FATE | Never too soon for bugs to be "late." |

"When they come by with your prize for this one, Dortha," Mom wrote, "don't forget us little people." Though Mom loved receiving suggestions for corrections on her own entries, she didn't feel comfortable in a critical role herself. "You never really know what the judges will go for," she said to me. She wrote "Like these a lot" next to entries from various Robins:

ALARM	To ensure that bugs have "bought the farm."
NEVER	For bugs, this stuff is DEADly clever.
NO!	When bugs just simply have to go.
THUNDER	So "bugs end" up six feet under.

BARBARIAN   *Stops bugs at border, and germs*
                    they're carryin'.

Rather than critique the other contesters, Mom offered encouragement, although her responses were often as indecipherable to me as some of the entries I used to place in the slack-jawed category. When I glanced at her half-finished letter to the Robins while she made lunch in the kitchen, I couldn't understand a word.

Mary Ann, am positively green with envy over your free Pfaff. Emma, I'm really pulling for you to win that car—tire slashing is such a dirty trick! Dortha, I just knew that SiamEASE would win something. My "bathroom" line for Armstrong was "Mom's on bathroom Queue T!" but I fouled up my own keying (unintentionally sent two with identical names) and I'm not sure if that's the winner. I thought it was a cinch for endless duplication. The other was "Re-treads won't tire me!"

None of this made sense until I saw Mom's notes and the other contesters' letters sticking out from the Skippy labels. A "Pfaff" was a brand of sewing machine. Apparently, Dortha had won another television—seventh prize in the Armstrong One-Step Floor Care contest—by filling in the last line with a Red Mitten:

✏➤

**Washing . . . Waiting . . . Waxing . . . Waiting
That's ancient history!**

With Armstrong One-Step Floor Care
It's SiamEASE for me!

Mom's last line to the Armstrong poem—*Mom's on bathroom Queue T!*—hadn't won, nor had her *Swish! Wash-waxsimile!* But her reference to footprints appearing before the wax was dry (no longer a problem with the quick-drying Armstrong) was *Re-treads won't tire me!* It won Mom ninth prize, a Kodak 8mm movie camera.

Seeing all this conveyed in the coded language of the Round Robin, I felt a new respect for my mother and her colleagues. Competing against tens of thousands of other contesters throughout the country, not to mention contesting groups in our own area—such as the Versatillies in Fort Wayne and the Lima-Writes in nearby Lima—these women had a desire for victory that rivaled that of the greatest generals. Most of them won almost as much as Mom did (thus far in her astounding career, my mother averaged one win for every four entries she submitted) and eagerly awaited the next battle.

The Robins had so many stories to exchange that the letters zipped around the circle quickly. Mom, not wanting to slow things down—and not trusting Pokey to usher the packet through on time—walked hers down to the post office to mail off to the next person on the list. One day while she was gone, Pokey delivered an official-looking envelope addressed to me. In all of my fifteen years, I had seen my name on an envelope only once before—last year, the summer of 1960, when Mom won a year's subscription to Dell Comics in my name with this poem:

Other heroes
Wax and wane
But Tarzan's still
The one for Jane.

It was a thrill seeing my name typed on an envelope again, this one from the Ohio State Safety Council. I knew that the letter was intended for Mom, so I waited for her to come home and open it. Sure enough, it announced that I had won the Northwest Ohio safety slogan contest—that is, Mom's entry under my name had come in first. "What did you win, Mom?"

"*We,*" she corrected me, "won fifty dollars."

"What was the winning slogan?"

"You were brilliant, Tuff, as usual. Your entry was '*Stay Alert and Stay Alive.*' "

A week later, the State Safety Council awarded me the first prize of $50, and a photographer from the *Defiance Crescent-News* took a picture of me and the second-place winner. I did my best to look intelligent enough to have written the slogan, but I got the feeling that the middle-aged woman who came in second doubted my credentials. In the newspaper photo, she looked down at me with a mixture of disbelief and anger.

"Maybe she thought her slogan was better than yours," Mom said. "Hers was '*Alert Today, Alive Tomorrow.*' It doesn't sound quite as good. Without a verb, there's no punch."

"Maybe she didn't like coming in second to a teenager," I said.

"Her expression might have nothing to do with you," said Mom. "It could be that her hatband was too tight."

I looked again at the photo. I knew my friends would see my picture in the paper and I felt that surge of exhilaration Mom must have experienced almost daily since her first win. Mom was far from feeling exhilarated, however:

We've been having another of our periodic runs of evil luck, finance-wise, and I do believe everything in the house is broken, including that infernal clothes washer.

Mom was careful about portraying our financial state as "normal" for a big family, but you could tell the Robins understood the situation perfectly. They also loved household crises and home-repair remedies. What's wrong with the clothes washer? Betty wanted to know. And had Mom heard of the new contact lenses? Even if they were lost or broken, Dortha wrote, they could be insured.

Of the six kids remaining in the house, everyone but Dave wore eyeglasses, probably because we liked to read so much. Mom said it was a good thing we didn't enter contests because the fine print on the entry blanks was microscopic enough to ruin anyone's vision. The Ryan kids caught her contesting fever anyway. Betsy wrote a poem that won the $100 first prize for Defiance fourth graders in a poetry contest sponsored by Catholic Daughters of

America, and Barb's poem won the $50 second place for sixth graders. The two of them were flabbergasted by the large cash prizes, and Mom instantly opened savings accounts for them at the First Federal.

My mother wasn't really surprised at these wins. She had been showing us how to write rhymed verse for years. Her teaching method was simple and inviting. She would leave an open notebook on the dining room table with the first line of a poem written on an otherwise blank page. Anyone in the house was encouraged to add a second line to rhyme with the first. Then Mom would add a third line and wait for someone to add the fourth.

Mom and Betsy wrote this poem when Betsy could barely write:

Mom: March is a month when kites fly high.
Betsy: They run from the wind across the sky.
Mom: I think that when a kite looks down
Betsy: It sees the sights all over town.

Even Aunt Lucy caught the contesting bug. Her entry in the "Why I Shop at the A&P Food Market" contest "was so much better than mine," Mom told the Robins, that she gave Aunt Lucy her prize, a motorized barbecue grill. Of course, my parents didn't want a barbecue anyway. Dad never stepped into the backyard for any reason, and Mom was afraid Mike would find a secondary use for red-hot charcoal briquettes.

For his part, Mike, now an eighth grader, decided to enter a writing contest sponsored by the Catholic Knights of Ohio. He struggled over his essay for many weeks, even while sleeping. One night he stumbled downstairs in mid-dream to Mom and Dad's pitch-black bedroom. "Mom?" he called from the doorway.

Mom shook herself awake, expecting a medical complaint, such as a stomachache. "Is that you, Mike?"

"Mom, I need your help," he said, his worry audible in the dark. "Should I write 'Oh,' 'Oh shit,' or just leave it out?"

Mom took a moment. She knew Mike was dreaming on his feet and wouldn't remember swearing, let alone write it in a religious essay. "I think I'd just leave it out."

"That's what I thought," he said, and sleepwalked back to bed. His essay, "The Power of Prayer," won first prize, a new black Schwinn bicycle. A story calling him "a budding writer" appeared, along with his photo, in the *Crescent-News* and in the *Catholic Knights of Ohio Messenger*.

Let me tell you, Birdies, this boy Michael has enough nervous energy to light a small community. I do believe he wrote most of that essay in his sleep, though he doesn't ever calm down, even at night. I'm thinking of taking away the Wheaties. He doesn't need any—just chloroform. As a writer, though, he's got the knack!

The other boys weren't as confident writing essays, but when it came to sports, they were born experts. Gulf Oil sponsored a weekly football pool, and both Dad and Bruce hustled down to Defiance's lone Gulf gas station for entry blanks. The premise was like that of any weekly sports pool: Entrants tried to predict the winning teams and scores for upcoming weekend college and professional games. The top prize for the most wins each week was three hundred gallons of gas. The runner-up won twenty-five gallons.

For days, Dad and Bruce sequestered themselves in the dining room, poring over football statistics on the teams, players, player changes, coaches, past scores. "In other words," they liked to tell Mom when she passed by, "no guesswork." This systematic approach, they felt, took care of everything but the fantastic upsets that sometimes happen in sports. They filled out their entry blanks separately, even secretively.

The first week Dad submitted ten entries, Bruce— with characteristic exuberance—fifty-one. The day after the games, they checked the winners list taped to the window of the Gulf station. Neither one of them won a single gallon of gas. "So much for research," Dad said.

"It'll pay off eventually," said Bruce, with the patience of a born contester. (Heaven knows he had heard Mom say it enough times.) "Either that or we should just fill out a blank for every conceivable combination of wins. We could use the names of everyone in the family, like Mom does for her contests."

Dad wasn't convinced. "To cover every possible combination," he said, "you'd have to fill out a thousand entry blanks. Even *this* family doesn't have that many names in it." The second week, Dad submitted twelve entries, Bruce ninety-two.

Don't know if I told you son Bruce and the Master of the House have been competing in the Gulf football pool, trying to win free gas. You'd think they were preparing for a final exam in Greek. A couple of years ago, before the state outlawed it as gambling, Dick won almost $400 in two weeks on the same type ticket. He sent in only one ticket per week—you had to pay so much, according to how many teams you estimated scores on—for three weeks, but his research was very thorough. His dad haw-hawed like mad all the time he was filling out the form, but yelled just as hard as anyone when we listened to the scores those Saturday evenings and found that Dick had actually won. The whole thing would have bored me to death, but then the menfolk think *I'M* crazy, too!

A few days later, my father and brother pounded into the house in mid-argument.

"What's the matter with you two?" Mom demanded.

They turned to her at once, both of them shouting like six-year-olds. "I won twenty-five gallons of gas in the Gulf football pool!" said Bruce. "I sent in a lot of entries, so I used all of our names. Today they hung the winners' names on the gas station window, and 'Barb Ryan' came in second. That was my entry."

Dad blew up. "It was *my* entry!" he yelled, his blue eyes bulging in anger. "I entered in Barb's name, and my 'Barb Ryan' won."

"*I* won?" Barb asked, confused. Her small, high-pitched voice floated in from the dining room, where the younger kids were listening to the big fight from the farthest corner.

"No," Bruce said. "Dad and I used your name on two different entries."

"Oh, I can't believe this!" Mom said, shaking her head. "The two of you are going to have to work it out—but not by fighting! Isn't there some way to figure out which entry won?" Mom knew it was probably hopeless. Even she couldn't always determine which of her entries had won a particular contest.

After thirty minutes of grumbling and complaining, Dad and Bruce agreed to split the gasoline, twelve and a half gallons each. They even had the gas station attendant split the twenty-five-gallon certificate in two. Bruce disappeared after that. To avoid another fight, he began to work more nighttime hours at Max's poolroom downtown.

Meanwhile, the next Round Robin had arrived, and Mom was anxious to read the other members' handwritten critiques on her bug spray entries. Dortha was the kindest editor. "Most of these too clever for the 'likes' of Chi Donnelley," she wrote, referring to the judges at the Donnelley company in Chicago. "Save the concept for a contest judged by D. L. Blair. They appreciate wit."

Betty White was good on form and the most

direct in her criticism. She had taken a correspondence course on how to contest, and was quick to share her knowledge with other members of the group. "No, no, no!" Betty wrote next to Mom's last entry to name a new bug spray (*BARRAGE—SURE, like running your motor inside the garage!*). "Never use a weak word like 'the' when you can use a more power-ful one—like 'locked,' 'closed,' 'sealed,' or even 'shut'—instead."

Mom, veteran that she was, instantly realized that Betty was right. "The point," she told me, "isn't to omit articles of speech—that could ruin the rhythm, you see—but to substitute words that create a more lasting image in the judges' minds." Still, Mom stuck to her original idea. "If I changed 'the' to 'shut,' it takes the emphasis away from the rhyme of 'barrage' and 'garage.' I think I'll leave it be." I reread the line several times. The amount of thought that had gone into the entry belied its simplicity. Contesting looked a lot easier than it was.

Dortha was now more adamant than ever that Mom find a way to get to an Affadaisies meeting. The next one was set for the following Tuesday in Payne. Since Bruce had recently passed his driver's test and now even had the required gasoline, he was the man for the job. Desperate to go, Mom told Dad that she and Bruce would have to use the car for the drive to Payne. "All right," he said, "but let him use his own gas. And I still think it's *my* gas, by the way." So Mom, relieved and excited at once, accepted Dortha's invitation.

I'm dyin' to get to come see you girlie birds, but old wheel-less wonder me will have to rely on the driving skills of son Bruce. I only hope he can drive as well as he eats. For someone downright scrawny, he can really put it away.

The next Tuesday, Bruce filled Dad's car with twelve-and-a-half free gallons of gas and drove home to pick up Mom for the trip. As she brushed her hair one last time, she looked around the messy house, piled with comic books, schoolbooks, encyclopedias, marbles, paper dolls, baseball cards, doll clothes, pillows, blankets, crayons, crumpled Kleenex tissues, and rugs in a well-mixed, two-foot layer all over the floor. "I probably should have cleaned the house before we left," she sighed, "but what's one more day? Besides, we're not expecting visitors."

Just as they started out the door, six-year-old Dave pushed through them coming the other way, puffing with the effort of carrying a large burlap bag filled to bursting. "Whatcha got there, Davey?" Mom said, leaning over for a better look.

"It's a surprise, Mom!" said Dave, beaming as he unfolded the top of the bag. "It's for you!"

Mom couldn't believe her eyes. "Holy Moly!"

The bag was filled with hundreds of tulip blooms, every color of the rainbow.

"Davey!" Mom exclaimed. "Where did these come from?"

"They grow all over, Mom! I picked them from in front of Druhots' house, in Mrs. Desch's backyard, Mrs. Zipfel's, Mrs. Bidlack's. They were *everywhere*, even in *our* backyard. You love flowers, so I pulled the tops off for you."

"My Lord," Mom said sadly, just as the first grief-stricken neighbor arrived at the front door.

"Did you see what your son did to my beautiful Stop-the-Car tulips, Evelyn?" asked Mrs. Simonis, close to tears. "I sent all the way to the Netherlands for those bulbs."

"Stop-the-Car?" Mom said, as Dave hid silently behind the door. "What do they look like?"

"A purply peach," said Mrs. Simonis, wringing her hands. "Purple on top, peach on the base." Mom peered into the burlap bag. There were dozens of purply-peach blossoms. Mrs. Simonis took a peek, too. "Oh my stars!" she gasped, clutching her hands over her heart.

Mom exhaled deeply. "I'm as sorry as I can be, Jean," she said. "Davey didn't understand how hard you worked at growing them. And if I may say so," she added, looking hopefully from the bag into Mrs. Simonis's face, "they're the prettiest ones here!"

The intended compliment was lost on Mrs. Simonis, who continued to stare sorrowfully at my mother. Mom tried again. "We're so sorry, Jean. Davey! Tell Mrs. Simonis how sorry you are!"

Dave squeaked, "I'm sorry," not moving from behind the door. The quiet apology barely traveled the foot between his hiding place and Mrs. Simonis.

"If Dave hasn't already picked mine from the backyard," Mom continued, "you're welcome to go dig those up. They aren't from the Netherlands, but they're pretty in a basic American sort of way." Mrs. Simonis didn't respond. In a daze, she slowly walked away.

Mom turned to Bruce. "Of all the luck!" she said. "Something tells me I'm going to be hearing from a lot of bereft gardeners. I'll have to stay home today."

Bruce's mouth dropped open. "But, Mom, I put

all my gas in Dad's car. How am I supposed to get it out?"

"For the love of Pete," she said. "Go tell him that you put *his* twelve and a half gallons in the car and that he should give you the certificate for his half in exchange."

The rest of the day was devoted to the dearly departed tulips. Former owners of the blossoms arrived in droves as word of Dave's deed spread through the neighborhood. The house, at least, was bright and beautiful. Mom got the kids to fill every bowl we could find with water. We floated the blooms—320 in all—on top. Our front room looked like a busy funeral parlor.

Mom and Dave spent four hours receiving grieving gardeners. "I just *knew* I should have cleaned the house," Mom groaned. All was not lost, though. She wrote this poem, later selling it to a Catholic magazine for $5:

Real Thing
She tosses a pillow,
Poses a book,
To give her home
That lived-in look.
Six children spare me
Such sly biz:
My home looks lived-in
'Cause it IS!

That week, Mom received an assortment of small checks in the mail—$1 for a poem sold to *Precious Blood Messenger,* another dollar for a rhyme in a Lutheran Sunday school magazine, and $2.50 for a story about Bruce's big feet (size 13) in the *Boot and Shoe Recorder*. With the $5 for her "Real Thing" poem, she was able to finish paying for the two raincoats she had on layaway for Betsy and Barb and half of a pair of eyeglasses, leaving just two pairs unpaid for.

It made Mom happy that we didn't have to rely on the Lions Club for our glasses anymore, but glasses themselves seemed to be going out of fashion for people who could afford contact lenses. Every teenager in the world, Bruce included, now wanted contacts, but they were beyond the reach of our family pocketbook. Even the cost of insuring them was more money than we had to spend.

Dortha, sympathy over the contacts issue with your daughter. I had quiet fits when Bruce decided he wanted them after he'd worn glasses since he was about six, suffering surely at least fifty separate and various breakages in the twelve-year interim. Why a kid who's worn glasses that long suddenly decides he'll look so much better without them, I don't know. You wouldn't think he'd look natural even to himself! The sad thing is that insurance on contacts has gone so high as to be almost prohibitive. The last company over here who still had a moderate rate discontinued it when one of their clients dropped hers in her dessert at a fashionable soiree and unknowingly ate it.

Almost forgot—Got my check for the $5 poem. Also got $15 from Charm Craft greeting card company, for a birthday card idea. Every little bit helps! Leaves me a little puzzled, though, since at present I have at least seven places where all twenty bucks should go. Problems, problems!

The Robins loved Mom's spirited anecdotes, but beneath her rousing "Every little bit helps!" they sensed a false cheer. It was no secret that the Ryan family was hanging by a string.

CHAPTER FOURTEEN

Going, Going,
Gone

If our finances were on the edge before, the tulip episode tipped the family into the abyss. Mom walked down to the bank and withdrew the $50 she won for the safety slogan so she could give $5 to each afflicted neighbor. "Seems like I barely get the check cashed before the money disappears," Mom said forlornly, and not for the first time, as she counted out ten $5 bills. As usual, the words were barely out of her mouth before she had written another poem, this one earning her $3 from *Grit,* a national newspaper of verse and short prose:

Going, Going, Gone
We can't take it with us . . .
That much we all know.
My trouble's been keeping
The stuff 'til I go.

Mom wrote these poems quickly and efficiently—"a veritable writing machine," she called herself happily—because now instead of waiting for bills to come in, she had plans for every penny she made. She continued paying Dick's car insurance and sent clippings from the *Defiance Crescent-News* to the Robins, who savored every word.

Dick Ryan Unbeaten: Latest word on the Ryan boys of Defiance in the minor leagues has Dick hurling the Decatur Commodores to a 2–0 victory over Clinton in the Midwest League. . . . Dick is now 4–0. Brother Bub Ryan won his first game with the Montgomery Rebels in Alabama after pitching the last 4 innings—1 hit, no runs, no walks.

Bruce, too, was making a surprisingly steady income racking balls after school at Max's Card and Pool Room, where owner Max Sheik had taken Bruce under his wing. "If your mother hadn't had so many boys," Max said gruffly, "I wouldn't have any employees at all."

And with Dortha and the Round Robins around to share the excitement of winning—and the suspense of waiting—a commonplace win turned into exhilaration when her last line entry in the Lever Brothers "Million-Dollar Contest" won tenth prize, a set of cooking pans:

**A million dollar contest and who could ask for more
A golden opportunity is knocking at my door
To try good Lever products and be a winner
"too"**

Wise wives demand the Lever Brand, "No!" "just-as-goods" in lieu!

Knowing Dortha had sent entries to the same contest, Mom made one of the rare telephone calls they shared together (a call to Payne, twenty-five miles away, was considered long distance). "Dortha," she said breathlessly, "I just won the pots and pans from Lever. Did you get anything?"

"The mailman just left," said Dortha. "I won the carving set, twelfth prize."

"For what?" Mom said. "What was your last line?"

"Impress as chef and charmer and score high in Home IQ."

"Not bad," said Mom, "considering they were judged by Donnelley. It's hard to be clever without being *too* clever, but small wins like this always manage to get my heart pumped up again."

"Have you heard from the bug spray contest?" asked Dortha.

"Not yet," Mom said, "which worries me a bit. As we know, 'no news is good news' everywhere but in the contest biz." The bug spray win, both knew, could bring in some serious money.

"Did you see that Paper Mate pens launched a new one?" Dortha asked. "It's really a pip."

"No," said Mom, aghast. It was rare for my mother to miss the announcement of a contest. "What is it?"

"Supplying the last line to a jingle," said Dortha, "but the thing is"—and here Mom could hear the excitement in her voice—"the big prize is ten thousand dollars in credit. Face it, Evelyn, that's a lot of baseballs."

"Credit?" Mom said, disappointed. "You mean

they hold the money until you buy things? Dortha, I can't pay bills like that." Like many Midwesterners who had lived through the Depression, my parents distrusted the very idea of credit.

"Sure you can!" Dortha sang out. "It's like money under the mattress and just as safe. Besides, you'll love this one—we have to write all our entries with a Paper Mate pen."

"We do?" Mom said. "Darn! Of all the writing utensils in this house, I don't think a one of them is a Paper Mate." And then she thought it over. "How would the judges know if I used another pen?"

"Oh gad," said Dortha, "a corporation like that probably has a chemist in the mail room, checking all the incoming entries. You don't want to mess with the rules. The only reason these companies sponsor contests is to get us to buy whatever it is they're selling. You'd better bite the bullet and buy a Paper Mate."

"I will," said Mom, grabbing a Ticonderoga pencil. "Now give me the first lines of the jingle."

"All right, but you have to promise me you'll make the next Affadaisy meeting, okay? I won't even chance some problem with you getting a ride. I'll pick you up in Defiance myself and we can drive back to Payne together."

"Fine, anything you say," my mother laughed. "Now what's that jingle again?" And as soon as she hung up the phone, Mom started in on the Paper Mate jingle:

For school room, bank or office
Doodles and documents, too
Use a dependable Paper Mate

"In a word," it's the "write" pen for you!

> Evelyn Ryan

No blots on the name, or on you!

> Evelyn Ryann

No penchant for skipping to rue!

> Evelyn L. Ryann

No misstery writer are you!

> Evelyn Lenore Ryann

Each refill bestows life anew.

> Mrs. Evelyn Ryan

The "mark" of a penman's Buy-Q.

> Mrs. Leo J. Ryan

Small expense means an ex-pensive you!

> Mrs. Leo Ryan

Find skipping has skipped to m'lou.

> Mrs. Leo A. Ryan

A day later, Mike and I helped Mom stuff envelopes. "Hey, Mom, I love this 'skipped to m'lou' entry," I said. "It's almost as good as 'a penman's Buy-Q.' That's a play on 'IQ,' right?"

"Good one, Tuff," Mom sniffed—she was coming down with a bad cold. "You're catching on."

"I like the 'no blots on the name or on you,'" said Mike. "But how do they know you've used a Paper Mate to fill out the blanks? You could've used *any* pen."

"Oh yeah?" she said. "What if the pen leaked and made a blot on the entry blank? The people at Paper Mate would know I hadn't used their non-blotting pen. What then?" She paused to blow her nose.

We were interrupted by a chirp across the room.

Sure enough, Barney's tiny bird head peeked out at Mom from the potted plant on the windowsill.

By now even Dad loved Barney, our very own sparrow, who had grown so adept at flying that he would soar up the basement stairs into the house in search of Mom, his favorite human being. He liked to sit on the end of the ironing board as she worked, sometimes perching on her shoulder, but his favorite spot was the top of her head. To him, Mom's hair was almost as soft as the cotton batting in his shoebox downstairs.

Mom had begun sneezing explosively because of her cold, and each blast catapulted Barney a few inches into the air above her skull. "Oh Lord," Mom said sadly as she dialed the phone, "I have to call Dortha to cancel. With this cold, I can't even think about going to the Affadaisies meeting." She could, however, contemplate the side of the Kleenex box, and the contest advertised there was just the remedy Mom needed. First prize was $30,000 in publicly traded stock. She spent the afternoon sneezing and writing last lines to this jingle:

Kleenex is so handy
I use it every day
Costs so little, helps so much
Big blows! Sore nose? Passe!

Mrs. K. J. Ryan

My come-to-blows mainstay.

Mrs. Kelly J. Ryan

Throw it <u>and</u> germs away.

Mrs. Evelyn Ryan

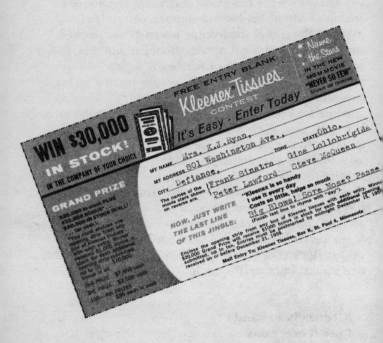

Does lots in tot's sick bay.
>   Evelyn Ryan

Thru "tug-a-long" relay.
>   Mrs. Kelly Joseph Ryan

<u>*This*</u> *"Teacher's Pet" rates "A."*
>   Mrs. Kelly Ryan

Rx: Blow, then throw away.
>   Evelyn L. Ryan

Very little ironing got done that day. After finishing her Kleenex entries, Mom moved on to the Dole pineapple contest—

✐

Dole pineapple chunks are <u>just</u> as they'd be
If I was Dole and Dole was me.

—when she heard Pokey coming up the walk to the mailbox. The Round Robin circulated separately from Affadaisies meetings,· and Mom's thoughts perked up at the thought of another batch of letters. She walked out the porch door to meet Pokey halfway, her mind still on Dole entries:

✐

Dole pineapple chunks are Dole-icious cut <u>bite-size</u>,
For sweet, cocktail, salad, conveniently <u>right-size</u>.

"Hello, Vernon," said Mom, smiling. She never called him Pokey to his face.

"Afternoon, Evelyn," Vernon said as he rifled through his leather mailbag. When he looked up from his letters, his gaze froze. "Uh . . . Evelyn?"

"Uh-huh?" Mom said.

"You probably already know this," he said, his

feet shuffling shyly, "but you've got a bird on your head."

At this, Mom raised her hands slowly to the sides of her hair and felt the unmistakable feathered body resting on top. "Oh sure," she laughed. "I guess I forgot for a minute."

Vernon smiled, but never stopped staring at Mom's hairline.

"He fell out of a tree a while back," Mom said, trying to explain away her embarrassment. "He's been with us ever since."

"I knew there must be a reason," said Vernon, handing Mom the day's mail as he backed slowly down the front steps. "It's just not often that I see a bird riding on someone's head."

Back in the house, Barney still nesting high in the strands of her hair, Mom chuckled as she looked in the mirror. "I can't believe I walked out there with you on my head, Barney," she said. "By tomorrow, everybody in town will be calling me the Bird Lady of Defiance."

Just through the door from school, Barb delivered the punch line. "The good news, Mom," she said, "is that you'll no longer be known as the Dead-Tulip Lady."

Mom laughed in mid-sneeze. "Oh, anything but that," she said as she stood at the ironing board unwrapping her new Paper Mate pen. An hour later, Barb passed Mom busily writing more Paper Mate rhymes, steam hissing up from the board like a humidifier.

For school room, bank or office
Doodles and documents, too

Use a dependable Paper Mate
Well spent is its small cost to you.
Mrs. Evalyn Lenore Ryan

What's "right" to the "point"—it comes through!
Mrs. Kelly Ryan

Makes its "mark" 'cause it always comes thru!
Mrs. Leo Jay Ryan

It's plainly "write" usage to you.
Evelyn Lenore Ryan

Two hearts are its "copy-right" cue!
Mrs. Evelyn Lenore Ryan

The Robins kept track of each other's ailments as meticulously as they researched contesting, and Mom, who referred to herself as "the accident-prone Ryan of all time," felt some relief chronicling her bad cold and one pratfall after another.

Pulled my sacroiliac out of plumb again lifting huge flower urn off mother-in-law's grave; knocked into end of eavespout on roof while replacing the storm windows with screens and cut my head open; cut several dozen assorted fingers peeling various eatables lately; fell victim to the twenty four-hour virus just at suppertime on my favorite TV night and had to go to bed; and caught cold sitting on the bleachers for two hours watching Davey play Bunny League baseball. Darned good thing Dave's team won or I'd have been in an evil mood! Gotta hand it to my daily swallow of sea water, my daily vitamin-and-iron pill, my daily apple, and my daily tablespoonful of apple cider vinegar. Just can't beat them thar old home remedies, nohow.

The Round Robins' trademark enthusiasm was abruptly suspended by the news that Emma had nearly died in a recent thunderstorm. Every time a howling summer storm knocked out the electricity in her neighborhood of Goshen, Indiana (about one hundred miles from Defiance), Emma's husband had to call in the local fire department to help pump her iron lung by hand until power was restored. If Emma were left alone for even a few minutes without power, she would die from lack of oxygen.

But the latest storm had felled trees and power lines and knocked out the phones, leaving Emma helpless and alone. Her sons were in school, and her husband at work, so until they were able to get home, Emma's neighbors—aware of her situation—spelled one another in what Emma called "the hand-pumping derby." Everyone agreed it had been a close call.

Of course all my complaints pale in comparison to the storm that knocked out your electricity, Emma. Glad your guardian angel was on duty when your iron lung lost power. I can just imagine how exhausting hand-pumping can become after awhile. Have you thought of setting up an alarm system so an outage will ring a bell in the fire station?

Mom knew better than to worry about Emma, who had, after all, lived in the iron lung for fifteen years and was "accustomed to the occasional mishap" by now, as she said. In some cases, she was the most daring Robin, having introduced the group to a competition announced in *True Story*, a magazine known for titillating "true-life" tales. Entrants were asked to read a fictional story and invent a title that best described it. The first month's story was about a working mother who felt guilty leaving her children in the care of someone else during the day. Mom sent in many entries, several under Barb's name:

My Moonlighting Money Couldn't Buy Mothering
Mother Was Prodigal with Her Bounty but a
    Miser with Her Love
My Mother Gave Us Everything—But Herself

These were, according to Dortha, "just corny enough to win."

But Mom's characteristic pluck almost deserted her late in the summer of 1962 when, along with the latest Round Robin, two more letters arrived, one from Dick and one from Bub. Writing from New York, Dick said he had been released from the Detroit Tigers and drafted by the army. "Released?" Mom cried out in disbelief while reading the letter. "Released and *drafted*?" Dick had injured his arm a month earlier while playing football with other members of the team. Further pitching had so aggravated the injury that the coaches took him out of the rotation. A few weeks later, he was quietly let go, and his days as a professional baseball player were over. Dick's best friend had also been drafted, and the two of them were on their way to Fort Gordon in Georgia for basic training.

"I can't believe it," Mom said feebly. "An entire career down the drain because of a game of football?" She was as close to tears as I had ever seen her. We stood around silently, trying not to cry ourselves.

Bub's letter was equally shocking. He had been so unhinged at Dick's release from the team that he quit on the same day that Dick left. "It's just not a very stable life, Mom," he wrote. "I can't expect to raise a family without knowing whether they're going to jerk the rug out from under me like that." (Mom knew he wanted to marry Jannie, his high school sweetheart.) With the help of a couple of buddies in the Tiger organization, he was moving to Los Angeles to enter the police academy. So he, too, was out of baseball—and planned to live a long way from Defiance.

"Los Angeles? The police academy?" Mom's knees started to buckle as she grabbed a chair and sat down hard. "I just can't believe it." We tried to comfort her, knowing it was no use. Mom was a person who set her sights on a goal and never varied in the direction she chose. She did not win contests because of luck, she always told us. She won because she wanted to, because she was determined to. To see her own sons—each so gifted at the one sport everyone in the family loved—lose an opportunity as golden as the one the Tigers had offered, was beyond her understanding. "Unbelievable," she sighed again.

In a few hours, her disappointment ebbed as she thought of the turmoil Dick and Bub must be going through. Both of them had dreamed since childhood of pitching for the Detroit Tigers. Dick had delayed going to college and Bub had postponed marrying Jannie to devote themselves to pro baseball. Now, in a heartbeat, it was all over. And here they were, trying in their letters to sound adult about it, as though moving on was the mature thing to do. Well, Mom thought to herself, maybe it was. They were young men, capable of making their own decisions and living on their own in the world.

"I guess they'll finally learn how to do their own laundry," she said wearily. "And pay their own car insurance. That's good, I'm sure." Barney chirped from the ironing board. "Pretty soon," Mom muttered to her feathered buddy, "it'll be time for you to fly away, too."

Contesting by now had become more than a potential source of income. Writing entries distracted my mother from bad news, and it was Mom's way of putting her brain to work at something productive—something she felt contributed positive energy to the world. Turning from Barney, she picked up the Paper Mate again, this time adding more exuberance than she felt:

For school room, bank or office
Doodles and documents, too
Use a dependable Paper Mate
Spencer'd be (p)envious of you!
> Mrs. Leo B. Ryan

Your "John Henry" won't cause cries of "Who?"
> Mrs. Leo C. Ryan

Make the "grade," with its aid, lifetime through!
> Mrs. Leo D. Ryan

"Wears" well—clips to mink or muu-muu!
> Mrs. Leo E. Ryan

As style—"right" as Adolphe Menjou!
> Mrs. Leo F. Ryan

"Adolphe Menjou, Mom?" Barb asked.

"He is a *famous* actor," Mom said, flipping over Dad's frayed (and only) white shirt, "and stylish, too."

When Dad stepped in the door from work that day, he was already in a bad mood, and disheveled to boot. Bits of grass and evergreen were plastered to his face and work clothes. He threw his lunch bag onto the table. "That ratty chicken nearly killed me!" he shouted. "What's the matter with him?"

"What happened?" said Mom, not the least bit surprised. She knew it was only a matter of time before Charley went after the wrong person.

"The little weasel flew head-high out of the bushes and knocked me flat. You better get rid of him before I kill him myself."

"Just settle down," Mom said, her voice rising. "You're not to touch a feather on his head!" Mom's sudden ferocity stunned Dad into silence. "I've already talked it over with Aunt Lucy," she said. "There's an egg farm near her house, and they're always looking for more chickens. Charley can be king of the roost there and live with his own kind for once."

None of us felt that Charley had our best interests at heart. After all, he clawed and bit us at every opportunity. Still, we had no desire to do him harm. "But, Mom," Barb said, twisting a pigtail in worry, "Charley thinks his kind is *cats*."

"Believe me, Barb," Mom said, "Charley will be in chicken heaven on that farm."

When Dad heard the news about Dick and Bub, he sank to a chair in disbelief. Little bits of evergreen still stuck to the back of his head. "I had a feeling something was wrong," he said. "Neither one of them's written for a while." He looked across the table at Mom. "Can't we do something?" he asked.

"They've got their own lives to live now, Dad," said Mom. "They'll be all right."

"I didn't want them to be *all right,* Mother," he said quietly. "I wanted them to be the *best.*"

Mom reached out to rest her hand on Dad's arm. "They *are* the best, Kelly. It doesn't matter what they do. We just have to let them go."

Dad sighed, ambling out to the kitchen. Mom went in search of her Paper Mate:

For school room, bank or office
Doodles and documents, too
Use a dependable Paper Mate
No lapse, no perhaps; neat, theme-through!
> Mrs. Leo G. Ryan
Each one writes "like a millyun" or two.
> Mrs. Leo H. Ryan
Smooths abcdarian's debut!
> Mrs. Leo I. Ryan
To smoo-o-o-th little stINKer's debut!
> Mrs. Leo K. Ryan
To brighten your ballpoint-of-view!
> Mrs. Leo L. Ryan

"Oh, Mom," said Betsy, "I love that 'ballpoint-of-view.'"

"I'm afraid it's the only one in this batch that's worthy of sending in," Mom said.

"Let *them* decide!" Betsy said jubilantly. "Isn't that what judges *do?*"

Mom looked down at her youngest daughter, born fifteen years after Lea Anne but at that moment apparently the smartest person in the house. "You're right, Bets," Mom said. "We wouldn't want to underestimate those judges."

As if the news from Dick and Bub wasn't heartrending enough, the house and its environs seemed about to fall apart from the strain:

The decrepit washer is acting up again—it runs only HOT water 'til it empties the tank; the brakes went out again on the old jalopy; plus, the car needs a new starter; the TV set broke down this morning; and the refrigerator handle finally fell off completely.

We can probably live without the TV, the refrigerator handle, and the car, but without that WASHING MACHINE, we are a mere load-of-clothes away from The Grapes of Wrath around here.

Another doozy of a storm roared through Friday night (and I sure hope this one didn't travel across the state line into your territory, Emma!). There were two jolts that sounded like atomic explosions. One tore a three-foot hole in the ground right beside the house—spewed mud clear over the roof onto the other side!

A fourth letter in the mail that day lightened Mom's emotional load a bit. It was an affidavit from the Real-Kill pesticide company. An "affy," as everyone in the house knew, meant that Mom was probably in the running for a major prize in the bug spray contest. All she had to do was sign the form, get it notarized, and mail it back to Real-Kill. She would then be one of several candidates awaiting further word on who won what.

Let me set you straight, gals—I sent that affy back so fast it probably met itself coming. Haven't heard a word since. If I get one of those ice crushers I'm gonna hit somebody over the head with it, preferably me. I just might have fouled things up a bit—the letter was addressed to E. L. Ryan. I, like a nut, signed the affy MRS. E. L. Ryan—I remembered on the way home from the mailbox. Hope they don't give me a lesser prize just because I added the "Mrs." Can't remember which entry I sent as E. L. Ryan, but am sure I had some not-so-good ones signed Mrs. E. L. Ryan. Argh!

Betty, hope YOUR affy from Watchmakers of Switzerland turned into something fabulous. Your luck has been wonderful lately. Your refrigerator and stove sound like the Ryan retiree-age appliances. When the door handle of our fridge came clear off, we had just finished stowing the week's vittles inside. Took us hours to figure out how to get 'em back out again in time for dinner.

Every Robin knew the feeling of waiting on tenterhooks for responses to affidavits. It wasn't common practice, but a few companies sent affys for minor prizes (like the ice crusher), and this drove contesters crazy. "An ice crusher!" Mom had exclaimed when it arrived in the mail. "What was last prize? A block of ice?"

Another time, an affidavit Mom received from

Kraft Foods turned out to be for a clock radio, not the $10,000 first prize she was praying for. She was happy with the clock radio and used it in the kitchen for years to tune in to radio contests hosted by the lone radio station in Defiance, WONW. "But frankly," she admitted to well-wishers, "I would have preferred the ten thousand dollars."

A week later, Pokey ambled up the porch steps with "a decided spring in his step," Mom would later tell the Robins, and soberly delivered the good news. One of Mom's pesticide entries had won third prize, an RCA color television worth $540, according to the letter. Mom's emotions had bounced up and down so often in the past few weeks that it took a few moments for the news to sink in.

"Does this mean I don't have to sit on the floor to keep the picture from flipping?" said Betsy.

"Well I sure hope so." Mom laughed. "Listen to this, kids," she said, reading from the letter. "They want me to specify my choice of finish to be sure it matches our 'decor.' "

We had to laugh at that. "How about 'Early American Refuse'?" she chuckled. "Or 'Scarred Scandinavian.' "

"Just be truthful, Mom," said Mike. "Tell them it's 'Cracked and Splintered Old Stuff.' "

Sometimes it took only a single win like the TV to inject our household with winning energy. Dad and Bruce renewed their separate attempts to win the Gulf football pool, stepping up the number of entries each week to ensure better results. One weekend, Dad submitted 15 entry blanks, Bruce 155. And this time, one of them won.

"Mom! I did it!" shouted Bruce, running into the

kitchen about ten steps ahead of Dad. "Betsy won three hundred gallons of gas!"

Betsy looked pleasantly surprised. "I did?"

Bruce smiled down at Betsy. "Well, not exactly," he said. "I used your name in the pool and came in first." Just then Dad knocked Bruce from behind, sending him flying across the kitchen table and onto the floor. "You liar!" Dad boomed. "I won that gas and you know it! I won the twenty-five gallons under Barb's name, and I won this three hundred gallons under Betsy's!"

Mom grabbed Dad's arm, then whispered menacingly, "If you even *think* of hitting him again, Kelly, I'm calling the police!"

Dad turned away in defeat. Bruce pulled himself up from the floor, clearly unnerved but quietly determined. "That's it, Mom. I'm going to Los Angeles. I can live with Bub."

Mom was taken aback. "Los Angeles?"

Bruce dabbed at his nose, his hands shaking. "I'm going to sell this gas to Max Sheik, down at the poolroom. He told me that if I ever won the whole thing, he'd buy it from me. I'll use the money to buy a train ticket."

For the third time in as many weeks, Mom felt herself sinking into a chair. She knew Bruce was right. The fights with Dad were the most compelling reason to go, but there were others. Defiance offered few job opportunities for high school graduates, and neither Mom nor Bruce wanted him to be working at Max's poolroom in ten years' time.

"I guess you've thought about this for a while," she said, resigned.

"A long time," Bruce said. "I want to go, Mom.

Bub can help me find work, and college is cheaper in Los Angeles than in Defiance." This was true. Defiance College, a private school, had become far more expensive than state universities in California.

"Well, if you've got the money to go, then you should. There's no telling when or if we'd ever have the money to help if you tried to do it later."

"I'll stick around until later in the fall. . . ."

"No," Mom said firmly, though her voice was shaking. "You've made the decision that's best for you." She looked at Dad, then back at Bruce. "You should go now, while you have the money to do it."

Bruce sighed. "Okay. Bub says the sooner I establish residency, the cheaper school will be for me."

Forty-eight hours later, the Ryan family stood inside the elderly Baltimore & Ohio train station in Defiance, three blocks from home. After hearing thousands of trains roar by our house, this was the first time any of the kids had ventured inside the station. The miniature Victorian structure hugging the iron rails that cut through town had seen better days. Paint peelings curled down the wall above the water fountain. The curved wooden bench had been worn smooth, though it was solid enough to hold the weight of eight of us. Oddly enough, the air inside the ancient station house felt fresh and new, almost electric with opportunity.

The trip from Defiance to Los Angeles cost $148. This was $2 less than the $150 Max Sheik had paid Bruce for the three hundred gallons of gasoline. Mike, Barb, Betsy, Dave, and I sat morosely off at one end of the bench, still not accepting Bruce's imminent departure. Mom and Dad stood next to

Bruce, his single suitcase (the same one he had taken for the weekend in New York two years before), and a grocery bag full of food Mom had packed for the three-day cross-country trip.

"Twelve peanut butter sandwiches, six apples, five bananas, a family-sized bag of cookies, and a toothbrush," Mom said, smiling. "Should be enough for three days, even for *you.*"

"I'm really low on cash, Mom," said Bruce. "I only have a couple of bucks."

"Money is the one thing I don't have," she said. "I still owe the eye doctor for two pairs of eyeglasses, including the ones you're wearing. But you won't need any money for the trip—you've got all this food—and Bub will pick you up at the station in Los Angeles."

When the shiny blue-and-silver passenger train coasted to a stop next to the rickety platform, it appeared to be trapped in the wrong century, like a rocket standing next to the OK Corral. There were very few passengers going west that day, and after Bruce climbed aboard, the train pulled out quickly. We waved good-bye to the sleek behemoth and the figure of our beloved Bruce, who seemed lost and forlorn, though standing squarely on the threshold of his future. Even Dad was misty-eyed.

We would later learn that Bruce arrived in Los Angeles weak with hunger, having eaten all twelve sandwiches, six apples, five bananas, and the bag of cookies before the sun had set on his first day of travel.

Bruce left for California to live with brother Bub, the cop. After he's in residence there six months he can attend Los Angeles City College for practically nothing. Even good old Defiance College, right on our doorstep, is $800 per year just for tuition now. Will probably be even higher next year. The house has been like a morgue ever since. Only five kids left! It doesn't seem to matter how many you have—whenever one of them goes it leaves a big hole!

After Bruce left, the house felt somber for days. Mom took to carrying her Paper Mate pen wherever she went, "just in case inspiration strikes."

For school room, bank or office
Doodles and documents, too
Use a dependable Paper Mate
No blotters need jotters pursue!

> Mrs. Leo M. Ryan

Acclimates to isle or igloo!

> Mrs. Leo N. Ryan

Not your fault if mail don't go through!

> Mrs. Leo O. Ryan

Like the SeaBees, this outfit "can do"!

> Mrs. Leo P. Ryan

"Writes through butter" is utterly true!

> Mrs. Leo Q. Ryan

"Gee, Mom, two inner rhymes—'blotters-jotters' and 'butter-utter'—not bad," I said. I was beginning to feel fluent in the language of contesting, and I liked flaunting the vocabulary. "And you worked part of the company name into 'acclimates'—that's got to impress the judges."

Mom smiled at me from the pile of envelopes and

stamps. "Why, Tuff, I do believe we should anoint you the first Junior Affadaisy."

Reassured once again by watching our mother working as usual on her contest entries, the Ryan kids were also distracted by the impending Great Liberation of Barney ceremony. Now that Barney had grown to full, healthy adulthood, he could fly as well as any wild bird. He liked to perch on the windowsill of the dining room window, entranced by the doings of his sparrow cousins in the backyard.

Mom had always said that Barney was a temporary boarder. She knew he wouldn't be happy living indoors all his life, especially in wintertime, when the basement was cold and lonely. So on a sunny day in early fall before the first leaf had fallen, she carried Barney out into the middle of the backyard and set him on the ground. The rest of us stood several feet back, not wanting to interfere. Barney hopped about in the grass and attracted the attention of a flock of sparrows in neighborhood trees. They swooped down en masse, lighting on the ground around him and chirping.

Out of nowhere, a strange cat shot forward from the bushes. The sparrows retreated to the trees—all but Barney, who thought every cat was as harmless as Mammy. When the cat turned in Barney's direction, Mom was prepared to jump in, but she didn't have to. The flock of sparrows dive-bombed the cat, chasing him back into the bushes before landing in a protective circle around Barney. After a few more minutes of chattering, the flock rose up from the ground in a cloud of flapping feathers. This time Barney went, too, and as we watched from the lawn, the flock circled once over our heads before soaring away. "Good-bye, Barney!" everyone cheered, waving as the flock grew smaller in the distance. We stayed for a while in the yard, looking up at the empty sky, when it suddenly hit us. Barney was really gone. "We'll never see him again!" cried Dave. Betsy put her arm around his blocky little body. "We might, Davey," she said. "*Any* sparrow we see from now on could be him."

In the next letter, every Robin commiserated with Mom. "Now here is the empty-nest syndrome if I ever saw one," wrote Emma, "except that in your case it's the empty*ing* nest. Few mothers are as familiar with this phenomenon as we Birdies, I must say."

But there was one more bird to go. The time had come for Charley to find his own way "in this fowl world," as Dad liked to say. On the day Aunt Lucy drove to our house from Bryan to get him, Charley knew something was up. Ordinarily, at the first sound of a door shutting, he shot up out of the greenery to chase after whoever emerged from the house. But today, no amount of door slamming could get him to come out from under the front bushes. Mom finally had to reach into the evergreens to get him. She was the only human being he wouldn't bite. Despite our numerous scars, we hated to see him go. The fact that he loved our mother and nearly killed our father several times seemed about as logical to us as the world would ever get.

Mom coaxed the clucking bird into the cage that Aunt Lucy had brought with her and snapped the metal door shut. Peering into the cage, Mom couldn't disguise her worry. "Evelyn," said Lucy as she placed the cage in the backseat of her car, "think of this as Charley's first day of kindergarten. He's got his whole life ahead of him. Plus, he's about to meet a hundred adoring hens at the egg farm. He'll be ecstatic." Lucy got in the front seat and put the car into gear. "By the time we turn the corner," she said, "Charley will be looking forward to his new adventure." Mammy leapt into Mom's arms as Lucy pulled away. They could both see Charley's beady red eyes staring back at them from the bars of the cage. Mammy, who had watched two litters and one sparrow leave home, seemed to know that this was Charley's turn. But Mom lingered in the street, staring after the departed rooster for a long time. "I hope Charley *likes* chickens," she said.

In the next group of letters, the Robins were effusive in congratulating Mom on her big TV win in the bug spray contest. Betty White, who had criticized Mom's entries ("No, no, no!"), was, if not contrite, at least capable of self-effacing humor. "Stick with me, kid," she wrote, "and you'll go far." Mom laughed. Never one to take criticism poorly, she filed it away as resource material for the next contest.

And besides, Betty offered advice that, coupled with Mom's innate Rube Goldberg talents, helped keep alive an appliance that should have been long dead.

Betty, you were right. The valve on our clothes washer was plugged. Cured it myself just this morning by shutting off the hot water completely and whacking and whamming the darned thing until the cold water broke through. To heck with the servicemen after this. Always DID want to take a sledge hammer to a few of these contrary appliances! Emma, maybe that's something to try when you lose electricity in the next storm. . . .

Mom was more concerned than she let on during the oddly lit, deadly still days Midwesterners have come to call "tornado weather." For several days, she had sniffed the air and cocked her ear to what she called "evil voices in the wind."

"In the old days," said Mike, "they'd burn you for a witch." But sure enough, the kitchen radio began broadcasting warnings that tornadoes could touch down at any moment.

It was in this particular eye of the storm that Paper Mate announced the winners of its jingle contest. To the family's astonishment and sorrow, not one of Mom's entries won a thing.

"And you used their stupid pen every time!" Mike complained.

Everyone in the house thought Mom got rooked. "Those judges must be nuts," I said. "How do you keep entering contests when they keep missing your best entries?"

"Well, I'm sorry, too, when I lose," she said. "But you know, writing for me is like working in the garden. You can be proud of what you've done whether someone else likes it or—"

"I don't care!" I heard myself shout. "You're better than any of them! You stand here day after day and—" To my astonishment, tears were rolling down my face. "It's not fair!" I blurted out. "They should have let you win!"

My mother set the iron down and turned to face

me. "Tuff," she said, "just who is the 'they' in all this?"

"You know—the judges." I looked away.

"And why do you care about them?"

"Because they have all the power! They make the decisions! They miss all the best stuff! You should protest! You should *do* something!"

"Well, let's say we protest, and there's a big review. Let's say all the contestants who lost want the judges to look at the entries all over again. And let's say the judges agree to do that, even looking at my entries first, and they *still* award the prize to somebody else. What then?"

"I don't know," I said, frustrated. "I just think those guys are wrong to say your entries aren't good enough. I know your entries are *better* than good. One of them should've *won* something!"

"Are you sure you're talking just about contests?" she asked. "Remember, these judges are professionals—they're hired to judge my poetry or jingles, and that's okay. But I have a feeling you're talking about another kind of 'judge'—people out there who think they can pass judgment on someone like me and you, and that's not okay."

"You mean—"

"I mean some of our neighbors, or the police, or Father McCague, or a few of the nuns at St. Mary's. They think we're lesser people because we don't have a lot of money. Do you agree with them?"

"No. You know I don't care about them."

"Remember when the nuns at St. Mary's thought you were 'dumb'? You went on to prove how smart you were to the teachers who really count, didn't you?"

"Yes, but, Mom! We should have told those nuns off! They pushed us around and we never did anything wrong! It's just like—just like—"

"Just like what? Like Dad?"

I jumped up. "Yes! Just like Dad! They're all like Dad! Why don't we ever get to stand up to Dad?"

Mom nodded, as if she had been waiting for this question for a long time. "Because, Tuff, 'standing up' to your dad would mean nothing. In fact, you'd be wasting time and energy you should be spending on your own life. You could spend hours every night fighting with Dad about whether he's being 'fair' to us—or you could do what you're doing: getting good grades, planning for college, saving your own money."

We both sat at the table now, looking out the window into the yard. "Sometimes I hate him, Mom."

"I'm not surprised. Considering what we all go through every night, it's normal that you would. But try to think harder about what it is you really hate."

"What do you mean?"

"A long time ago I figured out something that made life a lot simpler. Don't let yourself be judged by others, and don't judge other people."

"Someone judged *you*?" I said. "Why?"

"It doesn't really matter why," she said, "and it was a long time ago. But it sure made me think twice before judging anyone else, including your dad. I don't even like to judge my own contest entries. I like the feeling of being actively engaged in something that might one day bring in a little cash."

She got up and wandered closer to the window. "And let's not forget," she said, frowning at the fast-moving storm clouds headed our way, "how lucky we are to even *have* an active life."

She was thinking of Emma at that moment, just as all the Robins worried about her when tornadoes were anywhere near our tri-state area, and this time rightly so. As the storms tore through the Goshen area, Dortha called Mom to say that Emma's day bed—which moved up and down to keep her breathing—had collapsed, and she had been moved into the iron lung, which she typically used only at night. Again the hand-pumping brigade kept Emma breathing until electricity was restored. "Enough about me," Emma wrote later in her cavalier manner. "Are you all safe in your storm cellars when these dang twisters come calling?"

Mom was only now breathing easier because the tornadoes had missed my sister Lea Anne's house by a mile on either side.

As far as spending the night in the cellar is concerned—the southwest room of our basement was never cemented, has original dirt floor, and is plentifully populated with spiders, centipedes, and the like. Makes you feel crawly even opening the door. ALL of us would almost rather be blown away than have to spend any time there.

Eventually, Mom followed the Robins' lead by including more updates about her personal life. At first she kept these stories light, showing how her grown kids gave her material for a good story, like this old-fashioned anecdote she submitted in Dick's name to the "Humor in Uniform" column in *Reader's Digest:*

Newly assigned to Military Police Training at Fort Gordon, Ga., my married buddy inquired pensively of his Commanding Officer why he wasn't allowed to live off-base with his wife in nearby Augusta.

"Son," explained the C.O., with an exaggerated show of patience, "if the Army wanted you to have a wife, they'd have issued you one!"

But despite my mother's perky writing style, the Robins knew that with Bruce gone, Mom was feeling uncharacteristically low. For the first time, she confided in them that Dad was "a mite jealous" of her success as a contester, and that he was feeling pressure from some of his coworkers at the machine shop:

Believe it or not, there are a couple of guys who work in Hubby's department at the Shop who go into a full-blown green-eyed snit every time they hear I've won something new. The rest of the fellows, thank goodness, derive an unholy joy out of baiting them, and have probably credited me with winning a great number of things I never even heard of!

Small glimpses inside each Robin's life became so frequent that sometimes Mom read the letters too fast. When Emma wrote of buying a new summer outfit, Mom asked what color her new dress was.

Emma, if your trials this past summer don't rate you a seat to the host's right at the Heavenly board I'll fricassee that defunct Playtex girdle and eat it! Hope the storms are over and your new dress proves to be a delight.

In the next Round Robin packet to arrive in the mail, Emma answered Mom's question about her new outfit. "It's not a dress, Evelyn," Emma wrote. "It's a sunshine-yellow iron lung to replace the aqua one I've been using since I first got polio. The yellow makes me feel so cheerful! Why don't you come with Dortha when the gang comes to see me next week? Then you can see 'my new outfit' for yourself."

"Come hell or high water," Mom said, "this time I'm going."

PART FIVE

CHAPTER FIFTEEN

Hell and

High Water

*L*ittle did my mother and I realize before we started out for Emma's house in Goshen, Indiana, that hell *and* high water would come along for the ride.

I had just gotten my driver's license, using Aunt Lucy's 1957 aqua-and-white Chevy for the test. The car was in perfect condition—far better shape than Dad's old '54, especially on long drives. I only wished Mom and I would be driving Lucy's car to Indiana. In Dad's car, for some reason, air blew straight through the grille, past the engine, and directly into the cab, at whatever speed the car was moving. The faster we went, the harder the breeze blew inside. Highway driving was the worst—passengers in the front seat were pummeled by a fifty-five-mile-per-hour gale wind.

I knew nothing about car engines and even less

about car chassis, so I tried to fix the problem by stuffing rags into the most likely holes beneath the dashboard and glove compartment. It was late September and a few fallen leaves crunched underfoot on my way back to the house. The air felt crisp, with a decidedly cool edge to it, but with any luck, the day would warm up and we wouldn't mind whatever spikes of wind got through the cracks.

Mom spent the early morning making lunch for Dad and the kids—bologna and cheese sandwiches and a huge bowl of everyone's favorite dessert, cherry Jell-O with a layer of marshmallows floating on top. Then she wrote out instructions for supper, just in case we weren't yet back from Indiana: "Kelly—heat up some fish sticks, make a salad, finish up the Jell-O." She didn't want him to go off the deep end and make a vat of his navy bean soup, which everyone hated.

At 9:00 A.M. I said, "Okay, Mom. We'd better go. It'll take us two hours to get there and two to get back."

"After all the mishaps that have kept me from going to these meetings," she said, "I can't believe I'm almost out the door. Have you seen the map?"

"I put it in your purse," I said.

"Have you seen my purse?" She laughed, not kidding. The most common item in the Ryan Lost and Found was Mom's purse. She had a habit of picking it up and putting it down, never remembering where. As an antidote, she had acquired larger and larger purses over the years. But as Mom quickly proved, a large purse was just as lost as a small one.

"Here it is," I said, carrying it into the living

room. "You left it on the front steps with the empty milk bottles." Just then the phone rang.

"Don't answer it, Mom," I said. "We're two seconds from leaving."

"I can't just let it ring," she said. "It could be Lea Anne or Dick or Bub or Rog or Bruce." Dad had already picked up the receiver, so we started out the door. "Mother!" he called out. "It's for you. Somebody from the Toledo *Blade*."

"I'll wait in the car, Mom," I said. "Tell him we already subscribe."

The "somebody" from the Toledo *Blade* turned out to be a reporter who wanted to write a feature story on Mom and her winning ways. "Mrs. Ryan," he said, "another staff member tells me that in the past week, you've appeared in *The Blade* three times. You won two caption contests and appeared in Dr. Benjamin Fine's syndicated column, 'Your Education Forum.' Is that right?"

"Ah!" she brightened. "You *noticed!*"

The previous week, Mom had won a fifteen-volume set of Compton's Pictured Encyclopedia for a question she submitted to Dr. Fine's national column. Her question was on a subject dear to her heart: *Is mathematics overstressed in school, to the detriment of language?* (Dr. Fine's response: Balance in any endeavor is a delicate matter.)

She had also won $1.11 each for finishing two separate statements: "Security is . . ." and "Futility is . . ." for Charles Schulz "Peanuts" drawings. Mom's entries:

Security is *a pillowy layer of miniature marshmallows atop a bed of cherry Jell-O.*

Futility is *trying to appear poised while eating corn on the cob.*

It was a good week for my mother, moneywise. In addition to her *Blade* credits, Mom also sold a humorous anecdote to the *Chicago Tribune*. She was paid $10 for this true story about Betsy being away from home for the first time, at Girl Scout camp:

✏━━

It was 9-year-old Betsy's first day at camp, and she scrutinized the middle-aged camp counselor closely. Finally Betsy mustered the courage to approach her. "You know," she said, "you look just like my mother except you have your wrinkles in different places!"

"And if I'm not mistaken," the reporter went on, "your daughter Barbara wrote a piece on her recent trip to Alaska that's about to be printed in the Travel section."

"Oh," Mom said, "I think there was a bit of a misunderstanding there. Barby's only eleven and has never been to Alaska. As I explained to the Travel editor when he called, my daughter wrote that article from the comfort of the davenport, using library books. She didn't know, you see, that you're supposed to actually *visit* the place you're writing about. The editor was very nice about it, though. He complimented her on the piece."

There was a short silence on the other end of the line. "Well . . . uh . . . Mrs. Ryan," the reporter said, "how did *you* get started? What was the first contest you won?"

"Why, contests have appealed to me from the time I was a little girl," Mom replied. Then she remembered that I was waiting in the car. "I'm so flattered you called," she said, "but I was just on my way out the door. Could we do the interview another time?" The reporter agreed to call later in the week, and Mom practically skipped her way out to the car.

"That was a reporter," she said cheerfully as she climbed into the passenger seat. "He wants to hear all about my wins." Then she looked down at the floor. "What's Mike's undershirt doing jammed into that gap in the floorboards?"

"Mom," I said as I carefully backed the elderly blue-and-white Chevy into the street, "I have taken the trouble of plugging the holes that turn this tub into a frigid wind tunnel on the highway. I ran out of rags. Actually, I thought Mike's shirt *was* a rag. It has as many holes as the car does."

"I don't doubt it," Mom said. "But as long as there's more fabric than air, I try not to throw them out." Then she stared dreamily out the window as the two- and three-story nineteenth-century homes of Washington Avenue floated past. "You know, Tuff, when I was a girl, my first love wasn't contesting. It was the newspaper."

"What newspaper?" I stole a quick look across the front seat. This was my first out-of-town drive, and it showed. I sat rigidly behind the wheel, my eyes like magnets on the road. I envied Mom the passive luxury of her passenger seat.

"Well, first of all, the seven newspapers my aunt Clara and uncle Frank subscribed to."

"*Seven?*" I asked. Even the two papers tossed on our front porch every morning and afternoon were more than enough reading for most people. "Where did they come from?"

"Every small town had at least one newspaper in those days. Remember, this was 1915 or so, and there were no TV's, and no radios either, at least in our part of the country. The only source of information people had then was the newspaper."

The day seemed to be warming up, though we had barely crossed the mud-colored Maumee at the north edge of town. Taking a peek out the driver's window, I could see the river was running high for this time of year. Stately cottonwood trees lining the banks stood in a foot of churned-up, silt-colored stew. The milky-brown currents of Midwestern rivers were dirty and unseemly to a lot of people, but not to me. When I looked at the river, I thought of the creamy coffee my mother drank every morning.

Eyes on the road.

The seven papers Mom's uncle Frank and aunt Clara read were mostly Republican-owned, but they subscribed to a few Democrat newspapers, too. "Not to mention," Mom said, "a German-language paper for immigrants like my grandparents, and a Whig paper."

"Wig?" I said. "A newspaper about—"

"No, *Whig* with an *h,* as in the political party of the same name," she said. "The party died out in the mid-1800s, but it still had its fol-lowers. According to Uncle Frank, people had to have a variety of news sources to be well-rounded, so he subscribed to them all."

Passing the Defiance city limits, Mom and I cruised into the flat green farmland of northwestern

Ohio, where the horizon sat like a distant pancake on the road. Driving in the Ohio countryside was a straightforward thing. Except for the routes that followed the rivers, most roads were laid out in a grid of straight lines and right angles. I was still worried that my inexperience might cause an accident, but it wouldn't be because of an unexpected curve in the road. I was beginning to relax a little, and the air in the car now felt almost balmy.

Mom gazed out the window, still in her dreamy mode.

"I can see their parlor room as plain as day," she said, "even after fifty years. I haven't changed much since then." Mom continued as she peeled off her pink cardigan sweater, "Anytime somebody came to visit, they'd find me in the middle of the living room floor reading the Sherwood *Chronicle* or the *Defiance Crescent-News*. That's where all the early contests used to be advertised, and that's where I got hooked."

I couldn't remember a time when I was alone with my mother like this. Away from the house, the kids, and Dad, she could sit back and concentrate on something other than laundry or lunch. "I guess you spent a lot of time at Frank and Clara's," I said.

"Well, I lived with them for the first three years of my life, you know," she said, adjusting Mike's shirt in the floorboards to let in a little outside air. As we passed an old sunburned farmer rolling along the berm of the road on his dusty green John Deere tractor, I couldn't help noticing that he wore a wool scarf and gloves. Mom saw him, too. "I wonder if he has circulation problems," she said. Why else would he be so cold when we were more than comfortably warm?

Mom's life, I knew, had begun tragically. Her own mother died a few minutes after giving birth to her. Her father was so grief-stricken that he sent both his daughters to live with relatives.

"The whole town of Sherwood went into mourning when my mother died," said Mom wistfully.

I had heard this story before but never knew the details. "How did she die exactly?" For some reason, I had never asked this question, perhaps because the whole subject was too sad, too scary. I could never imagine life without my own mother.

"Mom had spent the morning cutting out dresses—she was a seamstress, you know. In the afternoon, she lay down on her bed and went into labor. She did everything like that—calmly, methodically. My sister Enie's birth four years earlier had been uneventful, and so was mine, or so Dad, Aunt Clara, and the doctor thought. After I was born, they closed the bedroom door so she could rest," Mom said. "She bled to death in her sleep. People said Dad was never the same after that."

Who could blame him, I thought, as we sailed past acres of golden wheat and tall fields of feed corn drying on yellowed stalks. The wheat was ready for harvest, if a surprise rainstorm didn't get to it first. I thought of Orren and Minnie Lehman, happily married for fourteen years, with no reason to suspect that their marriage wouldn't continue for another half a century.

Caught up in Mom's tale, I glanced slowly from the windshield to the speedometer to make sure I wasn't driving over the limit. My eyes froze on the temperature gauge. "Mom," I said, "the car's overheated!" I had been so busy listening that I hadn't noticed that the temperature had shot way above the "H." The needle was practically vertical.

"Oh my Scot," said Mom, leaning over to look at the gauge herself. "I wondered why that farmer we passed looked so darn cold when we were on the toasty side. Now what?"

"We're only a mile from Sherwood," I said. "There's a gas station there."

Mom knew that better than I did. She was born in the tiny hamlet of Sherwood, barely a smudge on the map, population five hundred. "Well," she said, "I don't think we're supposed to keep going when the engine's that hot, but I don't think we have a choice either."

I kept on driving.

"I wonder if the CraMotte family still runs the Hi-Speed Garage on North Harrison," Mom said, as if our melting car was the last thing on her mind. It took an eternity for the leafy green outskirts of Sherwood to appear on the horizon, and by that time a few lungsful of smoky steam had worked their way from the radiator into the passenger compartment. Mom fanned herself with one hand. "Kind of warm for September, isn't it?" She laughed.

We rolled into the Hi-Speed station, tripping the bell that announced the arrival of cars at the pump, and the young attendant strolled out of the doorway just as Mom and I emerged from the steaming car. "Overheated eh?" he said as he lifted the hood. Billows of steam engulfed us all, but I could still read his name tag, "Joe."

"Yes," I said, worried that it was all my fault. "It couldn't be because I plugged up the rusting holes in the floorboards, could it?"

Joe waved away the steam with his arms. "Nah. Nothing you do in the passenger compartment could overheat the engine," he said.

"We were doing just fine," said Mom, "and then we weren't. By the way, are you a CraMotte?"

"A CraWhat?" said Joe, looking over the engine. "Here's your problem," he said, pointing to a spot behind the radiator. "The fan belt's gone. How long you gals been driving without it?"

"No idea," I said. "The car overheated before I even noticed a rise in temperature."

"Well," he said, "you won't be going anywhere soon. It'll take at least an hour for the radiator to cool down enough for me to open it. Might as well make yourself at home."

Mom turned in my direction and sighed. "I'm beginning to suspect that I'm just not intended to visit my contesting friends," she said.

"It'll only take an hour for everything to cool down, Mom. Joe will put on another fan belt, and we'll be in Goshen in plenty of time."

"If you say so," she said, as disappointed as I had ever seen her. This was, after all, her first outing since her trip to New York two years before. She looked around the garage for a place to sit down.

"Hey, Mom," I said. "Let's walk into town and visit the cemetery behind your old house. We haven't done that for a while." Her face lit up, and we walked across the tarmac to the sidewalk leading into Sherwood proper. Something about her expression lifted my spirits, too. Her stride was quick and purposeful—I had to trot to keep up—as if she were marching into her future instead of her past.

CHAPTER SIXTEEN

Mrs. Etchie

In the early 1920s when Mom was a girl, Sherwood was a prosperous village with well-maintained two- and three-story houses and a small commercial district surrounding the train depot. The decline of the railroads after World War II claimed many small towns like this one. As Mom and I meandered down the deserted main street, we found an old-fashioned food market and a hardware store open for business. Aside from Joe at the gas station, we had yet to see a single person. "I know it's hard to believe now," Mom said, spreading her arms to encompass the street scene, "but this was once a bustling community."

We stopped in front of a squat concrete building, obviously empty. "This was the town hall, where the post office, firehouse, and town jail were housed," she said. "*The Chronicle* had its newspaper office

The 1931 Sherwood High School graduating class in its entirety. From left: Mom (valedictorian), Helen Smith, Ruby Musselman, Maxine Miller, Hazel Musselman, Juanita Sohn, and Beulah Henderson. Whenever Mom looked at this photo, she said, "I should have thought to ask Beulah what she was wearing to graduation."

here, too." She peeked through the slats of a boarded-up window. "You can almost see it."

I looked in over her shoulder. "Looks pretty dark in there."

"Oh, it was a cavernous and gloomy room all right, but lively. The paper was written, typeset, and printed by Mrs. Etchie, Seth, and me. It was one of the last hand-set newspapers in the country."

I knew Mrs. Etchie, Mom's step-grandmother, had published (and written most of) the Sherwood *Chronicle*, a weekly newspaper that in its heyday had a circulation of a thousand readers—not bad considering the town never had more than five hundred inhabitants. The paper was a four-page, six-column journal of small-town life, with local items, ads, excerpts reprinted from other newspapers in the area, and a feature column written by my mother. Before Mom came on board, *The Chronicle* had a staff of two: Mrs. Etchie —a.k.a. "The Editor"; and Seth, the printer, who never began or finished a day without a burning half-inch stogie clenched between his teeth.

At first Mom did nothing but set type. At seventeen, she was reputed to be the fastest and most accurate typesetter in the region, working with a single stick on which she placed each letter of type, retrieved with unerring speed from the slim drawers of Mrs. Etchie's ancient wooden printer's desk. Each completed stick of type was laid out by Seth in the forms for each page.

"That Seth, he was a corker," she said. "When ads came in late, he had to typeset them himself, with no one there to proofread, and the man just couldn't spell." I knew where this was going. "The worst typos," she said, beginning to chuckle, "were advertisements—in really large print, mind you—for 'Peanus Butter' and 'Men's Dress Shits.' Of course, the whole town was horrified."

Every kid in the Ryan family had heard this story before, all of us falling into fits of laughter no matter how many times she told it. The thought of obscenities appearing in a newspaper, especially in my mother's puritanical era, nearly doubled us over. Mom never tired of the story either. "Mrs. Etchie and I enjoyed those typos so much we started looking forward to reading our own paper." She laughed, wiping tears from her eyes, "even though we thought we had written every word in it!"

By the age of twenty, Mom started writing "Columnings of an Amateur," her weekly twenty-inch column of town talk, anecdotes, and philosophical meanderings on life and the world in general. Her flowery humor was a perfect fit for the 1930s, and she emulated Walter Winchell's style of omniscient-sounding gossip, even when reporting a wedding anniversary.

Our most hearty and effusive congratulations to our august mayor, Mr. Shong, and his worthy wife, who, so we read for ourself in the Washington News *last week, have been parking their spearmint on the same bedpost for twenty years. In this day and age, an anniversary like that calls for a medal. Lindbergh, they tell us, got one for flying the ocean, and it didn't take half that long.*

Soon Mom developed a voice that bounced from the formal to the personal with conversational ease. She could tease and joke with the people of Sherwood and still invoke a self-deprecating humor that made readers feel they were a part of *The Chronicle* staff.

Our decrepit old press went on a rampage last Thursday and kept us all working until after six o'clock that evening, and you, dear readers, are not entirely blameless. To begin with, you people who will just bring in your advertising copy at the last minute (your conscience will tell you if you are one of these) caused us to be forty-five minutes late in starting to print.

The federal government had become a favorite target by 1933, the middle of the Great Depression. President Roosevelt had created the National Recovery Administration (NRA), which, among other things, asked American farmers to reduce production of many livestock crops. Mom loved to tweak such mandates and give her despondent farm readers a rare chuckle:

Even the chicken industry seems to have gone the way of the hogs, wheat, and corn, the production of which has been curtailed because of government edict. The Editor relates with great chagrin the story of her N.R.A. hen, who had been setting religiously for the past three weeks upon a bevy of eggs, and has now hatched out every third one.

Across the street from the town hall and *Chronicle* office sat a one-story gray brick building with a cracked front window. "This used to be the Bee Hive general store," said Mom as a sheet of old newspaper blew by. "The whole village shopped here."

It is reported that Mitzi, the dog everybody knows, caused quite a commotion Saturday by chasing an itinerant chicken into the crowded aisles of the Bee Hive grocery, whence it fled squawking and cackling amongst a veritable sea of legs of surprised customers and frantic clerks, only to elude pursuit and ensconce itself on a bale of dry goods, where it brazenly proceeded about the business of laying a fresher egg than has ever been in any store in town before. . . .

Mom's penchant for writing breathless and nearly endless sentences was, her editor step-grandmother used to say, "unequaled in all of Sherwood."

"I can't believe the Moats family still sells cars," Mom said as she peered into the window of the circa-1920 Moats Ford dealership, one of the few stores in town still operating. "They've been in the business since Henry Ford started making cars." Once again, not a person could be seen inside.

At the weekly drawing at the Bee Hive grocery, Saturday night, a certain village housewife by the name of Mrs. Moats was heard to confide to a second bystander that she would feel highly elated if she were fortunate enough to draw one of the prizes—no matter how minor—just so it wasn't one of those cookie jars intended for that purpose. She had several of those at home. But what one wants isn't half so important as what one gets, so before the passing of many minutes, the lady's name was called off and she was awarded a cookie jar, as a token of the divine favor of Lady Luck. That in itself was unusual, but it never rains unless it pours, and before the evening was out the lady had won six of the despised jars altogether. All this to forewarn prospective buyers of a new Ford car: Check the trunk for cookie jars.

Sherwood might have been small, Mom wanted me to know, but it had also been thriving. "Aside from the Bee Hive grocery and the car dealership," she said, "Sherwood had Musselman's grocery store, Newman's drug store, a lumber company, Hackman's bakery, Heller's clothing store, a produce market, a dry cleaner, and a funeral parlor."

"Was there a movie theater?" I asked, looking at the few remaining buildings along the street. "Could you afford going to the movies during the Depression?" For all the Ryan kids, including me, life without movies didn't seem worth living.

"Oh sure," she said. "They cost about five cents, and almost everyone had a nickel, even though people's assets were frozen by federal mandate. That meant the banks had closed and stayed closed. The idea of going to the bank to withdraw your own money had become a long-lost dream, a capitalist fairy tale."

✎➤

It never fails. Just as the bank is about to open, the alarm goes off and I wake up.

"Going to the movies in those days," Mom said, "took our minds off the Depression. Dad wouldn't let me go to the Sunday night shows—he thought that was sinful behavior for the Sabbath—so I had to sneak out of the house."

As Mom's column became more popular and her confidence grew, she spoofed everything from the federal government to her own father. Orren Lehman may not have known she was sneaking out to the movies on Sunday nights, but he certainly learned about it when he spread the weekly *Chronicle* open the next Friday to find his young daughter offering tips on how to get back into the house in the dead of night:

It is well to begin immediately one enters the door by swinging the left foot in a wide arc to the fore as a purely precautionary measure. . . . You should know by this time how easy it is to jar the dipper out of the water bucket. The wisest move to make next consists in taking three or four short steps at a slight angle in the general direction of where the stove should be. Grope around with your left hand until you touch it. Is it still hot? If so, your burned finger teaches you to stay strictly away from that corner. . . .

Half a block from the business district, Mom and I came upon the corner house where she was born, a small Victorianesque house with a wraparound porch and modest garage-sized barn in back.

"Do you remember this house, Tuff?"

"Only vaguely," I said. "I can barely picture your dad and stepmother."

"See those front steps?" Mom said, lost in memory. "They're falling to pieces now, but I can remember sitting there every afternoon with Enie, waiting for Dad to walk home from the train station. One time in the

*M*om in 1934, during the time she wrote for the *Sherwood* Chronicle, *playing tennis with her friend Beulah Henderson.*

1920s he ordered a god-awful green-and-yellow pin-stripe suit from the Sears Roebuck catalog for $5.35. The color was so peculiar," she laughed, "and the material was so cheap, that whenever one of us spotted Dad walking down the street in that suit, we'd say, 'Here comes ol' five-thirty-five.' "

Across the street was Mrs. Etchie's old house, now a green-shingled rectangle bordered on two sides by a precariously tipped veranda. We turned right down the side street leading to the town's century-old graveyard.

Visiting cemeteries is a Midwestern ritual, but Mom took up the practice at a tender age. "When Dad remarried in 1916 and my sister Enie and I came back to live here," said Mom, "I was three years old. Enie was seven. We could see our mother's grave from the back porch. As little girls, we would reenact her funeral, reverentially laying a doll in our wagon and pulling it into the cemetery to her grave. And, oh, how we cried! We were so sad that she was gone. Especially me. I hadn't even known her. So I made Enie repeat everything she remembered about Mom until I felt I was remembering her myself."

"Like what?" I asked.

"Oh, little, everyday things. Enie told me that our mother's eyes were blue; that she sewed all of our clothes; that she loved butterscotch pudding."

"What about your stepmother?" I asked, as we picked our way through the oldest section of the cemetery.

Mom shrugged. "She just didn't have much of a sense of humor," she said. "To her, life was a cold, dark thing. But her mother, Mrs. Etchie, now *she* was a different story!"

The square granite headstone in front of us read "Josephine Etchie." Mom reached down to pull a weed from the grass on the grave. "How I loved this woman," she said. "At fifty, she became my step-grandmother, and from that day on, we were inseparable. We had an unusual rapport for two people so far apart in age. Maybe she was young for her years, or I was old for mine. Maybe we were just kindred souls."

"What did she look like?" I asked.

"Tall and gaunt," Mom said, "with eyes the color of root beer. She'd grown a bit stooped from so many years of bending over a type case, and she always carried a huge old-fashioned purse under her arm. It was more like a briefcase, really—and inside there was always a little treat of some kind for a little girl, and lots of mysterious papers pertaining to *The Chronicle*.

"There was only one thing Mrs. Etchie couldn't do," said Mom, "and that was win a contest of any kind."

"No kidding," I said. "She entered contests, too?"

"Well, she tried. Limericks, jingles, 25 words or less—you name it—she couldn't win it." Mom laughed. "I learned a lot about how *not* to win a contest from her."

"What did she do wrong?"

"For one thing, she very rarely paid attention to the rules," said Mom, "which is always certain death for contesting. And she never submitted the required quallies, or product labels, with her entry. One day at *The Chronicle* office, she got a very long letter from R. G. Dun Cigars explaining why her contest limerick hadn't won."

"The company took the time to write to contestants?"

"Oh yes. They had products to sell, you see."

> April 27, 1932
> Mrs. J. Etchie
> Sherwood, O.

Dear Madam: We are very happy indeed to have received your rhyme and letter in our R. G. Dun Prize Contest. However, you evidently misunderstood one of the principal rules of our contest, and that is to enclose ten R. G. Dun cigar bands from any size Dun cigar.

Naturally your rhyme was not read by our judges because you failed to enclose the ten R. G. Dun cigar bands. If you are unable to purchase Dun cigars in your city or town, we will be glad to send you the necessary ten cigars if you will enclose cash or a money order in the amount of 45 cents or 95 cents for whichever cigar you wish, as shown on the enclosed card. We will, upon receipt of this amount, send you ten R. G. Dun cigars. . . .

"Gee, you'd think Seth would have had plenty of cigar bands lying around," I said.

"Well, she didn't want to ask Seth. She was trying to win him a box of cigars in the first place. And she wasn't about to go out and buy ten cigars just to submit a limerick that had every chance of not winning anyway."

I laughed, knowing that although Mom wouldn't have bought the cigars either, she would have walked to the nearest bar and absconded with the contents of every ashtray.

"That's how life was with Mrs. Etchie, though," she said. "Always entertaining, even in defeat. Her mistake, if you could call it that, was thinking too much about what she could write and not enough about what the judges wanted. That made her a good journalist but a lousy contester. But she loved that letter. All this fuss about cigar bands kept her laughing for a long time."

"You were lucky that Mrs. Etchie came along when you were little," I said.

"Oh, I was," Mom said. "And you know, she never asked anything of me. She made the newspaper so appealing I felt drawn to it. I wanted to contribute to it. I hadn't thought of myself as a 'writer' before. It was the wonder of putting a newspaper together every week that inspired me."

"So now," I teased her, "you have the wonder of soaking labels off of peanut butter jars."

"Yes, wouldn't Mrs. Etchie get a kick out of that?" Mom laughed. "In fact, I think of her often when I'm working on contest entries. She taught me how to construct every word of that newspaper, one piece of lead at a time. I use the same approach in writing jingles, you know. I dismantle and recast the words, letter by letter, until they say what I want them to. It's as if Mrs. Etchie's spirit never left." Mom got up and brushed off the seat of her pants.

"But you *win* contests, Mom," I said. "Didn't you just say that Mrs. Etchie never did?"

"Well, it's all a matter of what you set out to do," Mom said, "and Mrs. Etchie always did what she set out to do."

We drifted out of the Sherwood cemetery back onto Harrison Street. It took five minutes to walk the length of town back to the Hi-Speed Garage, where Joe had some good news and some bad news.

CHAPTER SEVENTEEN

Such a Thing

as Destiny

Installed a new fan belt," Joe said sadly, "for all the good it's going to do you."

"What do you mean?" I said.

"I think the car got so hot the gears kind of melted together under the hood."

"Oh cripes," I moaned.

"You can still drive it," Joe said, "but you can't shift gears from inside the car anymore—the linkage is ruined. You'll have to pick a gear ahead of time and stick with it."

"What does that mean?" I said.

"I think I know," Mom said, "but that doesn't cheer me up any."

Joe wiped his greasy hand on his oil-colored overalls and grabbed a hammer. "Look here," he said. He lifted the hood and pointed to the gearbox and linkage underneath. "See those metal rods?"

Mom and I nodded numbly.

"There's one for first gear, one for second, one for third, and one for reverse. Right now first gear is engaged—it's in a different position than the others, see? But you can't stay in first. It won't get you anywhere very fast, and if you're driving in first for over a block, the engine's not going to be happy. Let me shift it for you."

Joe raised the ball peen hammer over his head and whacked one of the rods a mighty blow, moving it forward from the others. "There," he said, "now it's in third gear. Third gear is your best bet for country driving. Second gear for driving in town."

I stared at Joe uneasily, wondering if he would be our salvation or our doom. Mom stared at him in awe. Joe's approach to repair seemed modeled after her own.

"Does this mean we're going back to Defiance?" Mom said, with a look of disappointment.

"I don't see why," Joe said. "Whether you go on or go back, nothing's going to get worse. Just stay in third." We paid Joe for the fan belt and his labor. Once I learned how to ease the clutch out slowly enough so the engine could gain speed without dying, we lurched back onto the road to Indiana, hoping there were no small towns or traffic that would require a downshift between here and there.

We were less than five miles from Goshen when I spotted trouble ahead: road construction, backing up a long line of cars in our lane, most of them moving only about fifteen miles an hour, if that.

"Uh-oh," I said. "Looks like we'll have to slow down for a while." As we pulled up behind the line of slow-moving traffic, the car—still locked in third gear—started sputtering and lurching.

"I guess this is what Joe meant by 'town driving,' " my mother said, bracing herself against the dashboard with each lurch. "Third gear isn't cutting it."

"It sure isn't," I said.

"Pull over, Tuff," she said. "We're almost in Goshen, where we'll have to be in second gear anyway. Let's seize the moment."

Now we were in for it, I thought, steering the Chevy as close to the cornfield as I could without mowing down half the corn shocks on this side of the road. When we finally rolled to a stop, Mom had that familiar determined look on her face that meant she was going to get us out of this mess or win a trip to Europe.

"Doesn't Dad always keep a hammer under the front seat?" she said, rooting around under the front seat. "Aha! Here it is under Mike's shirt."

We got out of the car and propped open the heavy metal hood. "Let's not be hasty, Mom," I said. "Do you know which of those metal rods is second—"

CLANK! Mom whacked the gear into place with the eye of a jeweler cutting diamonds. "There," she said happily. "Now what was all the fuss about?"

I let the hood drop. "Joe would be proud, Mom," I said. We got back in the car and discovered that the quicker surge of second gear kept the Chevy from coughing its way down the road. We resumed our place in the slow-motion traffic.

For the next hour, whenever the lane opened up ahead of us, Mom got out and whacked us into third. Whenever we had to slow down for a while,

Mom took the hammer to the gearbox and whacked us into second. We had a system.

I thought my mother capable of any feat, mental or physical. "Mom," I ventured, "why did you stop writing your column in the Sherwood newspaper? You were so good at it."

"Well, I was twenty years old," she said. "I really didn't *feel* I was good at it, and over time the pressure got to me. Every week a thousand words, plus the typesetting. In a small town like that, not a lot of things happen to write about, so I was left to my own imagination. I just didn't have the confidence to continue after the first year."

It comes to our ears that our continued absence from duty has become the talk of the town. On every hand are we met by solicitous inquiries about the state of our health.

It wasn't the flu, Mrs. Shady Nook. It wasn't a strike, Mrs. Mud Creek. It wasn't even a vacation. It was just a breathing spell. We can't say funny things all the time. We are not the four Marx brothers. We are just another well that ran dry.

"So you gave it up?"

"Well, I had other plans. Right after high school, I went to nursing school with high hopes for a career—I loved taking care of people—but that horrible eczema I'd had from childhood came back with a vengeance. My hands were so blistered and swollen I had to come home. That's when I started writing as well as typesetting for Mrs. Etchie."

"Didn't you want to go on to college? You were the valedictorian of your high school class."

"Yes, well, the whole class only had seven people in it. I did get a partial scholarship to Defiance College, but it was still too expensive. I saved up my money, thinking I'd have enough eventually to go, but then I met your dad. We got married instead."

I shook my head. "I've always wondered why you got married so young. Didn't your father and stepmother—well, at least Mrs. Etchie—see how much promise you had as a writer?"

"Oh, yes, they encouraged me, but you know how young people are. Marrying your dad seemed like the right thing to do at the time."

Mom turned to look at me. "I want you to know that I don't regret any part of my life," she said, "including marrying Dad. I wouldn't trade any one of you kids for a whole illustrious career. Besides"—she smiled—"without the ten of you, what would I do for material?"

I smiled back, but it occurred to me that Mom always did this. Just when we got into the story of her life, she would make a joke or somehow distract us from the questions we asked.

"Look," Mom said as Goshen loomed into view, "here we are." We emerged from the highway construction into the outskirts of a city three times the size of Defiance. It was almost noon. "Time to slow down again." She seemed almost relieved to pick up the hammer and whack the melted gear into place.

When she got back in the car, I made one more stab at it. "Don't you think you left a great career behind, Mom? Do you ever think about that?"

"I'll tell you one thing, Tuffy. There's such a thing as destiny. Do you ever think about *that*? My mother had a destiny. So did Dad and Mrs. Etchie. Sometimes when your life seems most out of control, you know there's a direction. I don't mean you can't have free will—in fact, that can be the most important part."

"So you were meant to have ten kids?" I said.

"I feel that I'm doing exactly what I was meant to do in this life. I've never doubted it."

I sighed. It appeared that Mom had once again leapfrogged over some important aspect of her life. At the very least we seemed destined to get to Emma's.

Two blocks later, we arrived at Emma's two-story wood-frame house, only a few minutes late. Dortha met us at the door, along with four or five other members of the Affadaisies, and we were swept up in a cloud of contesting chatter as we walked into Emma's room.

"Welcome to Emma's ranch for contesters-in-a-slump!" Dortha said, grinning. "We call our little empty-headed retreat CASA-BLANKA!" At this, all the women erupted in laughter.

"Or," another woman cried out, "how about calling it the DESPONDerosa?"

"That reminds me, Dortha," Mom said. "What was that great highway safety slogan you told me about last summer? I've been chuckling over that one ever since."

"Which safety slogan?"

"Oh, you know, the 'seat belt' reference."

" 'Belt the ones you love!' "

The room exploded in laughter again. "And it

won!" Dortha shouted. At this, everyone doubled over.

Suddenly we were by Emma's bedside. Wearing a crisp, striped blouse with a high ruffled collar, Emma beamed brightly as Mom bent over to kiss her cheek. Everyone still chattering, Dortha wrapped her arm around Mom's shoulders and turned to me. "Do you know that your mother is the winningest Affadaisy?" she said, and I believed her.

Mom and I had agreed earlier that I would wander around town during this visit, and I took my leave.

As I walked out the door and down the street, murmurs of conversation, high-pitched laughter, and a few happy shouts followed me for half a block. Mom, I concluded, hadn't left her career behind those many years ago after all. She took it with her wherever she went.

PART SIX

CHAPTER EIGHTEEN

Rock Bottom

*M*om and I were still in the glow of our wild ride to Indiana and back when we arrived home at seven o'clock, a bit later than expected. We trudged up the sidewalk to the front door, toting between us a bushel basket of Winesap apples from a farm stand we had passed on the way home. A crash sounded from inside the house. "Uh-oh," I said. "Did that come from the kitchen?" I reached for the doorknob. "Maybe we shouldn't tell Dad about the car tonight. Tomorrow morning, he'll be sober."

I turned the knob, but the door wouldn't open. No one in Defiance ever locked their doors. Most people didn't even own house keys. "One of the kids must have locked it by accident," Mom said as we set the apples down on the steps. "Let's walk around to the back."

Our cat Mammy rushed out from the bushes to escort us along the pathway to the backyard. We could hear Barb, Betsy, and Dave somewhere behind the house singing one of their favorite songs in harmony: *She wore blue velvet. Wo, wo, wo. Bluer than velvet were her eyes.* Seven-year-old Dave, who had never heard of the word "velvet" but did have a classmate named Melvin, sang along in his own way: *She wore Blue Melvin. Wo, wo, wo. Bluer than Melvin were her eyes.*

When they saw us round the corner, they ran to meet us. "What are you kids doing out here?" said Mom. "It'll be dark soon."

"We went to the movies this afternoon, Mom," said Barb. "While we were gone, Dad locked us out of the house."

"He *what*?" Mom's face turned a light shade of purple. "I knew he didn't want me to go to Goshen, but I never guessed he'd try a stunt like this." She counted heads. "Where's Mike?"

"He stayed at the movies," said Betsy. "He likes to watch them over and over."

As the backyard grew darker in twilight, Mom sat down with a sigh on the back steps. "I suppose you tried the kitchen door, too?" she asked.

"Locked," said Barb, Betsy, and Dave together. "But," Dave said, beaming, "we have an idea."

"I'm *so* glad, Dave," said Mom, "because I'm fresh out. What is it?"

"The dining room window!" he exclaimed. "You can push me through."

"Yeah," said Barb. "We were waiting for you and Tuff to come home because you're taller."

We turned to the long window at the back of the dining room. It was open about a foot at the bottom. Dad must not have noticed. The windowsill was about six feet off the ground—too high to climb in without help. "It'll be like a circus trick," said Dave, excited at the prospect of breaking into his own home.

"It's not as though we have an alternative," said Mom. "Let's do it." Mom and I lifted my youngest brother over our heads and carried him like a surfboard to the opening above us. "Try not to make any noise when you land, Dave," said Mom, "so Dad won't hear you from the kitchen."

"Okay, Mom," Dave whispered.

We aimed his sturdy little body toward the wooden sill, which he grabbed and slithered across. The rest of us raced around the side of the house and ran into Mike coming from the opposite direction. He looked relieved to see us. "I couldn't get in," he said. "The door's locked."

"It shouldn't be anymore," said Mom on the run. When we got to the front yard, Dave stood, triumphant, in the open doorway. "Great idea, Davey," said Mom. We followed her into the house to the kitchen, where Mike and I set the bushel of apples on the table.

Dad, standing at the counter with his whiskey and beer, saw the anger on Mom's face and backed up a bit. I had never seen her so furious.

"Did you even bother fixing supper before you locked your kids out of the house?" she demanded.

"You're the one who went away today," he countered. "I'm the one who stayed home to do your job."

"And quite a job you did, too," said Mom, as she stepped around him to open the refrigerator. She took out the Jell-O and two boxes of frozen fish sticks. When she turned back to Dad, she was seething. "Kelly, I was gone for ten hours. If you resent taking care of your children for less than half a day, you might as well leave this house."

Suddenly Dad jabbed a burly arm in Mom's direction. At that moment, without thinking, all five kids in the room lunged at him, latching onto different parts of his body. I leapt onto his back, grabbing him around the neck like a bronco rider. Mike and Barb clung to an arm each, and Betsy and Dave clutched his legs. "No, Dad! No! Stop it!" we shouted while trying to strangle, sock, and trip him up. With his children hanging from him like oversized Christmas tree ornaments, he stumbled backward, butting up against the kitchen table and sending the basket of apples crashing to the floor. Such was my father's power that he could still lumber around the room, smashing fruit underfoot and dragging the weight of five frantic children with him.

As we pummeled away, Dad lurched forward and slammed against Mom, knocking the huge stainless steel bowl of cherry Jell-O free from her grip and into the air. Pinwheeling off him in the collision, kids landed in every corner of the room and watched as the bowl tilted as it rose, dumping its contents down the front of his chest. Some of it slipped into the neck of his sleeveless white undershirt, instantly staining the cloth blood red, before the bowl itself ricocheted off his skull with a loud atonal clang. Everyone but Dad was instantly reminded of Mom's latest contest entry:

For picnic or party, Jell-O's a boon—
Made by nine, all "set" by noon—

With taste and shimmer-shake appeal,
Jell-O jollies <u>any</u> meal.

The blow to Dad's head drained him of all belligerence, but he was still drunk. "My God, Mother!" he said, as he clutched his red-stained undershirt. "You've killed me!" Sinking quietly to the yellow linoleum foor, he leaned heavily against the cupboards beneath his drinking counter. Stunned into silence, no one spoke until a single miniature marshmallow rolled across the table and plopped off the edge.

"Death by Jell-O," Mom said. "Highly unlikely. And I want you to know that I am not about to wipe up the mess that you've made of this kitchen. You can clean it up yourself."

For once, Dad seemed to know he had gone too far. "All right, Mother, all right," he groaned, climbing to his feet. "Tuff, get me some paper tow—"

"Not on your life!" Mom said evenly. "You made the mess. You clean it up."

Seeing that the worst was over, Mike and I crept out from opposite corners of the room. Betsy and Dave crawled out from under the kitchen table. Barb came out from behind the refrigerator.

"And now seems as good a time as any to tell you, Kelly," Mom added, with masterful timing, "that the fan belt fell off the car and the gears melted together. In short, the car is ruined."

Dad's head whipped around, but he had used up his allotment of righteous anger, and he knew it. "Fine!" he said, dripping gelatin from his shirt and shoulders. "We'll just have to deal with it tomorrow.

Now hand over those fish sticks, Mother, and I'll heat them up for you."

He looked in our direction. "Don't you kids have anything better to do?" he said in all innocence, shooing us out of the kitchen. "If you keep walking on the floor, you're only going to make it harder to clean up."

Thankful to be out of his way, we sat in the living room with the TV on, listening to the sucking sounds of Dad mopping up the kitchen. Each of us felt different, stronger somehow—Mom because she had tasted freedom for a day and refused to let Dad take it away; the kids because as a team we had stopped Dad from hurting our mother.

Still, the sudden noise of the phone ringing a few minutes later sent us flying involuntarily out of our seats. Grateful for the distraction, Mom flew to the phone. It was Long Distance with a collect call from Bruce. "I'll accept the charges," she said. No one ever called our house from as far away as California, at least not collect. "Bruce!" Mom said when her fifth child came on the line. "What's wrong?"

"I've got money troubles, Mom," he said. "I don't know who else to ask. I signed up to go to Los Angeles City College," he said. "It's free, but the books aren't."

"Well, books couldn't cost that much," Mom said, trying to remember how much money she had stored in the closet. "How much do you need?"

"For the books, thirty dollars. But that's not the biggest expense."

"What?" she said. "Tell me."

"I need another hundred for emergency dental work. My wisdom teeth are impacted. The dentist says they have to come out right away. I'm sure you don't have much cash, Mom, but I don't know what else to do."

Mom was taken aback. "Goodness, Bruce, a hundred and thirty dollars—that's a lot of money, especially now with Christmas coming." She thought about it for a moment. "But nothing's as important as your education and your teeth. Let me see what I can do."

When she got off the phone, Mom walked into the kitchen, where Dad was still ankle-deep in Winesap applesauce. For a few months now, Dad had appeared to be spending more money than usual. He had even paid a few bills out of his own pocket. Mom had noticed, too, that the beer he'd been bringing home was Falstaff or Rolling Rock, slightly more expensive than Pabst. Even the label on his whiskey looked a little fancier—gold letters on a white background. There was no gold of any kind on Kessler's labels.

"Kelly," Mom said, standing in the muck surrounding Dad in the kitchen, "we need a hundred and thirty dollars for Bruce. He has to have emergency dental work and books for school."

Dad rested the mop against the counter and pulled out his wallet. Mom, mouth agape, watched him fan through the bills and pull out five twenties and three tens. "Where did all that come from?" she asked, dumbfounded.

"It doesn't matter, Mother," he said, turning back to mop the floor. "It's all gone now."

"I mean it—how did you get so much money?"

"Oh, never you mind," said Dad. "Just a little extra I saved up."

Mom knew she had no time to get a cashier's check. If she waited until morning, Dad would probably want the money back. She folded the bills inside three sheets of stationery and put them into an envelope addressed to Bruce. Then she told Mike to run it down to the mailbox outside the post office.

Mom felt relieved to bail Bruce out, but she wondered again about Dad's source of ready cash. Only a few weeks before, money had been scarce enough for Mom to worry about clothing the family. Even winter pajamas had been in short supply this year. Dave got Mike's hand-me-downs, Betsy got Barb's, Barb got mine. But that left Mike and me with nothing to wear to bed. Mom spent the $12 she received for two greeting card ideas on yards of flannel and sewed new pajamas for the two of us and a long pink nightgown for herself. She was especially proud of the nightgown, since she had never attempted to make one before. It was pink jersey cotton with white rosette piping, and it went all the way to her ankles.

Davey, meanwhile, decided that if Mom could win things by entering contests, he could too. He chose the annual NFL-sponsored "Punt, Pass & Kick" contest, in which kids of all age groups competed to throw and kick a football the greatest distance and with the most accuracy. Dave had little experience, and, with the older boys gone, he looked to Mom to help him practice. As the contest approached, they punted, passed, and kicked the football night and day.

A week after the Jell-O debacle, Mom stood at the front window, watching Dave punt a football alone in the street. "Uh-oh," she said, putting down her coffee cup, "that form is all wrong." She ran out the door, not bothering to change out of her new pink nightgown. "Wait, Dave," she said, taking the football out of his hands. "You can kick a lot higher if you start off on your right foot."

Dave looked confused. "Show me," he said. So Mom took a long stride with her right foot, then her left, and, as she related it later, "kicked that thing to kingdom come." The football sailed through the treetops for an eternity before bouncing to earth four houses down, under the train trestle. The *whomp!* of her bare foot connecting with leather was so loud and the kick so spectacular that neither one of them noticed her nightgown splitting up the side from hem to collar. Eventually Mom looked down to find herself half-naked in the street.

"Oh my Lord!" she gasped, clutching the sides together and making a run for the house as Dave, oblivious to her predicament, chased down the ball.

But then the day changed considerably. After getting dressed, Mom opened the daily paper to see a familiar name pop out at her from one of the back pages. Heading the list of "Local Homeowners Owing Property Taxes" were "Leo J. and Evelyn Ryan."

Mom closed the paper, having lost her appetite for news. "I should have thought of the property tax before I sent that money off to Bruce," Mom said, "but in all the confusion it slipped my mind."

By this time, yet another loss loomed, so gradually that few of Mom's cohorts in the Round Robin saw it coming. Contests of word skill—jingles and the 25-words-or-less variety—were beginning to lose ground to sweepstakes, which required nothing more than being lucky enough to have your name picked out of a hat.

"What a turn of events!" Mom said to Dortha one day on the phone. "I can understand why companies are starting to prefer sweepstakes—it's a lot easier to pick the winners. But I'd hate to see language skills dropped from contesting altogether."

"It may be," Dortha said matter-of-factly, "that we're on the verge of extinction. The sponsors are saying that judges are too slow and expensive."

"Don't scare me like that, Dortha." Mom laughed, but the thought chilled her to the bone. If jingles and 25-word entries disappeared, so would her income.

"Dr Pepper just announced a big one for next spring, Evelyn," said Dortha, "so there's hope. Don't let that one go by without a few dozen entries."

The contests offered that winter were few and far between, so when entry blanks for the much-awaited Dr Pepper contest began to appear in grocery stores in April, the Affadaisies scooped them up. The "Time of Your Life" contest offered thousands of dollars in cash, a new car, and a trip to Europe, but the rules were a little more complicated than Mom liked. Entrants were asked not only to supply the last line of a limerick, but also to calculate the exact, predetermined month, day, hour, minute, and second that company officials would dig up a buried time capsule. Clues to the time puzzle appeared on the inside of Dr Pepper bottle caps. This part of the contest wasn't meant to be difficult, just time-consuming. It was going to take a lot of work to track down all the clues.

"Okay, kids," she announced one morning at breakfast, "listen up! I want you to find a whole lot of Dr Pepper bottle caps."

"What for?" said Barb.

"The clues I need to enter this contest are printed inside the caps," said Mom.

"You want us to *buy* a bottle and drink it to get the cap?" said Betsy, thrilled at the idea.

"No," said Mom. "Wherever you go during the day, I want you to keep your eye out for vending machines that sell soda pop. When you find one, look through all the bottle caps in the receptacle under the bottle opener at the side of the machine."

"You mean like at school?" asked Dave.

"Vending machines are all over the place these days—school, the drugstore, the playground," said Mom. "Now this is the important part: Don't bring *all* the bottle caps home. Just the Dr Peppers."

"What will it say inside the caps?" asked Barb.

"There are five clues altogether," Mom said, "so we need a bottle cap for each clue—one for the *month*, one for the *day*, one for the *hour*, one for the *minute*, and one for the *second* the time capsule will be opened."

By the end of the week, the kitchen table was covered in bottle caps, including several Coca-Cola and Hires root beer caps that Dave thought were pretty. We helped Mom sort through the pile for clues. Some caps had no clues at all.

"Here's one," said Betsy. "It says, 'The month clue is "Ruby." ' " "Anyone have any ideas?" said Mom, who already knew the answer.

"I know!" I said. "Ruby is the birthstone for July."

"Correct!" said Mom, taking the cap out of Betsy's hands and putting it in her pocket.

"Here's the 'day' clue," cried Barb. "It's 'XXX.' What does that mean?"

"Roman numerals," said Mike. "Three X's stand for the number thirty. So the month and day are *July 30.*"

"Right again," said Mom, putting that cap away, too. "I told you that Latin class would come in handy."

"Here's the 'hour' one," said Dave. " '*Ten Little Indians.*' That must mean ten o'clock?"

"Yes, and what about the word 'little'?" said Mom. "What could that mean, if anything?"

"It would mean in the morning," said Barb. "As opposed to ten o'clock at night."

"I think so too," said Mom. "Okay," she summed up. "So far, we have *July 30, ten o'clock in the morning.* What about the 'minute' and 'second' clues? We have to have them all."

Half of the caps seemed to be blank, but Mike finally held up two caps. "Here they are. The 'minute' clue is '*Dozen.*' The 'second' clue is '*Golden Anniversary.*' "

"*Dozen* must mean twelve minutes," said Betsy.

"And *Golden Anniversary* is fifty years," said Barb.

"Nice work," said Mom. "Our answer is '*July 30 at 12 minutes and 50 seconds after 10 in the morning.*'"

"Can I have the rest of the bottle caps?" asked Dave.

With the clues worked out, Mom turned to making up the last line of the Dr Pepper jingle, using her

usual collection of aliases and variations on 801 Washington Avenue:

> **The "time of your life" you can win**
> **With Dr Pepper, the flavor that's in.**
> **It's distinctive and bright**
> **It's lively and light**
> *There's no time like NOW to begin!*
> > Mrs. Evelyn Lenore Ryan
> *Verr-r-r-y "big"—Texas saw it begin!*
> > Evelyn Ryan
> *Great <u>hot, cold</u>; you're sold once you begin!*
> > Evelyn Lenore Ryan
> *It quite <u>centsibly</u> fetes kith and kin.*
> > Mrs. Evelyn Ryan, Washington St.
> *It's "a case of" "Can't wait to begin!"*
> > Mrs. Evelyn Ryan, Washington Ave.
> *"Dr Pepper is OUT" spells chagrin!*
> > Evelyn L. Ryan

Watching Mom churn out these limericks, I began to feel a sense of dread. Still fresh in my mind was the disappointment I felt when she won nothing for similar efforts with the *Gypsy* and the Paper Mate pen jingles.

Mom saw me watching her at the ironing board. "I have a new 'business plan,' " she told me as she wrote. "I'm sending only a dozen or so entries. And only the very best ones."

Was she trying to make it easier for me? I was skeptical. "Don't your chances increase the more times you enter?" I said. "Something you think is just so-so might appeal to the judges."

"Yes, but here's my new theory: Maybe by sending in so many I dilute my own chances. Do you know what I mean? If I send *only* the best entries I'm capable of, then I might get the best results in return; in other words, a prize closer to the top."

My heart surged. Mom was so unfailingly upbeat about every contest entry she had ever written that I could hardly begrudge her the joy of switching strategy for this contest.

Just as she promised, Mom submitted only six more closing lines for the Dr Pepper limerick, and they all sounded like winners, with one possible exception:

The "time of your life" you can win
With Dr Pepper, the flavor that's in.
It's distinctive and bright
It's lively and light
Makes the scene from Miami to Minn!
    Mrs. Evalyn L. Ryan
"Live" for little! Here's how to begin!
    Evalyn Ryan
Quaff it down for a quick "Count-me-in!"
    Evalyn L. Ryan
Lets a gal "live" refreshingly thin!
    Mrs. L. J. Ryan, Washington St.
Voice your choice of glass bottle or tin!
    Mrs. L. J. Ryan, Washington Ave.
No "trydentical" drink rates as "twin!"
    Mrs. L. J. Ryan, Washington

"I like the inner rhyme of 'Voice your choice,' Mom," I said, "and the alliteration in 'Makes the scene from Miami to Minn.' But '*try*dentical'? I guess that's a Red Mitten."

"Yes," she said. "I made up that word just in case these judges appreciate such things."

"But what does the entry really say?"

"It says that other soft drinks may *try* to duplicate Dr Pepper, but they don't come close enough to be mistaken for the real thing. It also says that I'd sure as heck like 'twin' or *to win* this contest."

I looked back at the six-word entry. "It says all that?"

Mom popped the entry blank into an envelope. "Well, it better say all that or I just wasted a five-cent stamp."

At the post office twenty minutes later, I slid the latest batch of Dr Pepper entries into the out-of-town slot, along with an entry for Hormel's "Spam-ericks" contest:

The boat and the basket went over the dam
But Dad is our hero—he rescued the Spam!

I was still smiling over the Spam jingle as I ran up the front steps into the house, where the mood had plummeted dramatically. For a split second I thought I had walked into the wrong house. Mom would later call it "The Day the Mirth Stood Still." She hadn't yet recovered from making the list of local tax delinquents. Now another shock. She had just hung up the phone, was leaning against the dining room table, looking bleary-eyed and ashen. The remaining places were filled by Mike, Barb, Betsy, and Dave, who must have heard at least her half of the conversation. They looked as gray and drained as she did. "Sit down, Tuff," said Mom.

"What's the matter?" I said.

"I'd prefer not having to tell you kids," she said, brushing a wisp of hair out of her reddening eyes, "but if I don't, you might read it in the paper or hear about it in school. That would be much worse."

"Just tell us," I said.

"Cutter Murphy just called from the bank," she said. "If we don't pay them four thousand dollars in thirty days, they're going to take the house away."

Five jaws dropped in unison.

"What?" I said.

"Can they *do* that?" said Mike.

"*Why* would they do that?" said Barb.

"They can do it, and they will," said Mom. "Apparently, Dad took out a second mortgage a year ago without telling me. Now it's come due."

"They can't do that!" Betsy said firmly. "What's a second mortgage?"

"What's a mortgage?" said Dave.

"It's a loan of money," said Mom. "The bank will loan you money for a while, but then you have to pay it back. If you don't . . ." She paused, her eyes filling with tears.

"But, Mom," I said, "how could the bank loan Dad all that money without you knowing about it?"

Her fingers traced and retraced the geometric pattern on the top of the Formica table. "That's precisely what I asked Mr. Murphy. He told me only one signature was required."

"And what did you say?" I asked.

"I told him that if only one signature was required, then it should have been mine."

"But you should just ask Dad to give you back the money," said Dave hopefully. "Then you could take it down to the bank."

"I have a feeling that money is long gone, Davey. But I certainly intend to ask Dad when he gets home from work."

A suffocating gloom descended over the dining room table. Just days before, my mother had been unable to tolerate the overdue property tax bill of less than a hundred dollars. The second mortgage was forty times larger.

My mind raced for a solution, as my brothers' and sisters' thoughts kept pace.

"We could ask Aunt Lucy," said Mike. "She's the richest person we know."

"Lucy may be generous, Mike," said Mom, "but she's not rich. Even if she did have that much money, it wouldn't be fair to ask her for it."

"I could get my job back at Druhot's Bakery," I said, remembering the precious $36 I had put toward our Christmas presents. But even Mom couldn't stretch $36 into $4,000.

"You have to concentrate on school, Tuff," Mom said feebly.

"We could sell something . . . ," offered Barb before realizing the obvious, ". . . if we had anything worth four thousand dollars to sell." Mom and I exchanged fatalistic glances. The only thing we had of value was no longer of value. With its melded gears, the family Chevy languished at the curb, a one-ton, blue-and-white paperweight.

Dave had an idea, too. "We could ask Lea Anne and Dick and Bub and Rog and Bruce," he said. "They must have some money."

"Well," Mom said, "that's a thought, but they're all just starting out. They have barely enough to get by with themselves."

Our mother, the ultimate optimist, could see no silver lining. "All good ideas, kids," she answered, shaking her head. "I wish every one of them could work. This problem may be bigger than all of us."

"We'll think of something, Mom," said Betsy. "We have to try."

"That's what you've always taught us," offered Mike, "remember?"

"Never give up," said Barb.

"Yes, Mom," I said, trying to lift her spirits. "Even when you're losing, you can be a winner."

Mom had said the same things to us a hundred times before. Hearing us repeat them seemed to break through her fog. She looked at each one of us. We looked back at her. "You're right," she said. "Of course you're right. Let's all try to think of a way out of this."

At that, we drifted out of the room, shuffling off in different directions. I climbed the stairs to the tiny bedroom that had been mine since Bruce left for California. Right after we had moved into the house, Mom had repainted the cell-sized room, covering over the flowered wallpaper that made the space seem even smaller and more crowded than it was. Over the new paint job, Mom had hung cheap prints of flower arrangements and rainy Paris streets, making the room look both cheery and

ridiculous. She had made all the curtains herself—
great flowery swags of heavy material that kept out
cold and heat alike.

I thought about someone else sleeping in this
room, some other family living in this house, and
was overcome by the need to do something, anything. The only solution I could imagine was a miracle—that Mom win a contest immediately. I stood in
the middle of the room and prayed aloud, bypassing
the patron saints—intermediaries who I felt could
only delay my urgent message. I spoke directly to
God. "I know you can do this," I said. "You've done
it before, remember? So please just do it again. Let
her win a *big* contest. If you were saving one for
later, that'll be too late. Give it to her *now*."

Wrapped up in my own intense feelings, at first I
didn't register another set of murmurings coming
from the next room. I didn't have to open the door to
recognize the muffled prayers of my sisters next door,
offering their own spiritual appeals. *"Hailmaryfullof-
gracethelordiswiththeeblessedartthouamongstwomen."*
In my mind, I pictured heaven's switchboard operator
trying to keep up with all the incoming prayers from
our corner of Ohio. I hoped the old adage about
power in numbers was true.

When Dad got home, Mom was sitting in the
glider on the front porch, swaying slightly to and
fro, waiting for him. We heard no anger in her voice.
If anything, she sounded resigned. "When were you
going to tell me about the second mortgage you took
out on the house a year ago, Kelly?"

Dad stopped in his tracks. "It's due, huh?" was all
he said for a few minutes. "I had a feeling the day
might be creeping closer."

Mom was still hoping things weren't as bad as they seemed. "Did you spend it all? Is anything left?"

His eyes followed a dust mote floating in the late afternoon light. "No. It's all gone."

"On what?" Mom asked. "What did you spend it on?"

"Does it matter, Mother?" he said quietly. "I have nothing to show for it, if that's what you mean."

"Did you just drink it away? Did you drink our house away, Dad?"

Dad looked directly into Mom's eyes. "I was planning to pay it back without anyone ever knowing about it, Mother. My intentions were good. I paid some bills with it. And I wanted to have money for you when you needed it. When Bruce called, for example."

Mom sat up straight. "You know darn well that if I'd known you took out that loan, I would've marched the money right back to the bank. Borrowing money when you're already in the hole is not the way to get ahead."

"I felt like a drowning man, Mother," said Dad, trying to explain. "All these kids, no prayer of ever having a few extra dollars—"

"Kelly, you've jeopardized the one thing we have in the world—our *home!*"

They sat quietly, listening to the breeze move through the maple trees in the yard. "How long do we have?" said Dad.

"Thirty days."

"What will we do?" he said.

"I don't know, Dad," she said sadly. "For the first time, I have no idea what we'll do."

CHAPTER NINETEEN

Her Weight

in Gold

On each of the next six mornings, we watched Mom march out the door in her Sunday best for the walk downtown to the bank. She was determined to convince Cutter Murphy and any other officer of the bank who would listen to her that with a few months' grace period she could formulate a payment plan. They were having none of it. "We'd like to help you, Evelyn," said Cutter sincerely, "but our hands are tied. The rules are ironclad. The money is due in full—no installment plan, no grace period."

Dad was quiet, like a man entombed, with no more nightly blowups, though his drinking held steady. I continued my daily prayers, as did Barb and Betsy.

Brave as ever, Mom confronted the worst. Whispered conversations in the kitchen between my parents led me to believe that plans were being made to have Aunt Lucy take Barb, Betsy, and Dave until we got back on our feet again. The thought of not living with my youngest siblings upset me far more than losing the house.

Then just after lunch on the sixth day, the telephone rang. The cheerful jangle couldn't have sounded more inappropriate in a funeral home. I heard Mom pick up the phone, and, after a long pause, she began to speak, her voice surprisingly upbeat. This was enough to get me up and running down the stairs, followed by Mike, Barb, Betsy, and Dave.

We piled into the dining room, where Mom sat with the phone, waving in our direction, urging us closer. She physically lassoed us in with her free arm, and there we all stood, so close to our mother that we could feel her breath on our faces. Her eyes were glistening with excitement. We strained to hear the voice on the other end of the line, barely able to stand the suspense.

Finally, Mom said her polite good-byes and hung up. "Kelly!" Mom boomed in the direction of the kitchen. "Get in here quick!" Dad rounded the corner expecting to find something on fire. A bead of perspiration formed on Mom's upper lip, and she grinned at us feverishly. "It's way too soon to get excited," she said breathlessly, "but that was a detective from Toledo." I felt my heart flip in the center of my chest. "He says I'm being considered as a possible winner in the Dr Pepper 'Time of Your Life' contest."

A thin shaft of hope worked its way through the darkness hovering over 801 Washington. As the kids gasped and clutched at Mom's hands, Dad pulled out a chair to sit in before he fainted. "Is this like when you won the sports car, Mom?" asked Dave. "Is it a big prize like that?"

"I think so, Davey," Mom said.

"When will we know if you won something?" said Barb.

Mom put her hand to her chest, willing her breathing to slow down. "Let's try to be calm. I'm not sure if I won or what I won," she said, "but this detective is driving to Defiance *right now* to interview me." She fanned her face with one hand. "I had to stop myself from telling him I'd just run down and meet him halfway." She laughed.

"What if the prize is an ice crusher?" said Betsy. "What if it's a toaster?"

"Oh, Bets," Mom said, smiling patiently, "they might send me an affidavit in the mail for a prize like that, but they would *never . . . ever* drive an hour and a half on a two-lane road to ask me questions if I wasn't in the running for first prize."

"What *is* first prize?" asked Mike.

Mom jumped up. "Good question!" she said. She ran into the living room to look up the prizes in her notebook, and we soared after her like satellites.

"C'mon, c'mon," she said anxiously as she flipped back and forth in the book. "Here! This is it." She read the entry blank silently for a minute, then turned in our direction as if addressing a congregation. "First prize," she announced dramatically, "is more than just one prize. The person who wins this contest will receive *all four* of these prizes. First, two weeks for two in Switzerland . . ."

"Oooooohhh," we sighed.

". . . second, a new Ford Mustang . . ."

"Ahhhhhhhh." Another brand-new sports car to push up and down Washington Avenue!

". . . third, his and her gold watches . . ."

"Real gold?" Mike was almost salivating.

". . . and fourth, $3,440.64."

Silence filled the room. As we raced through our mental arithmetic, Barb was the first to call out. "Mom! That *has* to be our prize. It's almost the exact amount we need."

"And we'll have our own car again!" said Betsy.

"Wait, wait," said Mom. "Slow down, everybody. Don't assume too much. For one thing, this contest is being judged by D. L. Blair, the same judges who awarded me first prize in the Beech-Nut sandwich contest a few years ago. These companies almost never award more than one major prize to a single person, so that's disheartening. On the other hand, they're interviewing me, so that must mean something. We won't know anything until after the detective gets here." Suddenly she slammed her notebook shut. "Oh m'gosh! We have to clean the house!" she shouted. "We can't invite a visitor into this warren of clutter and grime. Quick! We only have a little over an hour!"

"What should we clean first?" I called out.

"Anything the detective might walk on, sit on, or see!" yelled Mom. "The whole first floor, starting with the front porch!"

She began barking out commands like a field marshal under siege. "Dad! Clean off the tabletops and every flat surface you can find! Betsy! Follow Dad around and wipe up whatever he cleans off! Barb! Get the broom and sweep the floors! Davey!

Take the old ratty magazine off the busted spring in the living room chair and replace it with a new one! Tuff and Mike, wash every single porch window, inside and out!"

Mike and I glanced through the open dining room door to the porch, whose windows consisted of two hundred small panes of glass. "But, Mom," I said, "there's no way we can do all those windows before he gets here."

"Just try your darnedest," she said. "Remember, he's coming over to make sure that I exist and that I wrote the entry. We want to make a good impression, don't we?"

"What are *you* going to do, Mom?" asked Betsy.

"I've got bigger fish to fry," Mom said, turning to the ironing board. "Somehow I have to weld this ancient girdle into shape one more time and hope the old girl still has enough elastic in her to keep me hemmed in for an hour."

"You're going to fill the house with the smell of burning rubber?" said Barb.

"Open the windows!" Mom shouted. "Let's get a breeze going in here. C'mon, everybody, let's get with it!"

The house going up in flames couldn't have caused a ruckus greater than seven people cleaning to beat the clock. Dad swept a single beefy arm across the dining room table, scooping up a towering pile of magazines, books, mail, and crayons. "Where should I put all this, Mother?" he asked from behind the unwieldy mountain of paper in his arms. Before Mom could answer, the stack toppled onto the dustpan Barb had just filled with dirt.

"Geez, Dad," said Barb. "Now I have to start all over again."

"Hide all that stuff, Kelly—out on the back porch, upstairs, behind any closed door, *anywhere* he can't see it."

Following behind Dad as instructed, Betsy wiped the dust and leavings Dad missed from the top of the table. "Betsy," Mom said, pointing to the far corner of the room, "dust off those knick-knacks and shelves while you're at it."

Betsy peered at the seven-foot-high cabinet, wondering how high she had to go. "Is he a short detective or a tall detective?"

"Assume tall, Betsy," Mom laughed.

Just then Dave passed by holding a single magazine in his hands. "This is the newest one I could find, Mom. It's only a year old."

"Good, Dave!" said Mom, melting a V-shaped piece of rubber onto a V-shaped gap in the girdle on the board. "When you get done with that, get the cookies out of the dryer and put them on a plate." Dave's eyes lit up. "And don't *eat* any of them. They're for the *detective*."

Dad walked by with an armload of loose clothing he'd collected from floors and furniture in the living room. Mom grabbed his arm on the way by. "Dad!" she said. "I almost forgot. Better run down to the store and pick up a six-pack of Dr Pepper."

Out on the front porch, Mike and I worked steadily down the rows of two hundred window-panes, he on the outside, me on the inside. In forty-five minutes, we had cleaned only the first hundred panes, and our panic showed. "We're not going to make it, Mom!" I cried out. "We need more people."

Mom shot out of the living room carrying a bucket of water and wearing her best dress—white with large navy-blue polka dots—a fake pearl necklace, and lipstick on her lower lip. "You missed your upper lip," I said.

"Well, I can either help you clean windows, or I can look presentable," she said, setting the bucket down. "I guess I better go back and see what else I missed."

Dad walked in the front door with the Dr Pepper. "Put one of them in the freezer," said Mom, "so it'll be cold for the detective. Hand the rest of them out to the kids and tell them not to drink it all at once. It's important that we're drinking Dr Pepper when he gets here."

With fifteen minutes to go, Mike and I still had fifty unwashed panes. I shouted into the house, "We're never going to finish in time! Can't we just pull the curtains?"

"No!" came the reply. "The curtains are in worse shape than the windows!"

At that, Mike and I gave up on washing the windows and began simply to wipe the top layer of dirt from each pane of glass. Sunlight streamed into the porch, and we looked through the windows at each other, genuinely surprised. "Gee," I said. "We ought to do this more often."

"Yeah," said Mike, "every twenty years or so."

With ten minutes to go, Dave, perched on Dad's shoulders and carrying rags, wiped cobwebs and their trailing streamers from the corners of the ceiling. Racing to dispose of their dust rags, Barb and Betsy collided in the doorway between the dining room and the porch, creating yet another maelstrom of flying dust and debris. "Seal off the dining room!" Mom ordered. "That stuff won't settle for hours! Then stop working and change into your good clothes—your go-to-church clothes!"

Five minutes later, we watched through the front window as a brand-new white Oldsmobile parked at the curb across the street. "Places, everyone!" Mom shouted like a veteran director. Every kid in the house headed for the chair with the busted spring. "Spread out!" she stage-whispered.

When the detective knocked at the door, he found a quaint Midwestern home cleaned to white-glove perfection. Norman Rockwell would have felt at home. Windows sparkled in the sun, floors shone, and tabletops revealed flat surfaces not seen since the Eisenhower administration. The ironing board had been put away for the first time in years, and just a hint of molten girdle lingered. Mike and I had stuck our water buckets and rags deep in the bushes by the side of the house, because the back porch was full to bursting with the stacks of paper and clothing Dad had ferried out of the house.

"Mrs. Ryan?" the detective asked at the door. "Mrs. Evelyn Ryan?"

"Why, yes," Mom said, smiling, so relaxed that we knew her girdle must have cooled considerably. "Won't you come in?"

The man introduced himself as Milton Feeney as Mom led him into the living room, where we sat waiting in our good clothes. I perched on the chair with the busted spring. The new magazine felt pretty much the same as the old one. We were all aware that the last time a detective paid us a visit, Mom won the Triumph sports car and the jukebox.

Mr. Feeney sat in the rocking chair and Mom sat on the couch facing him, the coffee table between them supporting five half-full bottles of Dr Pepper. "Would you care for a cookie, Mr. Feeney?" she asked, lifting the plate from the table. He had unlocked his briefcase and was busy rifling through the papers inside, so he said yes without looking up—a good thing, since the top cookie had a large bite out of it, tooth marks and all. Before Mr. Feeney's head reappeared from behind the briefcase in his lap, Mom snatched the half-eaten cookie off the plate and shoved it down the side of the couch. She glared accusingly at Dave, Betsy, Barb, Mike, and me as her eyes swept slowly around the room, each of us with wide eyes silently denying responsibility. "Dad," Mom called out sweetly, "would you get Mr. Feeney a Dr Pepper?" Then, as an aside to the detective, she added, "The kids just can't seem to get enough of it."

We stared at our mother in awe. This was so true. We rarely drank pop—it was too expensive. We drank Kool-Aid, which cost next to nothing, an advantage my mother was eager to point out in previous entries.

Kool-Aid ends folks' cold-drinks dearth.
Two quarts is only five cents' worth.

The questions started. Mr. Feeney wanted to know all about Mom—her age, the number and ages of her children, her past contest wins, her likes and dislikes (especially in regard to refreshing summer beverages). "Oh," Mom said, "I'm as bad as the kids about that. I love my Dr Pepper." Head down, Mr. Feeney scribbled away on form after form. At one point, the living room door opened, and the detective turned expectantly. When Mammy strolled through the crowded room to the back of the house, Mr. Feeney blinked twice. He looked at our mother questioningly. She smiled back. "Talented cat," she said.

The interview went on for a full hour, and Mom was in her glory. The last detective had interviewed not her but Bruce, whose taciturn "Yeps" and "Nopes" were a great frustration for the real prize winner. This time, Mom was so eloquent that Mr. Feeney couldn't write fast enough.

"And how much do you weigh, Mrs. Ryan?" asked Mr. Feeney, out of the blue.

Up to this point, the rest of us had been weaving in and out of daydreams, bored by questions centering on what contest magazines Mom subscribed to and whether she had written her entries herself. Hearing this latest question, we snapped to attention. Mom, for the first time, was silent.

Recognizing her embarrassment, Mr. Feeney said, "I know that sounds like a personal question, Mrs. Ryan. I don't know why it's here. Just give me an estimate."

"Well . . . uh," she said, nervously twirling her necklace between her fingers, "I'm sure they have their reasons for asking. Now let me think a minute. . . ."

We watched her face eagerly, wondering how eloquent she might be on this topic. Mom's *avoirdu-*

pois, as she called it, had edged up a bit in recent months. According to the figures on the Metropolitan ideal weight chart, her current weight of 160 was within acceptable limits for a person four inches taller. "Well, that explains everything," she had said to us then. "I'm not fat for my height. I'm short for my weight."

My mother never lied. She was so good with words that, given enough time, she could construct a response that was true, if misleading. "Why, when I stepped on the scale last June," she said finally, "I weighed a hundred and fifty."

Mr. Feeney dutifully recorded her answer. He didn't care how much Mom weighed. It was just another question to him. But the rest of us smiled broadly at our truthful mother.

Finally Mr. Feeney closed up his briefcase and rose to leave. "When the final decision is made, Mrs. Ryan," he said as he walked out the door, "you'll be notified immediately." We waved as he climbed into his Oldsmobile and drove away.

"How long does it usually take for them to decide on the real winner?" I asked.

"It's anybody's guess," said Mom. "It could take a week. It could take two. Even if I don't win," she said, looking around at her spotless surroundings, "at least I got a clean house out of the deal."

"But we don't have time to wait!" said Mike. "What about the bank?"

"Yes, Mom," said Barb. "Let's go down and tell them you're in the running! If you win, you can pay the whole thing!"

" 'If I win' isn't going to mean much to them, kids," she said. " 'If I win' is a long way from 'I *won*.' "

Mom went to see them anyway. By this time, the bank officers had gotten to know Evelyn Ryan so well that they were thrilled with the news that she might win the Dr Pepper contest. "We're rooting for you, Evelyn," said Cutter Murphy, "but there's nothing we can do for you unless you *do* win."

For the next several days, we froze in place every time the phone rang, letting Mom answer it. We asked friends not to call in the daytime, in case Dr Pepper was trying to get through. The level of anticipation rose and fell with every call. A week passed with no word. No one was sleeping well, and by the second week we were walking around the house like zombies. Between the excitement of winning the contest and the terror of losing it, time crawled by.

Meanwhile, Mom tried to determine which of her entries was in the running for first prize.

"When the detective called," she said, her notebook open to her Dr Pepper entries, "he asked for Evelyn Ryan. That should give me a clue. It's just that most of the entries I sent in were variations on that: Evelyn, Evelyn L., Evelyn Lenore, Evalyn, Evalyn L. I just have no idea which one got their attention."

"You could ask them," I said.

"Well, I'll be sure and do that if I ever hear from them again." She laughed. "I just hope they didn't disqualify me for fudging on the question about my weight."

Another week passed. By now we were so accustomed to eyeing the phone and willing it to ring that we jumped whenever it did.

With three days to go before the date of foreclosure, Mom jumped higher than most of us. In her frantic attempt to answer a morning call, she got all tangled up in a load of clean laundry. "Davey!" she cried. "Would you get that before I kill myself trying?"

Dave picked up the receiver as Mom struggled through the pile of towels and sheets on her way into the dining room. "Uh-huh," Dave said, frowning into the phone, then handed it to Mom. "It's Mr. Simonis," Dave said with a worried look on his face. "If he's calling about tulips, I didn't pick any more, Mom."

"I know you didn't, Dave," she said and then spoke into the phone. "Hello, Mr. Simonis."

"Hello, Mrs. Ryan," the unfamiliar voice on the other end of the line said, "this is John Simmons, vice president of advertising for Dr Pepper."

"Oh my word," said Mom, anticipating his message. "My son had you confused with a neighbor." She put her hands over the mouthpiece and whispered, "Dave! Go get everyone!" He ran off and within seconds had herded all of us, including Dad, to Mom's side.

"Mrs. Ryan," Mr. Simmons continued, "it's my pleasure to inform you that you are our first prize winner in the Dr Pepper 'Time of Your Life' contest."

"Oh, Mr. Simmons," Mom said as she leaned into the wall for support, "how I have awaited this call." She turned and nodded silently to all of us.

"I'm airmailing you a special delivery letter to confirm everything in writing, Mrs. Ryan, but I'm sure you already know that you've won a trip for two to Switzerland, a Ford Mustang, his and hers Longines watches, and cash in the amount of $3,440.64."

Mom wiped at the tears streaming down her cheeks. "How wonderful," she said with a composure we couldn't believe. "Why, these prizes couldn't have come at a better time for my large family." Mom was already in her gracious-winner mode.

"And another thing," said Mr. Simmons. "We want you and your husband to come to Dallas when we dig up the time capsule—all expenses paid, of course. Are you willing to do that?"

"Oh," Mom exclaimed, "I've always wanted to visit Dallas, Texas." She was elated. "Of course we'll come."

"Good," he said. "I'll send more information on that in the letter."

"Tell me, Mr. Simmons," Mom said, "do you know which entry won?"

"Don't *you* know?" he said.

"As it turns out, I sent in more than one," Mom confessed.

"Oh, Mrs. Ryan, I'm sorry. That's restricted information. I'm not allowed to tell you or anyone else. You have every reason to be proud, though. Your entry beat out more than two hundred and fifty thousand other entries in our contest."

"Goodness!" said Mom. *"Two hundred and fifty thousand?"*

"That's correct. And what are you planning to do now, Mrs. Ryan?" he asked.

"Well, first I'm going to sit down and cry for a few hours," she said, "and then I'm sure I'll do something exciting to celebrate. Thank you so much again, Mr. Simmons. You've brightened my day considerably."

With that, she hung up the phone, and an explosion of cheers and laughter filled the house.

Mom cried until she laughed; then laughed until she cried. She wasn't alone. We were stunned. Her latest win was a miracle of incredible timing and proportion. "Who would believe this?" I said happily. "It's just not possible. We're not going to lose the house. We might even come out ahead!"

"Oh for Pete's sake, that's right!" said Mom, trying to staunch the tears of joy with wads of Kleenex. "I've got to call the bank!" And she turned back to the phone.

"Evelyn," said Cutter Murphy, "how nice to hear from you."

"And for once, Cutter," Mom laughed, "it's nice to be calling you. As it happens, I just won the Dr Pepper contest we discussed earlier." Her formality astonished us. "It's about thirty-five hundred dollars in cash and a few other prizes, at least one of which we plan to sell to come up with the whole four thousand we owe you."

Cutter Murphy's gasp was audible two feet away from the phone. "I can't believe it. Congratulations, Evelyn. That's some kind of miracle you pulled off."

"I'll get you the money as soon as I get it," said Mom, "but I'm not sure when that might be. Probably within a week or two."

"Oh. Well, uh . . . we might have a problem there. The mortgage is due in three days, and as I've said, these rules are pretty much set in stone. . . ." His voice trailed off for a moment. "But perhaps we can make an exception. Your case is so extraordinary. Can you bring me confirmation of some kind that you expect to be receiving this money from Dr Pepper?"

"Oh, that's easily done," said Mom. "The vice

president of advertising just told me over the phone that he's airmailing me a letter of confirmation by special delivery."

"Good," said Cutter Murphy. "Bring it down to the bank before the three days are up, and you've got a deal."

Mom hung up the phone with a sense of accomplishment that made previous prizes seem like bingo wins.

"When does the Mustang get here?" asked Mike.

"Oh, Mike," Mom laughed, "we can't keep that. It's almost as small as the Triumph was. We'll have to trade it in on a larger car—a four-door."

"Well," said Mike happily, "it'll still be a *new* car." Aside from the long-gone Triumph, we had never had one before.

"And who's going to Switzerland, Mom?" asked Barb. "Can I go?"

"We won't be going to Switzerland anytime soon," said Mom. "We need money more than we need a vacation, and the cash prize won't quite cover what we owe on the second mortgage. I'll have to try talking Dr Pepper into exchanging the trip for cash."

"We can at least keep the watches," said Betsy.

"That's the oddest amount of money," said Dad. "Where would anybody come up with a prize of $3,440.64?"

"Remember that the theme of the contest was time?" asked Mom. "Hence, the 'Time of Your Life' contest. Switzerland is the time capital of the world, right? And the watches, of course, are timepieces. Even the Mustang comes with a clock on the dashboard. The cash prize signifies time, too. Ever notice that the Dr Pepper bottles all have '10, 2, 4' on the label? The $3,440.64 is meant to pay $10.24 for every hour of the two weeks in Switzerland."

"Time has been our theme, too," I said. "As in running out."

"Yes, Mom," said Betsy, laughing, "you won just in *time*."

"How *time*ly you can be when you try," Barb added.

We holed up in the dining room for the rest of the day, talking and laughing as the nervous energy we had built up over the past few weeks seeped out into the atmosphere.

"Mom!" said Mike, "we should call the newspapers."

"Oh, they'll find out soon enough," she said. "But I do believe I could splurge on a call to Dortha."

"Gad, girl!" said Dortha when she heard the news. "Isn't this your third big win? I knew you were good, but I didn't know you were *that* good."

"To tell you the truth, Dortha," said Mom, "I think there might have been some heavenly intervention with this one."

"Can you come to the next Affadaisy meeting?" asked Dortha. "I'll supply the hammer."

By the next day, everyone on the block had heard about Mom's win. Mrs. Druhot called to offer congratulations. So did Mrs. Zipfel. Even Pokey knew. As he ambled up the sidewalk, Mom met him at the bottom of the steps.

"I heard you won contests, Evelyn," he said, handing Mom the mail and wiping the sweat from the leather band in his cap, "but by the sound of the prizes, this one was a beaut. I want you to know I don't think there's anyone more deserving than you."

"Thank you, Vernon," said Mom, still in the glow of her victory. "And you've been a big part of it all. Without you delivering the announcements of my wins, I'd be nowhere. In fact," she said, looking quickly through the stack in her hands, "I'm waiting for a confirmation letter from Dr Pepper. I guess it hasn't come yet."

"I'll keep my eye out for it, Evelyn," offered Pokey. "Hey, tell you what I'll do—I'll check at the post office when I finish for the day. If it's there, I'll bring it over."

"You're an angel, Vernon. Thank you. It's coming airmail special delivery," she said, "just in case that helps."

But Vernon didn't come back that day, and when Mom spied him through the front window the next morning as he lugged his heavy leather bag down the opposite side of the street, she raced out the door to intercept him. "Whew," she said, catching her breath, "I didn't know I could still run like that."

Vernon shook his head. "Sorry, Evelyn," he said. "It's still not here. I've got everyone down at the post office waiting for it to come in."

"Oh dear," said Mom. She knew Pokey didn't understand why she needed the confirmation letter, and she didn't want to tell him that the bank needed proof of the win by tomorrow to keep from foreclosing on the house. "Well," she said, "I'm in sort of a hurry for it, so I appreciate all your help."

"Don't worry," he said. "Anything marked 'Air Mail Special Delivery' isn't going to go unnoticed."

By four o'clock in the afternoon, Mom had grown so worried about the letter that she couldn't even read the newspaper, let alone work on other contests or think about making supper. She wasn't hungry, and the kids weren't either, so we rocked in the front porch glider as Mom paced back and forth in front of us.

"Why don't you call up Dr Pepper, Mom?" I said. "They can phone the bank and assure them that the money's coming."

"Oh, Tuff," Mom said, stopping in mid-pace. "I don't want the folks at Dr Pepper to know about our troubles. I just can't figure where that letter got to. It was sent *airmail*, for goodness sakes."

"But tomorrow's the day, Mom. The bank has to see it by tomorrow."

We were startled by a knock at the front door, and through the sparkling-clean panes, we caught sight of Pokey's blue-hatted head. "Vernon!" Mom called out. "It's *you!*"

He opened the door enough to stick his head through. "Just wanted you to know," he said, smiling, "that neither rain nor sleet nor . . . however that goes." He held up a white envelope addressed to Mom.

She snatched the letter out of Pokey's hands. "This is it!" she exclaimed.

"Just one problem, Evelyn," he said. "You owe thirty cents in postage."

Mom looked more closely at the envelope. "Well, would you look at that!" Mom laughed. "They sent it airmail special delivery and forgot to put stamps on it!" Then she turned to the rest of us. "Who's got thirty cents? Anybody?"

She looked from one face to the next. No one had a dime. Mom was just about to ask Pokey for a loan when Betsy cried out, "Wait, Mom! What about the roll of postage stamps you use for contests?"

Mom smiled. "What about it, Vernon? Will you take six five-cent stamps?"

"Absolutely," said Pokey. "Coin of the realm! I don't see why not."

Mom tore the letter open. It was simple enough, yet we couldn't believe it no matter how many times we read it out loud.

Mrs. Evelyn Lenore Ryan
801 Washington
Defiance, Ohio

Dear Mrs. Ryan:

Once again, congratulations!

This will confirm our telephone conversation of a few moments ago during which I advised you that you are the First Prize winner in our "Time of Your Life" Contest. This means that you have won a Two-week Trip for Two to Switzerland, a new Ford Mustang, His and Her Longines Watches and $3,440.64.

Also, as discussed with you, we would like for you and Mr. Ryan to come to Dallas to attend the unearthing of the Time Capsule. If possible, we would like you to make this trip on Thursday, July 29, stay over that evening, assist in the digging up on July 30 and return to Defiance that evening.

If you will let me know your availability, we will follow through to arrange airline and hotel accommodations.

On behalf of all of us with Dr Pepper, including Mr. George Fruth, our good bottler in Napoleon, Ohio, we look forward to awarding you this First Prize. Please do not hesitate to write or call me if any questions come to mind.

Cordially,

John C. Simmons

"Oh, look!" Mom said. "It's addressed to 'Mrs. Evelyn Lenore Ryan.' Let me just check that notebook one more time to see if I can figure out the winning entry."

The "time of your life" you can win
With Dr Pepper, the flavor that's in.
It's distinctive and bright
It's lively and light
There's no time like NOW to begin!

Mrs. Evelyn Lenore Ryan

"Gosh," Mom said. "This line is so simple. I worried it would be duplicated all over the place. I thought for sure the winning line would be *'Verr-r-r-y "big"—Texas saw it begin!'* Texans have such intense state pride. You certainly don't find that kind of enthusiasm in Ohio."

"Let's face it, Mom," I said. "The Lone Star State sounds like a more exciting place than the Buckeye State."

"Not today it doesn't," said Mom.

The Dr Pepper Company flew Mom and Dad to Dallas to receive the prizes and meet with company officials. Mom beamed for the cameras as

*M*om, *happily in the spotlight in Dallas, Texas, after winning the Dr Pepper contest, even though "that gal ruined my hairdo when she squashed the cowboy hat on my head."*

she accepted the keys to a shiny new Mustang, and only for a moment worried that the TV crew in attendance might ask her to get in and start it up. (She hadn't yet told them she couldn't drive.) She was interviewed several times, and "every time I turned around someone stuck a Dr Pepper in my hand, so by the end of the first day I fairly squished with every step."

She even dug an honorary spadeful at the site of the Dr Pepper time capsule, at the exact moment we felt we had helped her figure out: July 30th at twelve minutes and fifty seconds after ten in the morning. The perfectly posed publicity photos, however, did little to hide Mom's distraction. A "Texas gal" at the airport had planted a three-gallon cowboy hat on her head with such enthusiasm that "my hairdo was squashed the whole time," she told us. "I don't think I took that darned thing off for two days."

Even Dad had a good time. He had never flown on an airplane before, and sipped discreetly from his flask without incident. Mom worried about him only once—on their first night, when Dad, looking forward to "a big Texas-sized steak," realized in disgust that the Dr Pepper people were leading them into the Ports o' Call restaurant, which specialized in Polynesian food. "No meat, no potatoes, no gravy?" Dad said, before Mom shot him a "don't you dare" look. After dinner, they went to see *The King and I*, starring Ann Blythe and Michael Ansara (who played Cochise on the TV show *Broken Arrow*). Backstage after the show, when Mom was introduced to Michael Ansara as the Dr Pepper grand prize winner, he grabbed her hand and said, "You *won?* I never win *anything!*"

*A*t **Dr Pepper** headquarters in Dallas, Mom stands next to her new Mustang and holds a bag of money marked "$3,440.64," plane tickets to Switzerland, and two gold watches.

Mom returned home to find that her fame had spread throughout our corner of northwestern Ohio. For a while, she couldn't walk into Goldenetz's or the Big Chief without being congratulated, and Dad reported that his coworkers at the shop had not only conceded that Mom was a gifted contester, they had clapped Dad on the back and congratulated him, too.

But when an ominous-looking envelope arrived in the mail with a return address of "City Hall," Mom slapped her forehead in horror. "Oh my Scot!" she said. "I forgot to pay the property taxes." Donning the same outfit she had worn during her many trips to the bank, she trudged downtown and was surprised to find apologetic expressions on the faces of the clerks in the tax collector's office. "Oh, Evelyn, we *hated* sending you the notice," they said. "Now tell us: What is Michael Ansara really like?"

Mom never won another major contest, but it didn't matter. The Dr Pepper victory brought a new sense of security to life in the Ryan house. From then on, we knew there could never be a problem bigger than Mom's ability to solve it.

A Truckload

of Birds

Life changed considerably at 801 Washington after the Dr Pepper win. One by one, the younger Ryan kids graduated from high school and left home. I wouldn't say that Mom pushed us out the door, but she let us know it wasn't in our best interests to hang around town. "Defiance doesn't have many opportunities," she said, "but there's a whole world of them out there waiting for you." We believed her.

As Mom and the Affadaisies had feared, contests of luck (sweepstakes) nearly obliterated contests of skill. To make up for the money and prizes she used to win, my mother hired on as a clerk in the downtown JCPenney store. It was the first job she'd held since working for the Sherwood *Chronicle* in the 1930s, and she didn't mind that her new career had nothing to do with language. "When you think about it," she said, "I've always been in sales. The only difference is that now I'm selling Fruit Of The Loom instead of Burma-Shave."

Even after contests of skill disappeared, Mom thought that her biggest "wins" were the college scholarships awarded to Mike, Barb, and Betsy. They filled in the applications, but Mom was the one who explained, in her own eloquent way, exactly why her children deserved assistance. As a result, Mike won a full scholarship to Washington University in St. Louis, and Barb and Betsy got full scholarships to Case Western Reserve University in Cleveland.

However, by the time the Ryan kids applied to renew their scholarships, college administrators jumped on changes in our household. Dad had retired by then, and since Mr. Ryan received a pension, Mrs. Ryan was employed, and "only" five of the ten kids lived at home, the college administrators uniformly responded, the Ryan students no longer needed as much financial help.

Mom wrote back to each school, breaking her lifelong rule of never burdening others with "family troubles." If going public about Dad was the difference between her children attending college and not attending college, she was prepared to stand up and tell all.

Out of reticence for disclosing family skeletons, I've always soft-pedaled words and phrases about our particular situation. Actually they've painted an incomplete picture and fall considerably short of "telling it like it is." I'm sure it must look to you that with only five out of ten children left to support, and with the added income from my part-time job, we don't need so much help anymore. Unfortunately, that look is deceiving.

The truth of the matter is that the applicant's father is an alcoholic. Supporting this costly habit has meant for years the rest of us have had to limp along on only a fraction of his income. Thanks to the kindness of relatives and friends who knew this, we've never actually gone hungry. But at the present time nearly everything we own is in a sad state of disrepair. House needs reroofing badly, siding is weathering, our stove, clothes dryer, and refrigerator are just barely working. We've gone without dental care until everyone needs everything done at once. We've made over clothing handed down to us by friends, and done without many essentials. Many times bills went unpaid until we had to pay overcharges for tardiness on them all.

The liquor bill has been a ruinous drain on my husband's paycheck. Drinking has wrecked his disposition and made study and homework next to impossible for our children. Yet all of ours have been top-notch students, and all but one so far have finished close to the top of their classes (two valedictorians, one tied for third, another was sixth). That's no small thing in a school the size of ours. Each of them is determined to get a college education (the older ones already have) and I'm telling you all this at long last because I feel it's not fair to them to hide the true circumstances.

During the time of the big prize contests I discovered a flair for writing winning entries, and would from time to time win appliances and enough cash to pay off some of the back bills. In this way we managed to keep our heads above water until we'd get behind again. But the days of contests are over and I took a part-time job to assume the responsibility of clothing the family and of paying book, supply, and incidental bills of our children still at home and in college. This has enabled my husband to put a little in the bank toward necessary home repairs. In his own way, he's trying. I'm afraid that the financial aid we're going to be able to give our children will be pitifully small. And I'm just praying they'll all be able to make it through college.

There. I've said it. Thank you for listening.

All scholarships were renewed in full.

Dad was diagnosed with diabetes in the mid-1970s. He quit drinking, but not in time to save his body. After his leg was amputated, he became dependent on Mom, spending most of his time in the kitchen in his wheelchair, listening to baseball on the radio. He died in 1983 at the age of seventy-five.

My father left a legacy of atonement that stunned my mother and all of their children. He told Betsy about his plans ten years before his death. "I go down to First Federal every month, Bets, and I just put this pension check right in the bank, see? It's a surprise for Mother. It belongs to her. You make sure she uses it. Will you do that for me?"

When Dad died, we discovered that he had saved over $60,000, more money than my parents had ever dreamed of having in their lifetime, and left it all to Mom.

My mother retired from JCPenney a few months before Dad died. After decades of living in a full house, she found herself alone, so for the next ten winters, she fulfilled a lifelong dream and traveled the country, visiting one or another of her children in Florida, California, Colorado, Texas, Virginia, and New York. "If I'd known how convenient all you kids were going to be, I would have had a few more," she liked to say.

As Mom grew older, so did downtown Defiance. Many buildings were boarded up. Some of their tenants (like Kuntz's Drugs and Woolworth's Five & Dime) had simply expired; others (including Mom's favorite shopping venue, JCPenney) had moved to the new mall on the north side of town. The downtown district may have been past its prime, but my mother wasn't about to admit the same about herself. If she needed something from the mall, she hiked the two miles there and the two miles back, stopping to admire the view from the library, the gladioli in a neighbor's yard, or the glint of sunshine on the river.

As she entered her eighties, Mom adapted to rather than re-paired the little breakdowns that regularly occur in a hundred-year-old home. Increasingly forgetful, she posted instructive notes around the house to remind herself and visitors how things worked. On the living room thermostat, REMEMBER TO TURN THIS OFF AT NIGHT; on the Venetian blinds in the bedroom, DO NOT TOUCH THIS CORD; on her old upright piano, DO NOT PUSH DOWN 2ND PEDAL FROM LEFT, UNDER PAIN OF DEATH.

In the summer of 1998, my mother was diagnosed with terminal cancer. The disease had already spread to every major organ in her body. According to the doctors, Mom had at most a month to live. Over the next two days, all ten of Mom's children returned home to spend the last weeks of her life with her at 801 Washington Avenue.

Already bedridden, Mom greeted each one of us with a horizontal hug and a kiss on the cheek. "I don't know how I got myself into such a pickle," she said, over and over again.

At first Mom was alert enough to retain her motherly role. "Dick!" she called out one morning as he left her bedside, "you've got a hole in the back of your shorts. We can fix that before you leave." As the days passed, her comments became more enigmatic. She seemed to be one page off in the dictionary. "Your hand is still crunchy," she said to Mike one morning.

At other times, she was entirely precise. When Lea Anne asked how she was feeling, Mom said, "I'm going up and down the grateful steps."

Working with hospice nurses, we ministered to Mom around the clock, doling out food and drugs and conversation. We exchanged her old mattress and bed frame for a hospital bed and watched her body grow smaller with each passing day. She began sleeping more, floating between this life and the next.

It wasn't easy watching our mother lose her hold on life. For one thing, life didn't want to let her go. For years, Mom had held her aging, fragile world together with not much more than a positive attitude and a sense of humor. Now as her health began to wane in earnest, her physical surroundings seemed determined to go with her.

The appliances she had won over the years—the large electric fan on the front porch, the clothes washer, the toaster, and the dining room clock—stopped working in the first two days we were home.

The thermometer hanging in the evergreens outside Mom's bedroom window registered only eighty degrees. Bruce and I bought a new one displaying the correct temperature—ninety-six. As he carried the old one away, thirty earwigs fell out of the housing on the back, and the dial rose from eighty degrees to ninety-six. "If you had left the earwigs in there," Mom said, "it'd still be eighty degrees."

Before dawn on the morning of the third day, the plumbing stopped working in the middle of a thunderstorm that also knocked out the electricity in the house. As the basement began to fill with water, Mike raced up the stairs in his underwear with his sleeping bag wrapped around him. Lightning blasts illuminated the inside of the house for a few seconds at a time—long enough for Barb, Betsy, and me to watch Mom's framed Poet Laureate certificate from the Toledo *Blade* fall to the floor. A moment later, a glass four-leaf clover that Mom had suctioned to the living room window also dropped with a crash. My sisters and I stared at one another. Betsy sat down in a nearby chair, which collapsed beneath her.

"Is everything all right out there?" Mom called from the bedroom.

"Everything's okay, Mom," Barb laughed. "The gods are toying with us, that's all."

Still, if it took ten people to handle the household that Mom had managed by herself for almost fifty years, so be it. We tried to see past minor troubles to the larger picture—keeping our mother free of pain and the house from crumbling around us. We had known her, of course, our whole lives—Lea Anne for 61 years, Dick 59, Bub 57, Rog 55, Bruce 53, me 52, Mike 50, Barb 48, Betsy 45, and Dave 44—and we took turns sitting by the side of her bed, talking to her whether she was alert or not.

"I can't quite figure out how far we are from Defiance," she said one morning.

"We're *in* Defiance, Mom," Barb said. "We're at home."

"Oh yes," she said. "It was a nice place to be. A saving place."

In the last week, Mom's body seemed to grow younger and more beautiful. In truth, she looked younger than any of her children. We sat around her bed, knowing the end was close.

"I'm worried about my truckload of birds," Mom said.

It took us a moment to realize she was referring to her houseful of children.

"I dreamed there was a collision, and none of them survived."

"We have never been in danger as long as you've been with us," I said. "Even after you leave, we'll carry you with us wherever we go."

Evelyn Ryan died in the early morning hours of August 29, 1998. She was eighty-five years old.

Though my brothers and sisters and I felt prepared for our mother's departure, we couldn't have been more devastated if her death had come as a complete surprise. We consoled ourselves at first by preparing for her funeral and then by going through the house in search of vital papers. We didn't have to look far. Mom's penchant for saving every shred of paper relating to her life meant that every chest, dresser, and closet in the house was stuffed.

Much to our surprise, the $60,000 that Dad had left Mom remained untouched. Mom had lived off the interest and her own JCPenney pension to preserve the capital for her children. And what a discovery we made in the cedar chest in her bedroom. From the moment the lid creaked open, we realized we had found our mother again. She had saved all our report cards from first grade on, every letter we had written home, every evidence of childhood victories—Dave's Punt, Pass & Kick award, newspaper clippings of Dick's and Bub's baseball wins, and copies of her letters to the boys at Tiger Town, even the Metropolitan Life Insurance chart of ideal weights she had tried so hard to fit into.

The chest also contained enough contest memorabilia to open a museum, all of it boxed and labeled "Do Not Destroy—Family History." This was a slice of American history: contest entry blanks, poems and limericks, win announcements on company letterhead, framable awards, Round- Robin letters, newspaper articles, publicity photos, and best of all (to us), the spiral notebooks—dozens of them—in which Mom had scribbled thousands of entries.

The chest housed an archaeological dig three feet deep, with the center layers dating to the 1950s and 1960s. At the very bottom, I found what must have been the first item Mom had slipped inside—a faded sixty-two-year-old copy of the Sherwood *Chronicle,* folded to reveal this small announcement:

MARRIED: Lehman–Ryan

In the presence of friends and a few members of the immediate families, Miss Evelyn Lenore Lehman, daughter of Mr. and Mrs. O. E. Lehman, was united in holy matrimony to Mr. Kelly Ryan, son of Mrs. Catherine Ryan of Defiance, at six o'clock Thanksgiving morning, November 26th, at St. Mary's Catholic Church at Defiance, with Father F. X. Gosser officiating. Attendants were Mr. Edmund Ryan, brother of the groom, and Mrs. Ryan. The bride was attired in a dress of dove gray crepe trimmed with insertions of net and soutache braid, with which she wore black accessories and a corsage of pink Ophelia roses.

"Mom and Dad were married at six o'clock in the morning?" I said. "On Thanksgiving day?"

"A dove-gray dress with black accessories?" said Barb.

And suddenly we knew. No wonder Mom never explained why she didn't go to college, or why she had given up writing her column for the newspaper.

"What's the big deal?" said Dave. "People have to get married all the time."

"It wasn't accepted back then," said Lea Anne. "Most women in that situation thought their lives were ruined."

"This explains everything," I said.

In the silence that overcame us, my mother's spirit seemed fuller, larger. Mom, once the bright and shining star of Sherwood and its newspaper, must have been scared to death—of marriage, of pregnancy, of disgrace. Somehow she overcame this stark beginning to create a life of abundance and promise for herself and for us. Hiding the truth from us meant that the woman who taught us to be proud, regardless of poverty or adversity, could never be our role model, or so she believed. But here was a woman who never showed the slightest bit of resentment or bitterness. In fact, the reverse was true. Mom delighted in life's innate hilarity, and her joy in living found its best statement through her gloriously understated "knack for words."

My mother continued writing almost until the day she died, her spirit and sense of humor unflagging to the end. A week before her death, I lifted a book from a chair at her bedside, and a small handwritten poem fluttered to the floor. It contained precisely 25 words:

Every time I pass the church
I stop and make a visit
So when I'm carried in feet first
God won't say, "Who is it?"

I read her poem aloud, and we laughed together. I remembered that fall day in 1953 when my mother won the first miraculous grand prize, Dick's new bicycle and $5,000, to buy the house we were sitting in now.

"I wouldn't worry, Mom," I said. "God will know who you are. You two go *way* back."

Lea Anne (oldest) is now a hospice nurse in Florida, where she lives with her husband of forty-two years, Bob Metzger. They have four children and nine grandchildren.

Dick lives in Los Angeles, tends bar, and plays baseball and softball in city leagues.

Bub, a retired Los Angeles policeman, teaches grade school in Virginia and lives with his wife of forty years, Jannie Sherrell. They have five children and eleven grandchildren.

Rog operates his own office-machine repair business in San Antonio, Texas. He has three children.

Bruce received his undergraduate and law degrees from UCLA. After seventeen years as an assistant attorney general for the State of Colorado, he is now an attorney in private practice in Denver.

I (Terry/Tuff) graduated from Bowling Green State University in Bowling Green, Ohio, with a dual major in English and journalism. I'm a technical writer and cartoonist, living in San Francisco.

Mike graduated from Washington University in St. Louis with a degree in political science. He also earned a degree in mechanical engineering from Chico State in California. Though he has worked as an engineer, Mike prefers the freedom of freelance house painting in San Antonio, Texas.

Barb received her B.A. in theater from Case Western Reserve University in Cleveland. She lives in Cleveland Heights, Ohio, where she works with her husband, Peter Menczer, restoring houses.

Betsy received a B.A. in English/theater from Case Western Reserve University, an M.A. and a Ph.D. in theater from the University of Illinois in Champaign-Urbana, Illinois. She has taught theater at the University of Iowa and at UCLA.

Her book, *Gertrude Stein's Theatre of the Absolute*, was published by the UMI Research Press at Ann Arbor. Betsy lives in New York State with her husband, Nick Mankovich, and their three children.

Dave married his high school sweetheart, Lucy Guillen. He is the only one of the Ryan kids to remain in Defiance, where he works at the General Motors Foundry. Dave and Lucy have three children and two grandchildren.

Dortha Schaefer turned eighty years old in the fall of 2000. She writes a local-color column for the *Paulding Progress*, a weekly newspaper in Paulding, Ohio. The former Affadaisies (from Payne, Ohio) combined with the Versatillies (from Fort Wayne, Indiana) to form The Contest Club. Its seven members meet monthly in Hicksville, Ohio.

AFTERWORD BY BETSY RYAN

My mother wrote from her own life, recording, embellishing, or ignoring as she chose, in the middle of everything. From the newsroom of her girlhood to the ironing board of her family life, the writing went on, shaping itself while she worked toward wildly differing goals. Whether for her cheeky column in her grandmother's newspaper, the fourth line of a breezy Birds Eye jingle, or the turn of phrase in a short story that might express, once and for all, the combined affection and horror we all felt for Charley the Chicken, it was a writing of humor and ease, rooted in her daily life and uniquely expressive of it. When many writers might retreat from the world for some needed solitude, she grabbed that writing pad and got it down, the prize won, the moment captured, the other hand on the iron.

But biography was not exactly her aim. She was more of a poet—someone who tinkered with words and shades of meaning and phraseology for the fun of it, someone whose search for the telling detail was a source of joy. In this way, she shaped her surroundings as much as they shaped her. And let's not forget laughter. She had an unerring sense of what was funny, coming as she did from a strict Methodist upbringing and learning through living to leave it well behind, and could double over from the effects of her own writing. It was a focal point for her talent, yes, but also a necessary release.

The thought used to cross our minds that Mom could have had a wonderful life writing advertising copy on Madison Avenue instead of raising ten children on no money in the middle of nowhere. But this was before we really knew her. We have learned from the things she left behind that hers was a remarkable life, defined most of all by the wish to include everything. From a child's poem or a paid-off loan note to her rural Ohio domestic life that allowed, or inspired, the perfect turn of phrase in a prizewinning entry, one thing was as important as the next, and equally absorbing. Looking through these things she left for us in the months after she died allowed us to see, piece by piece, what she was all about, and to appreciate the true extent of her accomplishment.

I have a recurring dream about my mother. She is sitting on her living room couch, holding this book in her hands. "This is wonderful," she is saying, with tears in her eyes. "But where did you find all of this material? Where did it come from?"

From you, Mom. It came from you.

ACKNOWLEDGMENTS

Without the memories and contributions of my brothers and sisters, this book in its present form wouldn't exist. Thanks especially to Betsy Ryan for her daily e-mails and insights on the subject of our mother, to Barry (Bruce) Ryan for his knowledge of beer brands and their prices, to Lea Anne (Ryan) Metzger for her memories of pre-1953 family life, to Fred (Bub) Ryan for his genealogic knowledge of the Ryan family cars, to Barb Ryan for her encyclopedic memory of Mom's flower garden, and to Mike Ryan for his knowledge on the physics of bullets. Thanks, too, to my other siblings, Dick Ryan, Rog Ryan, and Dave (Bongo) Ryan, for their continuous support of this book.

I'd also like to thank all the contributors to this book who live only in memory: Leo (Kelly) Ryan, Aunt Lucy and Uncle Dinny Moore, Uncles Bill, John, Chub, and Dan Ryan, Grandma Katie Ryan, Grandpa Orren and Grandmas Minnie and Lyrl Lehman, and Mrs. Josephine Etchie.

I have the best agent in the known world, Amy

Rennert, who made the book a reality. The bright light of her energy (not to mention how fast she talks) still keeps me awake at night. I also have the best editor a writer could ask for. Thanks to Denise Roy for recognizing the importance of ordinary-American history in the form of my mother's story and for her unflagging enthusiasm and hard work on my behalf.

Doris Ober, friend and manuscript consultant, was a help in more ways than one. It just so happens that in her second job out of college she was a judge for D. L. Blair, my mother's favorite contest judging company. It's quite possible that Doris selected an Evelyn Ryan entry in one of the two major contests she won that were judged by D. L. Blair.

Dortha Schaefer, my mother's best contesting friend, contributed greatly to my understanding of how contests and judging worked in the 1950s and 1960s. She patiently reviewed my drafts and offered support of a kind I could get nowhere else. When I told her I was working alone on this project, she said, "No, you aren't. You've got me." Thanks also to Betty White, another contesting whiz from the old days, for the search through her closets for memorabilia and for the stories of her wins.

Suze Orman shares my mother's philosophy that riches abound within us, whether we know it or not. Many thanks to Suze for showing us how to reveal inner and outer sources of wealth.

Thanks to my old high school pals, Connie (Sheik) Andrews, Craig Andrews, and Pat Walter, who filled in many missing details on the history of Defiance and its people, and who were as excited as I was at re-creating a shared past.

For readings of various versions of the manuscript and ongoing encouragement, thanks to Sylvia Mollick, Jodi Darby, Irene Ogus, Carolyn Cappai, Jan Montgomery, Marya Grambs, Peter Handel, Jeanne Allen, Marc Grant, Melissa Howden, Lynda Wiggins, Elaine Ryan, Norma Montgomery, Susan Krieger, Estelle Freedman, Julie Bertuccelli, Katherine Forrest, Marny Hall, Martha Mirabella, Lucy Hessler, Pam Lee, Bill Wright, Wayne and Linda Bonnett, John Goepel, Alice Spears, Jane Altman, Jett Psaris, Marlena Lyons, Jan Craig, Colleen Warner, and the Northglenn #1 Study Group of Lakewood, Colorado.

For bringing old photos back to life, thanks to Nick Mankovich and to Wayne and Linda Bonnett. Thanks also to Louise Kollenbaum for her unfailing artistic eye.

Special thanks to Pat Holt, who was there when the first word struck the page and pushed me to write the second word and all the ones that came after.

And to Betsy's sons—Gabe, Alex, and Chris Mankovich, who inherited the family's love of baseball and their grandmother's love of words.

To my high school English teachers, each inspiring in her own way: Mrs. Letha Davis, Mrs. Lorraine Andrews, and Mrs. Louise Barrett, with special thanks to Mrs. Bette Lacher, whose faith in my abilities was often greater than my own.

Most of all, thanks to the star of this show, Evelyn Ryan, mother (and hero) of ten.